T0339653

WITH A HEART
FULL OF LOVE

/

WITH A HEART FULL OF LOVE

Clara Taylor's Letters
from Russia 1917-1919
Volume 2

Edited by
Katrina Maloney & Patricia M. Maloney

SHE WRITES PRESS

Published 2022
Printed in the United States of America
Print ISBN: 978-1-64742-381-0
E-ISBN: 978-1-64742-382-7
Library of Congress Control Number: 2022900314

For information, address:
She Writes Press
1569 Solano Ave #546
Berkeley, CA 94707

She Writes Press is a division of SparkPoint Studio, LLC.

To David K. Martin, uncle and brother,
who first inspired us to gather her letters
and publish Aunt Teke's Great Adventure.

David Martin and Great Aunt Teke (Clara Taylor) in New York City 1956.
(Patricia M. Maloney)

CONTENTS

Clara Taylor in her YWCA uniform Arkhangelsk, Summer 1919
(Photographer unknown. Clara I. Taylor, personal papers)

Preface

by Patricia M. Maloney

My great aunt, Clara Isobel Taylor, stirred the imagination of family members with stories of her experiences in Russia from 1917 to 1919. She wrote letters to her father, her brothers John, Leslie, and George, her sisters Genieve and Mary, and her close friends at home. These letters give us a glimpse of her work for the YWCA and for the military men of the North Russian Expeditionary Force. We read about both challenges and joys. Clara struggled to learn the Russian language, and at the same time, she found satisfaction in going to market and bargaining for supplies. She grew frustrated with the political nature of the military mission, and found joy in planning parties to raise the spirits of gravely wounded men. There were great challenges to prepare meals in the midst of food shortages and an exciting ride on a reindeer sled. Her letters tell of sightseeing trips in the great cities of the north, church services in famous cathedrals, the interesting foods she ate, and, especially, the awe she felt at seeing the magnificence of the aurora borealis (northern lights) in the arctic zones. This sight impressed her a great deal, and she often told us about watching the magical appearance of the lights. She said that her travels through Finland, Sweden, and Norway were a highlight of the two years she spent on this adventure.

Clara was known to me and my brothers as "Aunt Teke" (pronounced "Teek"). One summer in the early 1900s, for reasons no one can quite recall, Clara, her niece Margaret Frances (my mother), and her nephew Muirison decided to give each other nicknames. Ever after, Clara was

"Teke," Margaret was "Tancie," and Muirison was "Tavey." These names, chosen in fun, became life-long affectionate labels. My mother was known as Tancie, even to acquaintances, for the rest of her life. I do remember her saying that Margaret Frances was a bit of a mouthful, and she greatly preferred to be called Tancie.

Aunt Teke had a strong, intense personality, and you can read some of that passion in these letters from Arkhangelsk. I remember the hour-long talks we had when we got together. Her conversations were crowded with intellectual topics, world and national events, and US history. She read extensively and remained interested in Russia long after she returned home. On one occasion, when she was visiting me and my family in Connecticut, we had a few friends over for dinner. Even after all these years, the guests at that meal recall her passionate descriptions of Russia and the strong opinions she held about many topics.

Aunt Teke was extremely inquisitive. She liked to ask young people about their goals, dreams, and future careers. She followed rules and expected others to do the same. She was a product of her era as well as being exceptional for pursuing a degree in economics and then opening her own financial services company specifically to help women. She was very supportive of her fellow workers. Her positive outlook lent itself to finding solutions to knotty problems, and that is evident in her letters home as she described her work in Russia during the Revolution.

The Taylor family was tight-knit and very supportive of one another. No one person over-shadowed another. James Muirison Taylor, the clan's patriarch, set the tone with his mellow personality and non-combative approach to the world. The choices and goals of each member of the family were respected. All seven of his children went to college, with his support and enthusiasm. At that time, the late 1800s and early 1900s, it was extremely uncommon for women to be educated beyond the high school level, yet each of the "Taylor girls" attended college.

My Aunt Teke was also very protective of those younger and less educated or experienced than herself. She was certainly not intimated by men! After she graduated from the University of Wisconsin with a degree in economics, in 1910, she took a job with the YWCA as an industrial specialist. She traveled around the Midwestern United States investigating the social welfare of workers and health conditions in factories. After several years of that work, she was well-prepared to investigate similar conditions in Petrograd and Moscow. She accepted a two-year contract from the YWCA to work in Russia as an industrial specialist. Originally Teke's role was to observe and interview Russian women in the industrial Russian complexes, survey the conditions, then submit reports. However, this part of her work in Russia ended up taking a back seat to other, more immediate concerns for women in revolutionary Moscow (see *Dearest Ones at Home, Volume 1*). Then, from the fall of 1918 through August of 1919, her second year in Russia, she was attached to the military mission, working to support the soldiers and officers of the Northern Russian Expeditionary Force in Arkhangelsk, North Russia.

When she returned to the United States in 1919, Aunt Teke worked for the YWCA for another couple of years. In 1922, she entered Columbia University and earned a master's degree in economics. She then established her own financial firm for women. During those years in New York City, she continued to have a very active social life. She supported the arts by attending plays and concerts. (We can see how much she enjoyed a spectacle in her descriptions of the theater and concerts she attended while traveling.) Teke sold her business and retired in 1957. Travel continued to entice her as she explored the United States and abroad. We have a stack of letters she wrote home from several of her trips, but she never again had to flee for her life as she did from Moscow in 1918. Aunt Teke finally settled down in La Jolla, California, in early 1960 and died there in 1968.

The two volumes we have compiled of Clara Taylor's letters and diary are our family's legacy from this amazing woman. We hope that you enjoy reading our Aunt Teke's own words about her extraordinary adventure, and that this record will enhance your overall understanding of the involvement of Americans in the Russian Revolution from 1917 to 1919.

Introduction
by Katrina Maloney

One hundred years after my great-grand-aunt Teke returned from Russia, my mother Patricia M. Maloney and I decided it was time to write up her story. We gathered together letters, her "line- a-day" diary, and a manuscript written by my uncle David K. Martin, who had interviewed Clara in the 1960s. For the two volumes of Clara Taylor's Letters from Russia, we transcribed the handwritten materials and added some historical background to help set the scene for the reader. The aim of this project was two-fold. First, we sought to produce a readable manuscript for our family in order to preserve the words of our ancestress. Second, as a broader goal, we wished to add to the primary source records of the American involvement in the Russian Revolution while also illuminating the history of women's roles during the Progressive Era.

Volume 1
Letters 1917–1918

You will find Clara's letters from September 1917 to August 1918 in Volume 1, titled *Dearest Ones at Home*. These include her accounts of traveling by train from her home in Illinois to San Francisco, then by steamer to Honolulu, Tokyo, and then to Vladivostok, Russia. After arriving on Russian soil, Clara and six YWCA colleagues traveled on the Trans-Siberian Railroad to Petrograd, arriving on the day before the infamous

October Revolution.[1] In December, the YWCA women left Petrograd and traveled to Moscow. Their job was to establish an Association to serve women in the city.[2]

The American women opened a YWCA house in Moscow with a grand celebration on December 30, 1917. There, for the next eight months, in a highly volatile revolutionary atmosphere, they taught home economics, physical education, English language, and other "improving courses" to both factory girls and mature women. We hear very little of the real danger the American women were in at that time through Clara's letters. (Although she does admit in a letter to her sister dated January 15, 1919, that the previous summer they had been in constant danger from the daily street battles in Moscow.) She is anxious at all times to assure her family that she is safe, even when there is shooting in the streets, not enough food, contaminated water, disease, and despair in the city. Clara started writing a "line-a-day" book in January 1918. These diary entries give us a better sense of the real emotions she was undergoing, but even those words, written as a record of day-to-day events, seem to carry a terse, stoic feel.

Volume 2
Letters and Diary 1918–1919

Clara's letters and diary entries, from the point in August 1918 when all foreign nationals were expelled from the interior of Russia, to the time she was safe at home in Illinois at the end of 1919, are found in this volume. During the second year of her Russian adventure, Clara and her YWCA colleagues are posted with the International North Russia Expeditionary Force. So, instead of teaching Russian girls and women, instead of conducting an industrial survey of factories in Moscow, Clara takes on duties to support the fighting men of the Expedition in Arkhangelsk Province, Northern Russia.[3] The military command was reluctant to involve women

---

1 The Bolshevik coup against the Russian Provisional Government occurred the night of November 7–8, 1917, Western calendar.

2 The YWCA had Associations or clubs in several different countries at this time.

3 "Arkhangelsk" is the English spelling of the contemporary Russian city, and will be used in these introductory essays to refer to the city and the Oblast (region). We have chosen to retain the various other spellings as written by each primary source when that source

(other than nurses) in the mission; however, while the YWCA staff was resting in Sweden in late 1918, the YWCA leadership in New York prevailed in their arguments that civilian women were needed to support the morale of the soldiers. Besides, the women were already close by. From October 1918 until their departure from Russia one year later, the women drew their salaries from the YWCA—they were not volunteers—and took their directions from the military command. Clara and her colleagues were assigned four areas of responsibility: to share information with the men from war maps and daily typewritten communiqués from Allied Bureau of Information; to create and manage a library of books, magazines, and papers; to organize weekly concerts, lectures, and films; to establish and maintain Hospitality Huts for the enlisted men; and to visit hospitalized soldiers. In addition, the women acted as hostesses at both the American and British Embassies, for parties and official visits. Clara tells her sister: "We are doing only army work, canteen, hospital, and acting as hostess to the whole Am. forces and officials here. Our very presence counts for a great deal." (See letter dated January 15, 1919.)

The civilian American women organized entertainments, concerts, lectures, delivered mail, baked pies, filled Christmas stockings, talked to soldiers, and soothed patients. Clara still felt strongly that she was "doing her bit" for the war effort, and even a serious bout with appendicitis could not quench her enthusiasm for the Russian people and the work she had undertaken. In the summer of 1919, Clara did somehow find the time to do some work for Russian women and girls in Arkhangelsk. As the troops were evacuating the city and there were fewer military duties to fulfill, the women taught English classes, set up educational programs, started a Girl Scout troop, and even took charge of forty Russian women prisoners.

For most of the their time in North Russia, especially after the Armistice, the YWCA staff believed that they would be returning to interior Russia "just as soon as the way is clear." But, in 1919, the Russia Civil War was showing no signs of abating, and the National Board of the YWCA announced that there would be no further attempt to establish Associations in Russia. Clara was saddened by that decision. She never changed her belief that what Russia needed was the best and brightest help

is cited (e.g., Moore and other military writers use "Archangel" and Clara either writes "Arkangel" or "Archangel").

from Americans "of the right sort." Her insights into the Russian character and their deep desire for friendship with Americans is touchingly portrayed in the letter to her sister Geney dated May 15, 1919. Clara had no illusions about the evils of the Soviet leadership, and it is interesting to me that she was ever considered a Bolshevik sympathizer. She had a genuine appreciation for the philosophic and humanitarian basis of socialism, which agreed with her deeply held religious beliefs. However, as she writes: ". . . no one with common sense believes in class warfare or sole rule of the proletariat. The methods used . . . have been criminal. What it has grown to be now is vastly different from what it was in the beginning. All of us devoutly wish now for the overthrow of the powers in Moscow" (ibid.).

This volume, like the first, has brief essays at the beginning of each section that give an historical framework around the events Clara relates. At the end of this book readers will find a longer essay about the international intervention into the Russian Civil War. Also included is a list of primary persons and a time line of the military events at each fighting front, in order to give a big-picture viewpoint.

Details about the American involvement in the Russian Civil War in this book have been taken from primary sources and recently published contemporary histories.[4] The following accounts are restricted to the military actions in the Murmansk and Arkhangelsk regions, with mention of world events that impact Clara's experience. Please note that the Russian Civil War (and concurrent international interventions) was an incredibly complex situation. I have tried to distill the main events to those that directly impacted Clara and her colleagues while they were in Northern Russia. Please see the bibliography for further reading about the conflict and United States involvement.

Foreign Intervention in the Arctic Regions

The International North Russia Expeditionary Force had two different theaters of action on Russian territory: in the Arkhangelsk Oblast bordering on the White Sea just below the Arctic Circle and in the Vladivostok area on the Pacific coast. Between late 1917 and 1919 there were six active fighting

---

4 Please see the historical essay at the end of this book for more details about why the US was involved in this conflict.

fronts radiating southeasterly and due south of the city of Arkhangelsk. There were scattered actions west of the city in the Karelia region; battles were also fought further west and south into the interior of Russia, along the Trans-Siberian highway, and in the Ukraine. Skirmishes all around the vast interior of the country were occurring simultaneously with the events Clara experienced. (Please see the map on page 14.)

Arkhangelsk was well-connected to the outside world, with consistent and fairly reliable communications in and out of the city. Clara now received regular cables and letters from home, and heard war news. Her letter dated November 1, 1918, noted in passing how she told the men "about the Dardanelles," which came under the control of the Allies at the Armistice of Mudros, on October 30, 1918. The YWCA women were in great demand as hostesses, as organizers, and as comforters. Their expertise in people management and their ability to organize disparate elements into useful work even against the greatest odds—without complaint—endeared them to the military command. These talents also made the American women great friends to the enlisted men who were the main priority of the "war work" in Arkhangelsk. Other American civilians in the region included men working with the Red Cross and the YMCA, journalists, diplomats, and businessmen. But for most of the year, Clara Taylor, Marcia Dunham, Helen Ogden, Catherine Childs (later Ryle), and Elizabeth Dickerson, two Red Cross nurses, Miss Gosling and Miss Foerester, plus Mrs. Davis, the wife of one of the Consuls, were the only American women in North Russia.

Letters were sent via various means, including diplomatic pouch, regular post, by the hand of friends traveling back to the States, and by dog or reindeer sled from icebound Arkhangelsk to Sweden. Clara's tone, the length, and the feel of these letters demonstrate the same dedication she held for her work and for the Russian people as expressed the previous year in Moscow.

The population of Arkhangelsk had blossomed from 40,000 timber traders and merchants to 140,000 people by 1917, with the addition of thousands of diplomats, military personnel, refugees, and international businessmen. During the time the YWCA and YMCA workers were in the city, there was a robust religious and artistic culture. Clara mentioned how the Russian people loved a spectacle, and she often attended the theater and musical evenings with her Russian friends. Importantly, there was also a solid infrastructure in place for telephone, telegraph, electricity, and tram services in the city and its suburbs. There was much to-and-fro across the White Sea from Arkhangelsk to the open seaport of Murmansk north on the Kola peninsula. The political situation in the city was somewhat volatile, it is true. However, the American women moved about in safety. Although there were widespread and severe food shortages in the region, Clara had enough to eat through her access to military, Red Cross, and YMCA resources. We hear less about the struggle to find food in Clara's letters this year, in contrast to the obsessive tone of her letters from Moscow.

From her weeks of rest in Sweden until her final departure from North Russia on August 23, 1919, Clara was well-connected and up-to-date, healthy, upbeat, exceedingly busy, more politically outspoken, and physically safe. She was not being shot at in the streets.

About the books

We have only minimally edited Clara's letters and diary entries: in these pages we hear the words she wrote to her dearest ones in her own voice. There are some diary entries that, in their incoherence, reflect her stress in dangerous times. (The Russian Civil War was bloody and brutal; Clara was right there in the middle of the conflict.) There are other entries that express her awe and delight for the natural beauty of the countryside or her genuine pleasure in dancing at parties. Because Clara tended to use either single quotation marks or no punctuation at all in her diary, we have italicized the names of ships, books, periodicals, and performances to make it easier for the reader. Where her handwriting was illegible, we have included this symbol [?], or ellipses to indicate undecipherable words. Her quirky spellings and abbreviations, non-standard punctuation, and family references are retained in these volumes. We have used occasional footnotes to clarify meaning or give explanations of terms, but the voice, tone, and attitude are all Clara's.

The events Clara Taylor witnessed during her years in Russia remained clear and poignant to her for the rest of her life. Clara was an extraordinary woman of strong character, deep love, a cheerful outlook, and endless fascination with intellectual pursuits. She never stopped having adventures.

And although her years in Russia were the time of the greatest personal danger, she never swerved from the conviction instilled by her family that the greatest purpose of her life was to serve others. On December 1, 1918, in a typical entry noting her work and the reaction of those she served, she wrote: "Began work at Sombola Hut with Mr. Bonte. The surprise of the men was delightful." It gave her the greatest pleasure to bring her presence as an American woman bearing smiles and a semblance of normality to the men "fighting without a war" far from home in a bleak frozen landscape.

Clara continued to travel widely but did not go back to Russia. This may have been due to the rumors that she was a Bolshevik sympathizer, which were started by the unfortunate Shelby Strother, a disgruntled American diplomat who was barred from some of the activities the YWCA hosted in Archangelsk. I was not able to confirm that Clara I. Taylor had a Federal Bureau of Investigation file, but my uncle told me that he believed Clara was blacklisted by the US State Department, preventing her return to Russia (David K. Martin interview with Katrina Maloney, 2013).

A note about censorship

The Espionage Act of 1917 gave the Postmaster General of the United States the power to block mail that he determined could interfere with military operations or support enemies of the United States. The Censorship Board (Post Office Department, Departments of Navy and War, the War Trade Board, and the Committee on Public Information) regulated all mail, cable, radio, telegraph, and telephone communications between the States and foreign nations. Letters that passed censorship were stamped with an official seal. Other countries handled postal monitoring in different ways. Soldiers writing home to Germany or Britain had their letters read by their superior officers; the Soviets had a wide-ranging and comprehensive censorship bureaucracy; the United States had a three-tiered system that scoured all letters written by soldiers (Demm 2017, para. 3.2.).

In her letter of February 23, 1919, Clara wrote: "Since letter 52 got cut up by the censor, I find it hard to write. I suppose there is much that I could write about that I don't, just because I don't want my letters hacked up." It is not clear which of Clara's letters were censored. Possibly, those that were sent through the diplomatic pouches were considered privileged and were read only by British officials, not by Soviet, British, and US offices. Letters were also was given by hand to various people who traveled out of Russia. For example, Clara's May 7, 1919 letter to Sis was given to Catherine Childs Ryall, who put it in a post box in London. Some may have been read by the US censorship office upon arrival in New York before being sent on to Illinois. In Clara's May 29, 1919, letter, she noted that none of the recent home letters she received were censored. Sadly, we do not have any of the letters or cables she received while in Russia. She destroyed them all just before leaving (see diary entry for August 6, 1919: "went thru truck and tore up all letters"). Although that was a highly characteristic action Clara took in order to protect others who might have been in trouble if her letters were confiscated, I can only feel a sadness that we cannot ever have the full picture of her extraordinary two years in Russia.

∾

On my writing table I have one of the copper candlesticks that Clara sent home from Russia. I have the portrait photograph taken in Arkhangelsk in the summer of 1919—the one where she is patiently modeling the YWCA uniform that finally, after so many delays, arrived just before she left Russia. The dress I wore at my high school graduation was a white lace frock she wore in the early 1900s. All my life I have heard about the amazing, extraordinary, larger-than-life personality of Aunt Teke, and it has been my privilege to compile these volumes. I never got to hear Clara's own voice recounting her Great Adventure, but I could hear her passion within the pages of her diary and letters home. I hope you can hear her too.

PART ONE

September 12, 1918 – December 5, 1918

Clara Taylor's original role for the YWCA in Russian was to conduct an industrial survey of the factory conditions in and around Moscow and report back to the YWCA's National Board. It was not until June 1918, after being in the city since the previous October, that she received permission from the Soviet government to inspect factories. She, an interpreter, and a government minder visited 22 factories within about 18 days. Her "Industrial Survey Report" was finalized during her rest and recuperation weeks in Sweden that September. Clara wrote the report as an internal document for the YWCA. To her dismay, she later learned that the report had been widely circulated within the US State Department. Clara notes in a letter home that she would have written it differently if she had known it would be shared with governmental agencies. Some of the supportive comments she wrote regarding the Soviets' organizational and philosophical approaches to manufacturing were taken out of context later in 1919. In fact, she was interviewed by "4 Secret Service men who apologized for interviews" upon her return to New York City in late 1919.[5]

Throughout the summer of 1918, the YWCA women continued to do the Association's work with Russian women to the best of their abilities. The city of Moscow was in turmoil. Cholera was widespread, as was the so-called "Spanish influenza." The thousands who died from those diseases had been weakened by months of food shortages and poor sanitation

---

5 See Clara's diary entry October 17, 1919.

within the city. The Bolsheviks sought to stabilize their power base, but, as Clara notes in a letter home dated July 7, 1918, skirmishes between the revolutionaries and their opponents continued like children squabbling in a sandbox. Clara writes:

> This morning almost simultaneously with the ringing of the church bells, the firing began. The counter-revolutionaries seized the post office, telegraph & telephone stations. For two hours it was truly awful. The Bolsheviks re-took these places with the use of three-inch artillery guns and machine guns. . . . This day's bloody affairs, I am sure, will not be attributed to either German or the Allies. It is a horrid Russian quarrel and probably confined entirely to Moscow.[6]

Because news from outside the city was restricted, the women could not know that the entire countryside of Russia was now embroiled in full-fledged civil war. Indeed, the United States itself had entered the conflict.

In August 1918, the YWCA women had no inkling they would step into the storm of battle in a few months' time. Now they nervously awaited permission from the Soviet government to leave the interior of the country. Their permission papers were repeatedly delayed. Clara's diary entries for the first week of August, 1918, give a hint of the pressure:

> . . . all Fr. & Eng. arrested. Great anxiety felt in our colony. . . . Conditions very serious. Permits not granted for us to leave city. Everybody tense with excitement . . . all packed and ready to leave but still uncertainty as to receiving permits. Spent all night at station with baggage . . .[7]

Finally, all foreign nationals were ordered onto a train from Moscow to Nizhny Novgorod (a large city on the Volga River 250 miles southeast of Moscow). There they spent twelve days until orders arrived to evacuate to Finland via Petrograd. Once they arrived in Petrograd, they were,

---

6 Maloney & Maloney 2014, 196.

7 ibid., 203.

again, detained for several days. Finally, on August 31, 1918, the group was allowed to cross over to Finland. They then traveled by train to Stockholm, Sweden. The American women, bank officers, diplomatic workers, and various other civilians rested in Stockholm for the next month. Clara was able to get a few housekeeping tasks accomplished, such as getting her coats interlined and shoes resoled. She ate well, took in the sights, completed and submitted her Industrial Report, and generally recharged for the next stage of what she expected to be her YWCA work with women. However, the next year proved to be a vastly different experience.

Events in North Russia

In the early summer of 1918, US, British, French, and Canadian troops with the North Russian Expeditionary Force[8] landed at both Vladivostok on the Russian Pacific coast, and, some 3,700 miles west, in the port city of Murmansk on the White Sea. The stated purpose of the western mission was three-fold: first, to protect the North Russia cities from Germany's plans to use the strategically placed ports as submarine bases; second, to attempt to draw off German troops from the fighting fronts in Europe; and third, to protect munition supplies from capture by the Red Army. American troops were told their task was to be "guard duty" in the city of Arkhangelsk. The reality was quite different. In fact, this mission, under British command, engaged in disastrous, bloody offensives against the Red Army in the hinterlands below Arkhangelsk. The men, while valiantly doing their duty, were confused and angry that the war they had signed up for had ended with the November 1918 Armistice, but they were still fighting someone else's war, far from home, in horrific conditions. The work to support the morale of the soldiers in this untenable situation was undertaken by Clara and her YWCA colleagues along with YMCA and a few Red Cross workers.

The reasons for the American military presence in the North Russian Expeditionary Force are complex and fraught. In early 1918, the Allied

---

8 The British press called the mission by various disparaging names, such as "Churchill's War", "The Great Russian Gamble" and "Whitehall's Folly". Russians referred to it as "The Foreign Intervention", and in the United States, the campaign in Arkhangelsk became known as "The Polar Bear Expedition."

Supreme Council at the Conference of Versailles decided to intervene in the Russia situation (which was seen to be teetering on the brink of chaos). The decision to commit US troops to the Mission was taken in July 1918 by US President Woodrow Wilson.[9]

Just as Clara and her friends were resting in Stockholm, the first US troops landed in Arkhangelsk. The 5,500 American men of the 339th Infantry, 310th Engineers, 337th Ambulance Company, and the 337th Field Hospital Company, under the command of Colonel George E. Stewart, arrived to conduct guard duty and support the White Russian Army against the Bolshevik Red Army on September 5, 1918.[10]

The circumstances and events of this little-known American mission are somewhat confusing. Please see this volume's bibliography for primary sources and contemporary explanations of the details that are beyond the scope of this short summary. I have striven to set the scene for the reader to better understand the extraordinary circumstances Clara found herself in, without going too deeply into the convoluted international relationships and confusing military maneuvers of the Russian Civil War.

World events during the last months of 1918 were extremely tense. In Moscow, Allied relationships with the Bolshevik government deteriorated in late summer. In France, the last offensives staged by the Allies in the Great War (WWI) were succeeding in breaking German lines. (From September 26 through November, the Battles of Meuse-Argonne were fought.) On November 11, 1918, the General Armistice was declared, ending the fighting on the Western Front in Europe. Other events on the world stage in November 1918 included the collapse of the Austria-Hungarian Empire with the abdications of Charles of Austria and Emperor Karl; Poland's declaration as an independent republic; the abdication of German Kaiser Wilhelm II, and the subsequent establishment of the Republic of Germany. The Bolsheviks declared themselves a Soviet State, and rescinded the

---

9 It is important to note that the US involvement in the Foreign Intervention was not sanctioned by the US Congress and only grudgingly acquiesced to by President Woodrow Wilson.

10 The NREF was under British command. The tensions created by conflicting loyalties and the perceived ineptness of the British leadership is well documented in the accounts by Moore, J., et al., 1920; Alberton, R., 1920; and Cuhady, J., 1924. Each of those authors blame President Wilson for sending too few troops into the conflict. (See the Bibliography for full citations.)

Treaty of Brest-Litovsk. US President Woodrow Wilson sailed for Europe to attend the Paris Peace Conference. The first cases of the Spanish influenza were reported from Haskel, Kansas, US, in April, 1918. A second wave of the pandemic killed 195,000 Americans in October alone. The flu also plowed a devastating course through soldiers demobilized from the European theater of war. Overall, 50 million deaths were attributed to the disease worldwide.[11]

In September 1918, as they rested in Stockholm, the YWCA women expected to travel from Sweden back into the interior of Russia in order to continue their work with women. However, that month, the YWCA leadership in New York changed their assignment to "war work" to be carried out in North Russia. The American YWCA women were attached to the military mission; now they were under the protection of the military and received their orders from Military Command. The six American workers who had been deeply involved in the support and education of Russian women, after a year of uncertainty and danger in revolutionary Moscow, now sailed via steamer to Arkhangelsk, Northern Russia, to become morale officers in an unpopular, poorly supported, and increasingly desperate mission.

Once they arrived in the city on October 17, 1918, the women divided up the war work. Elizabeth Dickerson was stationed at the largest YMCA canteen in the city, Helen Ogden and Marcia Dunham took on the creation and running of the YWCA Hostess House. This center was opened after much delay in January 1919 and was the only place in the city reserved exclusively for American servicemen (officers had their own clubs). The women served tea, coffee, cocoa, baked goods, and sandwiches. The house had several rooms, a piano, a Victrola, writing tables, and comfortable chairs for reading. Catherine Childs worked at the YMCA railroad canteen. Clara Taylor took on the establishment of a library for the Hostess House; canteen duty at the two YMCA Huts on either end of the city central (Smolny to the south, and Solombola to the north); and visiting at the three hospitals plus the *Kaylon*, a hospital ship moored in the Arkhangelsk harbor. Each of the women also did two- or three-week stints at a canteen

---

11 Reports of the total number of deaths vary. The 50 million figure is noted by the US Centers for Disease Control and Prevention website's page "1918 Pandemic H1N1 virus."

rail car traveling up and down the Vologda Rail Road front. Each was also in high demand as a hostess for the many social events put on by the Military Mission. There were teas, dances, lectures, entertainments—the social scene was bright, busy, and exhausting.

Clara also sat on committees, baked pies, played games, continued her Russian language lessons, walked all over the city, attended church, organized parties, and even had charge of some Russian women prisoners in the summer of 1919. All of the work done by the American women was highly valued by the enlisted men, their officers, the various diplomatic corps, and the local Russian people. An enormous amount of organization for the support of morale was undertaken in just three months.

We pick up Clara's story in August 1918, when she and the other foreign workers had escaped from Petrograd and were on the train to safety in Finland. After a lovely trip up through Finland, with "long interesting stops," and many wonderful sunsets, they arrived in Stockholm, Sweden on September 7, 1918.

Mentioned in This Section:

US Consular General Dewitt Clinton Poole (1885–1952), Special Assistant to the US Ambassador in Arkhangelsk; in 1919 oversaw American civilian evacuation as US Charge d'Affaires; University of Wisconsin graduate.

US Ambassador to Russia David R. Francis (1850–1927), in Russia from 1916 to 1917.

Raymond Robins (1873–1954), American writer interested in economics, labor, and diplomacy between the United States and Soviet Russia.

Mr. Anderson, YMCA war worker, captured by Bolsheviks, imprisoned in Moscow; then released and sent back to the United States.

Mr. Andrew and Mr. Wardivell, Red Cross workers, likewise captured and released.

Lloyd George (1863–1945), British Prime Minister from December 1916 to October 1922.

Sir Herbert Henry Asquith (1852–1928), British Prime Minister April 1908 to December 1916.

Theodore Roosevelt (1828–1919), US President 1901 to 1909.

Woodrow Wilson (1856–1924), US President 1913 to 1921.

Sir Edward Gray, Viscount of Faloden (1862–1933), British Foreign Secretary; with PM Asquith, involved Britain in the Great War.

Clara's Colleagues

Helen Ogden, YWCA cafeteria specialist and close friend of Clara's.

Marcia Dunham (often abbreviated "MOD"), the Executive Secretary for the YWCA's US Central Western region; recruited Clara for the Russian work.

Muriel Heap, YWCA worker who left Russia early in October 1918.

Catherine Childs, YWCA worker; married **Mr. Ryle** of the YMCA in November 1918 in Arkhangelsk.

Elizabeth Dickerson, YWCA physical education specialist.

Elizabeth (Bessie) Boies, Head of the YWCA work in Russia; had, along with **Clarissa Spencer**, instigated the YWCA Russian Association work in early 1917. Bessie and **Thomas Cotton** (Dartmouth College graduate, YMCA Secretary) were married in 1918. Her papers are archived at the Sophia Smith Library, Smith College, Northampton, Massachusetts.

Read Lewis, a close, lifelong friend of Clara's, employed with the US Information Bureau.

Jerome Davis (1891–1979), an American socialist, scholar, later a professor of Divinity at Yale University, labor organizer. He was a controversial figure who was in Russia from 1917 to 1918. A Bolshevik sympathizer, Davis quoted Clara's Industrial Survey Report out of context in some of his speeches, causing a great deal of trouble for her with the US State Department. (This report was a summary of her impressions and observations of Moscow factory life that she wrote in the fall of 1918. It was sent to the YWCA Headquarters and appeared in the Association's newsletter.)

Peter Pierce, US Consul at Murmansk, University of Wisconsin graduate, a good friend of Clara's.

Thom "Husky" Merrill, Dartmouth College graduate, YMCA worker.

Shelby Strother (sometimes spelled Strouther) is described as a "jolly Harvard man" early in Clara's acquaintance with him. Later he is found to be a difficult man who made trouble not only for Clara personally, but was also in conflict with Felix Cole, the American Head of Consular Staff. (See below, in the notes before Chapter Five for more about Strother.)

Significant Officials in Arkhangelsk

Colonel George E. Stewart (1872–1946), Head of General Staff.

Vice Consul Felix Cole (1887–1969), Head of Consular Staff, attended University of Wisconsin.

Vice Consul Robert Whitney Imbrie (1883–1924).

Crawford Wheeler, Head of YMCA work.

Lieutenant Cleofoth (sometimes spelled Kliefoth), and his wife, with the Military Mission, University of Wisconsin graduate.

Captain Lively, with the Red Cross.

Lieutenant Bricker, on the General Staff.

Colonel Ruggles, of the Military Mission.

Clara's Family

Father
James Muirison Taylor (1839–1921).

Mother
Adalaide Stewart Taylor (1840–1905).

Sisters
Mary F. Taylor, known as "Sis" (1871–1943).
Genieve M. Taylor, known as "Geney" (1874–1950).

Brothers and sisters-in-law
Leslie (1877–1934) and Elizabeth Taylor.
John (1879–1953) and Cora (1881–1982) Taylor.
George (1881–1956) and Trenna Taylor.
Sam (1869–1914) and Winifred Taylor.

Niece
Margaret Frances, known as "Tancie" (1909–2010), daughter of James and
Cora. She married David K. Martin and was the mother of Patricia M.
Maloney, grandmother of Katrina Maloney (editors).

Nephews
Muirison, known as "Tavey," son of James and Cora.
Sam, son of Leslie and Elizabeth.

Fritz (Fritzie) White, a young friend of the Taylor family, whose father was
in partnership with James M. Taylor (and later John) in their land abstract
business in Taylorville, Illinois. She worked for the YWCA in Terra Haute,
Illinois. She and Clara were very close friends, and Clara signed off as "your
loving sister" in her letters to Fritz.

Map of Russia, 1994
(Source: https://legacy.lib.utexas.edu/maps/commonwealth/russia.94.jpg)

Bessie Boies, Clara Taylor and Helen Ogden in their Moscow apartment, April 1918
after returning from Samara. Note the concern on Clara's face as she looks at Bessie,
and how ill Bessie appears.
(YWCA papers, Sophia Smith Collection, Smith College Archives)

Clara kneeling by a mountain of hand baggage at the Finland Rail Road Station in
Petrograd as the YWCA women were expelled from Russia, August 27, 1918.
(YWCA papers, Sophia Smith Collection, Smith College Archives)

The Finnish-Russian border at Beloostrov. This is the bridge over the Sestra River where
the Americans and other foreign nationals crossed over to safety, September 2, 1918.
(Picture postcard: "Beloostrov, Russia, crossing Sestra River (Rajajoki) and the Finnish–
Soviet border in 1920s" http://en.wikipedia.org/wiki/File:PK_Systerb%C3%A4cks_
gr%C3%A4nsbro.png)

Jerome Davis, Helen Ogden and Clara Taylor, laughing with relief to be safely in
Sweden after evacuation from Russia, September, 1918.
(Clara I. Taylor Papers, Sophia Smith Collection, Smith College Archives)

Chapter One
"I am sitting where I can guard three hatchways . . ."

Diary
August 30 – September 11, 1918

August 30, 1918, Petrograd
Friday. People again allowed to leave train. Word came of murder of Com. of Foreign Affairs. All hurried on train. In evening, RL [Read Lewis] & I visited Larva Alex. & Romanoff church. Had dinner at little French restaurant. Train left at 8 o'clock. CW [Crawford Wheeler] birthday spread[12] in box car.

August 31, 1918, Bela Osterof R.
Sat. Country flat but lovely. RL & I took long walk & had dinner together. In evening we walked & had spread in Eliz. compartment with Helen & Crawford.

MEMORANDA
Later. Russians ordered Am. to be held in Finland. But we were allowed to proceed. Captain Pierce of Military Mission is quite interested in our plans and in my Bolshevikism. Newspaper Arno dash Fleurot. Chas. St., Smith, Yarrow.

---

12 A "spread" is a meal with special foods on a special occasion.

September 1, 1918, Belo Ostrow, Rus.

Sun. Everything packed up. Inspection of baggage. Don, Husky & I got supper. Read & I took a long delightful walk in the evening. Countryside like N. Wis. & Minnesota. Had spread in Helen's compartment & played ghast [?] Lenin was shot but not killed.

September 2, 1918, Bela Ostrow, Russia

Mon. Husky Merrill, Dan & I got breakfast & coffee. Cold & gray. 3:30 we lined up & crossed the Finnish border as consuls called our names.[13] Took Laplos train to Dotcha. Gathered mushrooms. Everybody in gay spirits at being out of Russia.

September 3, 1918, Findland Dotcha[14]

Tues. Early breakfast of tea, prunes, nuts. Toni, Bess, RL & I walked to the Gulf of Finland. Wonderfully beautiful, picked heather & krurekuvek [?] berries. 10:30 left for Sweden. Children stolid & white-haired. Bol. tried to have our train stopped in Findland, but to no avail.

September 4, 1918, Findland

Wed. Train running on freight schedule which gives us long interesting stops. Country like northern Wisconsin. Flat, full of lakes & pines. Wonderful sunset. Hour at Kokkola neat little town, one story houses. Had big spread in our two comparts. very cold.

September 5, 1918, Tornio-Haparano Sweden

Thurs. Arrived at Tornio 9. All our Russian sec'y arrested at once. Tended baggage. Lovely clear, cold day. Good visit with Mr. Yarrow, newspaper man. Crossed to Harparand at 3—after big dinner left for Stockholm. Mr. Smith, RL & I watched georgous sunset. Dr. Huntington's [?]

---

13 Clara is referring to the Sestra River railroad bridge that was the national border between Russia and Finland between 1812 and 1940. In 1918, the Finnish border was only 18 miles from Petrograd.

14 A *dacha* is a country house. We have retained Clara's sometimes curious spelling habits. She often spelled Finland with a "d," as "Findland".

September 6, 1918, Traveling in Sweden

Fri. Crossed highest bridge in Sweden. Beautiful rolling country with lovely lakes & rivers. RL & I stood on rear platform most of day. Had nice spread with several of the men. Everybody feels wonderful let down after Russia.

September 7, 1918, Stockholm & Uppsala, Sweden

Sat. Arrived at Stockholm 9:30, visited Knight's Hall. Walked round castle, visited shops—bought ice cream soda—at noon took train for Uppsala—started shopping work and early appointments for Monday.

September 8, 1918, Uppsala, Sweden

Sun. Beautiful day in quaint, neat city. Attended Big Cathedral & walked about town. All had big dinner at hotel. Vesper meeting & supper together in evening. Everybody working on reports.

September 9, 1918, Uppsala, Sweden

Mon. Tended to relining of coats, hat, shoes & laundry. Worked like a Trojan on Report until ten. Hard rain all day. Mr. Foster lately from Am. gave report of news up to date. Paid last visit to the Doctors—Most of girls went to Stockholm.

September 10, 1918, Fritz's birthday, Uppsala

Tues. Worked all day on revising Industrial Report. Had dinner in the evening with the girls. Cold & raining. Every one feeling a little logy after rich food.

September 11, 1918, John's birthday Stockholm

Wed. Missed R. L. all day, visited Legation & consulate, tended errand, got ice cream soda. Saw changing of guards at Palace. ice cream soda—Returned at 6:30. Reception at Christian Assoc. Worked on Report until two thirty.

Letters

Sept. 12, 1918
Uppsala, Sweden

Dearest Ones at Home:

Just a hurried note before the big farewell dinner when thirty of us sit down to dinner before Mr. Cotton leaves for home.

I am well, wonderfully so, feeling fine and am sorry that we return to Russia so soon. It has been good to get out where things are not so disorderly and unhappy.

I will send a second letter tomorrow telling of our interesting departure. Life with me, as you can readily believe, is not monotonous. We were thirteen days coming from Nijni Novogerad [Nizhniy Novgorod] to Stockholm. We leave by Narvik, Norway for Arkangel. We will have a wonderful four days sailing in and out of Fjords.

I am sending things to NY which will be expressed to Mary. Please do not do anything with them until my next letter comes giving suggestions. Write NY and ask if they have copies made of my report to send you a copy. If they print it, as they may, send a copy with my compliments to Mr. Edward Ross, and John R. Commons, Ruth White, Lorian P. Jefferson, and Helen Kennedy c/o Public Library, Los Angles, Cal.

Please forgive this being short. I have worked day and night on the report, and getting shoes half soled, clothes cleaned and relined, fur coat shortened, and glasses.

Going to Stockholm tomorrow for several days.

There is no use writing more for such fun is going on at the table. Letter following—Love to all from

Clara

P.S. Sept. 18
Still no cable from NY or home. I felt sure I would receive some word. If only to tell me you all were well. Perhaps you have not heard from me, any oftener than I from you. I planned to cable when I knew what our plans

were. There still is question about our getting around thru Arkangel and in case we do not, of course it means returning to the USA.

This letter failed to reach the boat it was written for. Am sending special delivery to another Am. official who sails tomorrow asking him to mail it on the steamer.

Am enjoying Stockholm very much. It is a lovely city. My clothes are all ready for the next journey. Have not bought things that I wrote home for, as we were waiting for NY cable telling us whether things had already been sent.

We now plan to leave Monday, Sept. 23 for Narvik, Norway, but it is very uncertain. Several consular men, Read Lewis, and newspaper men and four Bank men plan to go also. So there will be quite a party of us.

I saw *Carmen* the other night and am going to opera again on Thursday, and I hope to the Ballet on Saturday. The city is gay with flags for the Norwegian king is visiting Stockholm.

I am sorry this letter failed to get off last Friday but hope eventually it reaches you. By the way letter 34 was never sent. If this letter reaches you before I cable my departure from here please cable. I want another word from home before getting back where receiving news is difficult.

This is a charming vacation and I am loving it, but all feel anxious to get back on our jobs.

Heaps and heaps of love to each and every one from your affectionate,

Teke

Sept. 13, 1918
Stockholm, Sweden
Written on train so please excuse

Dearest Family:

Oh that I could see and talk with you. Here I am in delightful clear, orderly Sweden. And how good it is to get away, for a brief breathing spell, from the chaotic turmoil of suffering Russia. As all letters go thru the censor, I will make my account brief.

About Aug 6 or 7 affairs between the Allies and the Bolshevik gov't became very tense, and relationships were broken off. The 10th all French and English, both men and women, were arrested. We were ordered all of us to get out of Bolshevik territory. We, the YMCA, bank men and ourselves took train to Nijni Novogorad where we lived on the train and on boats for twelve days. When orders came for our immediate return to Moscow, we left Nijni Sunday night Aug. 25 arrived in Moscow at noon the next day. At 2:30 a.m. Monday night, fourteen 1st class sleepers with all consular people (excepting Mr. Pool, Consular General), embassy folk, Bank men, YM and YWCA and newspaper and business men, along with the Italians—about 130 in all—left for Petrograd. There we were detained for three tense days.

Two of the days, Read Lewis and I spent sight seeing. The weather was fine, and Petrograd on a sunny summer day is wonderful. We visited the Winter Palace, gov't bldg's, saw the field of wars, St. Isacc Cathedral, and many other places of interest. While we were there, the minister of foreign affairs was shot, and every effort was made to detain us. One day many of our people were arrested. I am one of the few people who have not been arrested. Of course on examining our numerous documents with which we are all equipped, they very courteously release all Americans. On Sat. 31st we left Petrograd at 5:30 for Bela Ostrow[15] where we lived in our train until the afternoon of the 2d [Sept.]. We were a curious sight and procession. All our baggage after superficial inspection was carried half way across a road bridge, then we lined up and went to the bridge. In the centre of it was the Russian officer, Norwegian, Finnish and Am. Consuls. One by one our names were called and we walked into Finland. There we piled into a freight train with our baggage. We seven girls have 57 pieces which include food baskets, bed rolls, dunnage bags and innumerable hand bags as most people have gotten rid of trunks. We were taken out to a beautiful resort where we spent the night on the Gulf of Finland. For supper we went out and gathered mushrooms. Everybody was almost hilarious after the relaxation from regret and strain and fears in leaving Russia. For three days we journeyed leisurely on our special train thru Finland, stopping long time at towns for meals etc. So we saw the country quite thoroughly and several cities. Finland is like northern Wisconsin and Minnesota, with small glacial hills, rather more flat than hilly, lots and lots of lakes, with a wealth of pines and

---

15 Clara means Beloostrov, a small township located on the Sestra River's Karelin Island, which is now in the Kurortny district of St. Petersburg.

birches. We saw lots of irrigation [?] and heather, but not many other kinds of flowers. Russia is a veritable flower garden, but [there are] not so many birds with highly-colored plumage.

Thursday, Sept. 5 at 8 o'clock on a clear, crisp, cold morning we arrived in Tornio, where passports examined, and finally at 3 o'clock we, too, passed safely into Harpuando [Haparanda], Sweden. The Russians had tried to have us arrested in Finland, but fortunately the Finns gave us safe and hospitable conduct thru their country. At Harparando our baggage was passed and once more we piled into a special train which left at 8:30 [p.m.] for Stockholm.

Again we went rather leisurely so we saw the country which is very lovely and how we have eaten!! There certainly is a food situation here, but nothing compared with European Bolsheviki Russia. We arrived in Stockholm Sat. morning the 7th, where I bought a Scandinavian and Russian Boldakers,[16] had a glimpse of the city, and then all the YM and YW people came out to Uppsala where we have been for a week. Getting out reports, expense accounts, and having clothes fixed up. I am writing on the train on my way into Stockholm where we fix up our passports, get new glasses, and sight-see.

You will be glad to know that we will be in Stockholm for at least ten more days for rest and play and perhaps for two weeks. Then we go to Nrvik [Narvik], Norway for two days, where we take boats that will take us in and out the Fjords to Arkangel, back into Russia. It will probably be the middle or last of Oct. before we get back into interior Russia.

I have had almost no mail. 6 wks ago I had Dec. and Jan. letters. 3 from Sis, and 1 from Genieve. Send mail to Stockholm c/o Am. Legation, not consulate. People who come thru will bring it. Mark on envelope "for Russia." Besides at least once a month, send letters to* Arkangel and also to * Vladivostok. (*c/o legation). When we get to Arkangel, will cable address. We may be detained here much longer than we expect. So have each member of family write me Stockholm, giving brief outlines of past events, and future plans for this year as far as each knows. I am hungry for news. How are the boys effected by the draft law.

We are gorging ourselves with fresh fruits which we dared not eat in R. because of cholera. I am wonderfully well and in fine shape for this next

---

16 *Baedeker's* is a famous line of tourist's guidebooks.

year in Russia. All my supplies are holding out. We are glad to be out of suffering. I know how prisoners feel now when they are released. It was not until we got into Sweden, that we fully realized the scarcity of everything in Moscow and Russia. All of us want to return to Russia, even tho we are quite shut off from the outer world. Russia needs all the right kind of Americans and American stuff that she can get. Don't lose faith in her. Her plight is desperate and will continue to be so even after the fall of the Bolsheviks which is now only a matter of weeks. The counter Revolutions will be no better, and as yet there seems no immediate satisfactory gov't. Don't believe all you read in the papers. But don't think Russia can or will do anything in this big world war. She can't. It is impossible.

I am keeping a fairly good diary so will fill in the gap when I return home. Sis, have my white lace waist which is in box in attic cleaned and sometime send to me along with white georgette waist 40 size, like the white one, I gave you.[17] No hurry. Everything in Sweden is terribly expensive. I am not buying until we hear whether NY and our families have sent the things which we previously wrote for.

The Arctic Ocean trip is not cold. I am looking forward to it. Won't it be thrilling.

With a heart full of love to each and all from your ever affectionate

Clara

Sept. 14, 1918
Stockholm, Sweden

My Dear Fritzie:

I have sent two letters home. This is just an edition of some of the things I am doing in Stockholm. As you will eventually receive the home letters.

We have enjoyed being at Uppsala, where we spent our first strenuous days. All the YMCA and YW sec'ys[18] went there. An old, old University town. Where we worked on reports, accounts, tended to clothes, etc.

---

17 A "waist" is a tailored button down blouse patterned after a man's shirt. Also known as a "shirtwaist."

18 "sec'y" is Clara's abbreviation for secretary. A YWCA Secretary was an employee with

Uppsala is one of the oldest cities in Sweden, one of the first capitals of the country, and there is located the second oldest University in the world, the oldest being in Italy. There are about 25,000 students, men and women who attend. The campus is lovely. The buildings are old and academic looking, and some are very fine. All Sweden is divided up into twelve "nations" or States. Each has its own clubhouse with one of the Professors elected by them, as a Patron. So each student upon entering the University is automatically a member of the "nation" from which he comes.

Last Thursday afternoon, the Arch Bishop and his wife gave an informal reception for us. Their palatial home is very lovely. I loved especially the three big rooms filled to the ceiling with books. On Monday night he is giving a musical for us.

The old church at Uppsala is where the kings and queens are buried. It is large and very beautiful. I have been living in a pension where I have enjoyed watching the customs of the household. All our errands and fix up of clothes are about done, so now we will give ourselves a week of pleasure and sightseeing. Three of us are going to plan to go to Copenhagen for two or three days this week, if we can get permission to go. Otherwise we shall spend the time in Stockholm and places nearby. If we do not get away to the north after next week, I fancy that we shall look up Russian language teachers and begin our studying again. I fancy it will be the last of October or November before we get down into Vologa, Vialka or Interior Russia.

This brief breathing spell is going to be awfully good for us all, for the winter in Russia, I am sure, will be very bad in every respect. My heart aches for what people are suffering there. I fear greatly for the men folk . . .

[end of letter fragment]

Sunday Sept. 29, 1918
Stockholm

Dearest Ones at Home:

Here I am still in Stockholm and how I have loved it. I finished up all my

---

extensive credentials and job description—she was not strictly an administrative support person.

work at Uppsala on the 12th and ever since have been here where I have lived at the hotel and shopped and played.

Really, I feel just as tho I had been let out of prison. The joy and enthusiasm which I thought Russian misery had crushed have all returned. You all would be horrified if you knew how much time, yea hours, that I have spent in hotel dining rooms and cafes. Read Lewis and I have tried them all. It seemed wonderful once more to get into a place where there was music and people all looked well and were really happy and carefree. I have fairly gorged myself on fruit and vegetables. I have stored up in my system all that it may require of the things I believe a system is supposed to need from these things.

The food situation is serious here, you can't get good rich deserts, much sugar and very little bread. About half a Vienna roll is our daily allowance. But the variety here is greater than we were able to get in Russia, tho very expensive. We live fairly modestly, but spend what is equivalent to $4 a day on just food.

A cable from NY tells us that supplies have been sent to Arkangel on the Red Cross boat. So we shall live well. One thing family dear, we are all wonderfully well. We have enough to eat, tho the variety is very limited and you need not worry. Our supplies from America help out wonderfully. I am often ashamed of how well I live when really there is so much of hunger about me.

Well, Wed. Oct. 2 I leave for Narvik, Norway. Think of it, crossing the Arctic circle, will go by boat to Murmansk and Arkangel. We hope to get thru and down into Siberia. If there is a lot of war work to be done in Arkangel, I will be there all winter. Otherwise we will go south sometime in Nov. or Dec. whenever it is possible.

The Ambassador, many other gov't officials, 30 YMCA men will be in Arkangel. Quite our Moscow, Petrograd people, several Bank men and Red Cross folk. I really am thrilled with the novelty of the trip. We shall have to be quite soldiers in the way we travel and live. We have added more blankets, woolen stockings, mittens, underwear, hoods, etc. suitable for the climate. My coats were both interlined warmer than before. So I feel well provided for the trip. The sweater from home will be waiting for me there. Oh I can hardly wait to get there. Just think, dear ones, the last letter from you was written Jan 10th. I did hope to have a cable here. But of course you didn't realize how very little I have heard from you. . . . I wonder how many of my letters you have rec'd. Well, write directly to Arkangel until we cable differently.

I would have cabled sooner, but you see it looked as tho I would return to Siberia via the States. I have passage engaged now for sailing home Oct 5th, Marcia and I. But today's cable from NY advises us to go north. So tomorrow will cancel the state room order. So I waited until we should know definitely. I would much prefer Archangel way, for the other trip would have been so very long and so hard. And I don't want two weeks at home at this time to interfere with a longer vacation a year from next summer.

Well Stockholm is lovely. So clean, and orderly and really very beautiful. I have taken Inter-urban [rail] trips into the country, boat trips to resorts, besides "doing" the city. Last night at four, six of us took the Inter-urban to Saltsjaboden where we climbed the hills and rocks until 6:30, when we returned to the hotel and ate a wonderfully good meal, ordered second helpings on deserts. A week ago today 4 of us took the boat to Vaxholm for an eight hour trip, exploring an island, visiting a military post, and home by moon light, passing thru rocky, pine covered islands. This country makes me think of the Georgian Bay region. It is so lovely. And just now everything is radiant in colors.

I attended the opera a couple of times hearing *Carmen* and *Lowengrin*, and also hearing *Hamlet*. None were very good.

We have gotten a few magazines and papers here, and how we have devoured them. Friday night I read the Aug. 10th *New Republic* from cover to cover including the advertisements.

If I were you send for the *New Republic*. They are printing some awfully good Russian stuff. Especially for me, please get the copy of either last of July or 1st August with the Ransome[19] article, and put away. It is very good.

Send me clippings of what Raymond Robins is writing and saying, and comments. Also Ross' book when it is published. We are going to cable NY to send us books on various phases of the war. We know absolutely nothing of what is being written and thought. Here, of course we have gotten a few magazines. We need current event magazines like the *New Republic*, *Digest*, etc.

---

19 Arthur Ransome. "On Behalf of Russia: An Open Letter to America." July 27, 1918. *The New Republic.*

Here I have bought Caryly's *French Revolution*, 4 novels of H. G. Wells and book of short stories by Anthony Hope. Each of us have bought books, and in Arkangel we will set up a library for Americans where we can each benefit by the books of others.

I have had a curious change of heart about the Russian language. Now I feel more eager than ever to talk it, and I don't feel it is so impossible. I want to get back to my study of it. It has helped me some here. Elizabeth and Cora,[20] my advice to you girls is, to begin the children on German or French this winter. Before they get an idea of its being difficult. I most certainly shall take up both French and German after I get along further with Russian. The men here who are speaking four and five different languages, are those who had both French and German when they were grade [school] children. If I knew German I could read the Scandinavian newspapers.

Half of our party left a week ago for Narvik. Our party is divided into three groups. I go with the second. It has been good to be here, but I am very eager to start again. I have played long enough.

I am sending two things for the auto. Everybody here carries their own butter box and usually sugar. I have two, one for butter when we can get it, and one for some marmalade which I am buying. We are allowed to buy only a very small amount. There seems to be more food in Copenhagen than in any of the countries. I did want to go down there, but could not arrange it.

Do write me lots of home news. Is George effected by the Draft law? Where is Genieve, how does Fritz like her association work. Do you drive the car? Are you, too, limited greatly on sugar. What is your impression of the Russian situation.

It is difficult to prophesy what will be next, but I think personally, the Bolsheviks will hold all west of the Volga this winter, and if they do, the suffering in Moscow and Petrograd and vicinity will be something awful. For they are cut off from fuel and food and raw materials. I shudder to think what suffering of cold and hunger there will be. We still have six Am. friends that we feel concerned about. Mr. Anderson, a prisoner of war worker, is in Moscow prison. The Petrograd YM man is in hiding. Two Consuls down in southern Russia are said to be in prisons, and Major Wardivell and Mr. Andrew of the Red Cross are still in Moscow. Mr. Andrew has been too ill to move away.

---

20 Elizabeth and Cora were Clara's sisters-in-law.

Isn't the war news wonderful now. I do hope we are seeing the beginning of the end. All Europe is so weary with having suffered so much. The Swedish people feel so resentful that we entered the war. Everything is so expensive. I really don't know how people live. Stockings $4 a pair and woolen ones on [ration] cards only.

Tell John I would like a finance statement of how I stand. I am wondering how long it will take me to get square with the world. I will try to have all of Dec. salary deposited at home.

Just think a year ago today I was half dead with sea sickness aboard the *Nippon Maru*, our 2nd day out.

With heaps and heaps of love from your ever affectionate,

Clara

Sept. 29, 1918
Stockholm

Dearest Sis and Geney:

How I wish we could sit down and visit. We would just stop the clock and take no account of time. So many hundreds of things happen these eventful days that I would love to share with you.

Really during the last five or six months, I have had almost as much thrilling excitement as most people have in their whole life. Sitting in on a Revolution is exciting to say the least. All summer, there just being Helen and myself in Moscow, we were so on the inside of things in all phases of the work. And it was wonderful to be doing the Industrial Survey work, and getting hold of information which the gov't officials needed. My report has been sent to the [US] State Dep't. Had I any idea that it would have been asked for, I should have written it quite differently. Some day I shall write about the Bolsheviki Industrial Organization. I wrote the report with only the view of being useful to [the YWCA office in] New York, as one important phase of our work.

I am thrilled when I realize the tremendous work that anybody with ability will be able to do in Russia, when life becomes somewhat normal. But Oh, Girls, that isn't going to be for a long time. I prepare you for a horrible bloody pogrom of Jews, when the reaction comes and also of

Bolsheviki. Peace may come to the warring nations, but not soon in Russia. There, war will continue, and I am wondering if, when Germany finds her ambitions lost by this war—if after peace—she won't systematically strengthen herself in Russia. What a muddle the world is in. I often wonder what the Americans at home read about Russia. We nearly explode with wrath at some of the articles that have gotten thru to Russia.

Well I wish I could describe the intimate life we have with all Am. here. Our traveling in special trains makes for the most wholesome comradeship and I am so glad to say we have won the admiration of the men in being awfully good sports. No matter what the difficulties are, there has never been a murmur from us. And it is because we have proven ourselves so splendidly, that we are permitted to proceed to Arkangel. There we shall probably all do war work in hostess houses for the American troops. Helen is not returning to the States but will do war work in Russia. Two of our seven sec'ys will be married in the spring to two YMCA men. All the men have lots of fun at our expense. I know that I have caused sufficient amount of speculation for Read and I have been together lots during the summer, and very much since our evacuation began in August. But there is nothing more than thoroughly enjoying doing the same things. Life will probably be awfully interesting if I remain in Arkangel all winter. But when the other sec'ys come over for work, I will be in the first party to go [home]. Where I shall be, goodness only knows. Ekatreinburg, Omsk, Viatka or maybe Irkuts. If the Volga cities fall in Allies hands, I probably shall return to Nijni Novgorod. But send mail c/o of Consul or Embassy Arkangel and cable there also, for they will know my whereabouts when I leave.

In my box in the attic, Sis, is my leather case for traveling. I have needed it so much. Will you send when you send lace waist and new Georgette. If it doesn't cost too much, please send 4 yards of black meline for a scarf for the evening dress. That dress isn't very satisfactory. It needs relief from so much pink. 2 yds here or in Russia would cost $6–$8. Since Helen is remaining, I need another suit of silk and wool underwear, if you can send over to me. We are cabling the National Board for certain stock supplies such as handkerchiefs, stocking, etc. Geney, if at any time you see a pretty blue georgette like your dark blue, be sure and get it for me. In the spring I shall need one, as my velvet is too warm and too dressy for the kind of wear I should give it. When this blue silk goes to pieces, I don't know what

I shall do, if I cannot replace it. But maybe by spring things will change and it will be easier getting things. Our baggage problem becomes an ever-increasing problem.

When you must carry your bedding, and your food, and food stores and dishes every time you move, and more and more we are reducing to hand luggage. You can imagine what we look like. I have sold one trunk, but still have six pieces to look after every time I move. They are 2 enormous suitcases, one trunk, bed roll, dunnage bag, and food box and small suitcase. When I return home, it certainly will look like a Russian immigrant entering America. All that will be lacking will be the Samovar.

I shall need a hundred calling cards. I think the plate is at the Breeze office. There will be sec'ys coming from Am. I imagine within the next few months. Or YMCA and Red Cross supplies.

Sept. 30

Well, I have just returned from visiting a settlement where I saw and talked to an interesting group of cigar factory girls and have had coca and little cakes at a French restaurant. We all have eaten so much that we are uncomfortable most of the time. I am taking back a small box of apple butter.

I have boughten woolen hood, scarf, mittens and made all necessary arrangements for warm clothing. My white wristlets will be fine, Sis.

We leave here Wed. night Oct. 7; arrive Narvik Friday, leave Sat. night on boat going thru the Fjord to Kirkiness, thence to Murmansk and finally to Arkangel, hoping to arrive there about the 16–18th of October. We are not sure that we can come down, and if we cannot, Marcia and I shall return to Siberia by US and I shall get to see you all. Sometime about January first. Of course we are devoutly hoping to get thru. This trip will be a very great experience and qualify me for the Arctic Circle Club.

Poor Muriel Heap, one of our sec'ys, received a cable today, telling of her mother's death. She probably will go to France to join her sister and brother there. We are so sorry to see her go. She is one of the engaged girls. Her family should have cabled the truth to her several weeks ago for she has worried terribly, and two months ago her mother died. The first cable made us all suspect that it was not quite frank, and two days from now we would have been started north and cable connections not reliable until Arkangel.

Now girls dear, don't think that I am doing the heroic thing by returning.

I am perfectly safe, and will be in Russia. There is absolutely no cause for worry at any time. Even tho I will be where it is not possible to get mail or send mail. So do not worry for one moment. Am sorry to have to send for muff. They are terribly expensive here. The prices are unbelievable. I don't know how people live.

I will write again from Narvik. Do send me a cable at Arkangel before I get shut off again from the world.

A world of love to you both dear sisters, from your ever affectionate sister,

Teke

I am so grateful for all the shopping you dear ones are doing for me from time to time. I guess you think I don't know my own mind from one letter to the other, but Helen's remaining has made a difference in my needs as I bought several of her things which I returned. The box at Arkangel will give me more happiness that you can possibly imagine, for it is a direct contact with home. Send mail c/o of the Consulate in Arkangel.

I am writing Fritz on train to Narvik. The cable which I am sending today Oct. 1st. "Glorious month Sweden leaving October 3 Narvik, Murmansk arriving Arkangel 16. Warm equipment, plenty food/send mink muff. High spirits. Love."

Love dear girls from

Teke

Oct. 4, 1918

Narvik, Norway

Where is George this winter. Did my letter regarding things I send home get thru.

Dearest Fritz:

It is eleven thirty p.m. but I am going to get a letter started tonight for tomorrow is planned pretty full. Well, little did we think that when we were packing my things for Russia a year ago, that now once more I should be on my way there. The past month has gone so quickly and I know that it has done me a world of good being in Sweden. At first I was very much disappointed because I couldn't return on the first party, which sailed from here a week ago, but the extra time in Stockholm was worth the delay.

We—the four of us—and six YMCA men left Stockholm Wednesday night. The trip up to Boden was the same as when we came from Harparando. But I enjoyed it all again very much. This morning early, we ran thru the swampy rather bare and flat country, but by ten we came in sight of the mountains. From there until here it was glorious. The trees are golden, the grass and shrubbery red, with the highest mts. snow capped. Constantly beautiful clear lakes come into sight and finally the Fjord on which we shall sail out on. We went thru innumerable tunnels and snow sheds.

It took us a very short time to go thru the customs at the Border. The examination was very superficial, as of course a party like ours would have nothing dutiable or that would be confiscated.

Narvik is a quaint town built right in the mts. We visited the stores today, making a few purchases in food stuffs for our journey.

Tomorrow we will climb one of the mts. which towers just above our hotel. We intended going this afternoon but it was too rainy. Two more of our party join us tomorrow at noon, and at four thirty we take a small steamer until 6 a.m. Sunday morning when we take the big steamer. Just how long we shall be, I don't know, probably not more than eight or ten days. We had expected to go to Murmansk, first, but rec'd telegraph instructions that we probably would go straight from Vardo to Arkangel.

I am curious to see Arkangel. I have heard so much about it. Of course there are lots of British and American troops there now. We have heard many conflicting reports as to the number. If the way is not open down to Viathka [Volodga?], we may remain in Arkangel all winter, especially if there is war work to be done. Marcia Dunham and I will be the first to go down when the way is open. I sure do long to get back to Moscow, where so much work awaits us. It is just possible that if we cannot get thru, that two of us will return to Siberia via the States. In that case I might have Xmas dinner at home.

Today we saw our first Laplanders. They were small, stocky men, with curious packs on their shoulders and wear fur shoes. It is curious that it should be so mild here when you consider how far north this is.

Fritz, how goes the work, I know the people are just crazy about you. And I know there are parts of the work which you love and some that you do not like. On the whole, I think you will come to enjoy it more and more all the time.[21]

What great talk "fests" we shall have, when I return home. The next year and a half will go by rapidly. A year from May I want to start for home. I can see myself now going to the various conferences and talking about Russia.

Poor Russia, there is no place in the world where there is such keen suffering. My heart aches for all those who live east of the Volga. The world outside gets so little authentic news. It is almost like being interned in a prison camp. For weeks before we left, we had almost no news from the outside world. But in spite of the isolation we are glad to be going back. And surely there are still darker days to follow when the Bolsheviki gov't gives way. The counter Revolutionists will know no mercy. There will be pogroms that will shock the whole world. All classes of Russian people have much to learn before they come to realize that a permanent working gov't must include representatives of all classes. The Bourgeois still wish to be considered the representative class, the Proletariat say they alone are fit for gov't, and neither of these two extremes have much use for the so called Intelligentsia class, which truly has no other class in the world quite like it. It has a different meaning as used in Russia than anywhere else. They represent many fine people of the so-called middle class, and yet they cannot be compared with our middle class folk. Undoubtedly they are to blame for some of what is occurring now. I look for several more Revolutions before things settle down. The next five years will witness great political changes. I really think the time is passed for a Monarchy now. It was almost unbelievable how very little stir the killing of the Czar made. People had, of course, been thru so much, and the absorbing and terrifying problem to all is getting bread. Everything else, no matter how serious or important, becomes comparatively insignificant in the light of possible starvation.

Well, it rained all night and is still pouring. A heavy mist covers the

---

21 Fritz ("Fritzie") White was a close friend of Clara's and had begun working for the YWCA soon after Clara left for Russia in 1917.

mts. so we have had a nice fire and have been spending the morning doing a lot of personal things.

You will be glad to know that all my supplies are holding out splendidly. Soap lasts for ever here, because Russia is really very clean. Almost no smoke. So neither our selves or our clothes get grimy and dirty. Everything else is holding out very well. My blue suit which I bought just before I left is not satisfactory and I would have given much for a dark wool jersey cloth dress, for it would have been ideal for so much traveling and packing. I hope everything that I have now will be worn out when I come home, so I can buy just the most practical and suitable kind of things for Russia. I had the fur coat shortened and belt put on it. A fur lined coat is what we all should have had. How are your sisters Fritz? Give them my love and write me via Arkangel the news, both family and about your work. I have thought of you so very much.

The war is going to be over soon, I feel sure, and then everyone can settle down again to normal living, altho I feel sure that good permanent changes will come to America. We will make great strides towards democracy ourselves. Especially along Industrials lines. I am so eager to know what Raymond Robins is saying, so send me clippings from papers.

This is as much as any censor wants to read at one time. With a great heart full of love, sister dear, from your affectionate,

Clara

Oct. 9, 1918
Kirkenes, Norway

My Dear Ones at Home:

If you received my cablegram you are wondering just where in the Arctic regions I am tonight and how I am finding things.

To begin with the boat journey. We left Narvik Saturday Oct. 5 at 4:30 in a misty, cold drizzle. The mist was not so thick, however, but what we could see something of the beautiful wooded mounts on both sides of the Fjord. The mounts are not so grand as the Rockies, but beautiful in their foliage now, of all the rich colors of brown and yellow, that you can imagine. Sunday at four a.m. we were all up and dressed at Logdengen where we left the smaller boat to embark on the *Kacrou Jad*, a longer boat starting from further south. All day Sunday the sun shone. The highest mts were snow capped, and on both sides of the Fjord. It was wonderful at Harstad, where we stopped three hours. We climbed a small mt where we had a great view. It was mild so we had on just our ordinary coats. We have not had out our fur coats yet. Then the sunset. I shall never forget it. The reflection on the snow capped mts gave such unusual colors in reds and yellows. And the reflection on the water was remarkable. I know now that my appreciation of Art has been greatly enhanced. There are many water and mt pictures that I now can appreciate. We came into Tromson about seven. It made me think of Duluth as the city with its tiers of lights loomed up on the low mountainside. Then Sunday, being beautifully clear, the northern lights came out in such aweing splendor. At times, the whole heavens was lighted up with rays or paths of lights over the water. At one time, the light burst forth like sky rockets that burst into many sprays with delicate greens and pinks. Then a thick cotton-like wave curled across the heavens like an immense serpent.

Monday morning we stopped at a small fishing village, where just across the harbor loomed up a wonderful glacier. All that day we saw snowcapped mts and a number of glaciers. But the day for the most part was quite gray. We struck the open sea, when all were put to the test as sailors, for we are on a very small freighter. With very excellent cabin arrangements. Two of the men and I stood up in the bow for several hours. When and where we fed the fishes. I was not ill, however, and felt fine the rest of the day being able to eat my other two meals and keep them down.

Hammerfest was really a nice place, we reached there about 4 p.m. Read and I struck out on a mountain road and climbed up where we got a wonderful view, getting back about six thirty. All these towns are fishing towns for the most part. The ports never close and it does not get very cold. A little below zero. Most of the houses are big three story frame houses, with one main street, and several general stores. Always the harbors are filled with boats of every size and description. Those with riggings are the most picturesque.

Well, Tuesday, we none of us shall ever look back on with pleasure as sailors. We were still in port when we breakfasted. Then I dressed warm and went on deck. Altho we rode the waves, [they were] sliding, not whopping big ones. I felt fine, I spent several hours on the bow. It was curious, as long as I sang I was alright. I hummed every thing I knew, and improvised and composed. At noon we were again in port, and ate. Altho nearly everyone was horribly miserable and the northern-most cape in open sea was to be rounded. For two hours Don Laurie, Read and I held forth in the bow, where the wind blew a furious gale and where we got the benefit of the riding of the waves. The water was a steel gray, and angry looking, with choppy waves all white capped. The cape was a solid wall of barren, ragged, jagged rocks. Off to the north we could see North Cape. When darkness came, I had to go below. Everybody had gone to their cabins or were stretched out in the Dining Room salon. Read and I sat down to play cards but before we could even shuffle them, we decided it was too uninteresting and each took to our cabins. I stretched out on the couch instead of climbing up into my upper berth as I should have. I fell to sleep, immediately, a kindly way nature has of taking care of the utterly wretched. At ten when the maid called us for supper, (we were in port) I found the other three girls likewise dressed in their berths, and there we stayed until five this morn-ing. Several times in the night I awoke and wished that somebody would kindly remove my shoes for me, but I hadn't sense enough to ring for the maid. Read was the only one on board who was able to eat his supper that night. It was the only meal that I missed. Tonight poor Marcia is dreadfully ill, but I think she will sleep it off.

This morning Wed. at 5:30, Marcia, Read and I explored Vardo in the drizzling rain. We didn't mind a bit, for we all were so glad to be on land and to walk. We had hoped to get a boat there, an English freighter. But as there wasn't a single place in the town for us to stay and no boats, we came on here to Kirkenes. But while we were there in port, two camouflaged British freighters came into port from Archangel. Since we have been in more or less of a bay, we have had a calm day altho everyone is feeling a bit wretched. If we were on a bigger boat we wouldn't feel the constant throbbing of the machinery and the never ceasing pulsing motion. We came into port here at four and hope to get a freighter with its convoy some time within a couple or three days. Here it is mild as an early spring day. Misty and soft. The town as much as we have seen of it, looks like one of our north western 'mushroom mining towns'. It gives every evidence of being prosperous, with hopeful outlooks. A new iron ore mine was recently opened which has accounted for its rapid recent growth.

On the streets we hear Russian and French spoken. An English Vice Consul and an American Lieutenant have been looking after our welfare and advising us about things in general.

We saw quite a number of Laps in the street with their picturesque coats with bright red trimmings. Really, my high light brown boots cause as much attention and interest as these people do for me. Last winter in Moscow, I was always conscious that my feet betrayed me as being a foreigner when I wore these yellow shoes. My but they have been a joy, for only heavy boots can long withstand the cobblestone of Russia and these "sidewalk-less" towns.

Here in Kirkenes, our party of 14 are quite scattered over the town. We four girls have two rooms in the "big" hotel. We are on the 4th floor and may have to sleep two in each of the very narrow little white beds. The men are scattered about the town. Four, I fear, may sleep on the floor tonight. All come to our hotel for their meals, where the foreign consuls and various officials eat. 8 o'clock is late but usual hour for supper.

On the boat we have had good meals, but surely and certainly are bringing us back to what will be our Russian diet of meat potatoes and cabbage. We have had enough bread. We still must use bread cards everywhere. Tonight all of us are going to see an American moving picture show, altho all of us have "swimming" heads.

We all of us are longing to get to Arkangel soon and have the march over. If we get a big freighter it will be alright but if a trawler, Oh me Oh my! This crowd is delightful as no one has for a moment set up any false pretenses about sea sickness, all admit it, very frankly.

Thurs. Oct. 10

Well, the French movie was very entertaining and a good nights sleep has put us all on our land legs again. Marcia woke up feeling fine. It is raining, so think we shall not do much exploring. The streets and walks (there are no real sidewalks) are a sea of black mud. The men have gone to learn if we may go through the iron mine if we have time. We still hope the British freighters will come today. Two were due yesterday, their trawlers for convoy are awaiting them here. Another freighter came in from Arkangel last night so we are hopeful of getting out today.

Mr. Hatfield has just come in to announce that in an hour's time, all who wish may leave on a little train for the iron mine where we will spend three hours. The hotel people being willing to delay dinner from two until three thirty.

Oh family, I just wish that so many many weeks didn't have to pass before this reaches you. So you could know how well, and how happy I am and what wonderful very wonderful opportunities I am enjoying. Whoever would have dreamed when I left home for Russia of the great experiences that would be crowd into one brief year. Time has seemed short, but I have seen so much, events have crowded upon each other so rapidly, that I feel as tho I had lived a lifetime. I warn you, that everybody who left for Russia last fall has aged somewhat.

4:30 and dark

Well, I have had one glorious five mile walk out to the iron mine. When it came time to go, we loafed until we missed the train, so Read and I struck out. It was as balmy and soft as a spring day. I walked with my blue coat open and free and was too warm. The mts are low and rocky with very interesting rock formations. Lovely stratified rocks. Its quite shale-y about the mine. We couldn't find anyone who could talk English, so we wandered about looking into some of the open pits. Then we returned to the one little general store where they boiled six big eggs for us and gave us bread and butter. We had to bolt it up in ten minutes because we had to take the train which brought us back to Kirkenes.

Since dinner the three British freighters have arrived, and we have met the charming old sea captain. He is kindly, hospitable, but feels that he has very little in the way of accommodations to offer. But we have assured him that we are equal to anything. All we ask is space to sleep. We four women are to go with him, while the ten men of our party, with twelve Russian, two French men and several Swedes must rough it on the deck of one of the four convoy trawlers. They are little things and the sea is big, rough and cold. I truly feel sorry for them for we have suffered so much on the last little boat and these trawlers are only 1/4th the size. It doesn't seem quite right just because we are women, that we should always have the best and most consideration.

I wish you could see our zebra boat. I shall feel as tho I were with Captain Spike on a pirate boat. Oh I wish we had a lot of danties to give to our Captain host, he is so nice.

The British Consul has just told us that the Red Cross ship has safely reached Arkangel so my things from home will be there to gladden my heart. If you ever have chances to send me things always send some sweet chocolate. Not Hershey or Peters, but Bakers or other's sweetened chocolate bars. It keeps better and is better as food for our needs. Buy me goodies, raisins, figs, dates, prunes, chocolate, etc. and charge to my acc't or John can draw for it. Fritz's lovely date sticks would keep but I suppose that would take too much sugar. We never get fig cookies or crackers of any sort here, cakes and cookies yet belong to memory.

This will reach you about Thanksgiving time. It brings a heart full of love and greetings and a desire that you all should know that I am well, never was better in my life. For two months have done little else than play out of doors, am fit for any and all emergencies which may be before me in Russia and be sure that letters are being sent on every possible mail and I will cable often. And you family dear, send me cables often, for I rarely ever hear from you. And when we get down into Interior Russia news again will be difficult to receive. Send mail by Arkangel until Jan. and longer, unless we cable to the contrary. Am cabling you again on my safe arrival in Arkangel, there are 140,000 people there now.

A world of love to each and every one, from your ever affectionate one, now in the Arctic regions, lovingly,

Clara

Oct. 14, 1918
Arctic Ocean Onboard the *Clysdale*
Monday, one o'clock

My dear John:

Your imagination would certainly be put to a fine test if you could see where I am this minute. I am sitting where I can guard three hatchways in the first hole down. These hatchways lead to lower regions where there is a store of rum. A fine occupation for a YWCA sec'y!

This trip is wonderfully delightful. I am having the jolliest kind of a time. At four o'clock Saturday afternoon we were brought over with baggage to this curious camouflaged freighter. Us four women and 3 YM men and Read Lewis. The other four men are on another ship. After supper, the captains of our four big freighters and two convoys came out to our ship for a conference. So we all accepted the invitation of one of the other captains and rowed over to the other ship where the rest of our party is hospitably quartered. It was great sport descending the rope ladders down the sides of these giant boats. Of course they are all in darkness. They are so pirate looking anyway, in their present paint, that I felt as tho I really had joined Captain Kidd and was off to steal and loot.

The other boat had a piano, so we sang, and had a spread, returning to our dark ship at one o'clock.

Our captain had given us a stateroom where two sleep, while the other two of us girls sleep in the dining salon and very comfortably, too.

The four men sleep in the dining room of the petti officers when they are not on guard. This ship of ours, besides carrying rum, is loaded with high explosives. Just before the ship reached Kirkenes, the crew had broken into the rum and went on one grand jag. So our men were allowed to come on this ship provided they would do guard duty of the rum. Which means sitting down here. At night they have a lantern, and now, I am sitting right under the open hatchway where both light and air is good, and where there is no motion whatever of the boat. I am relieving one of the men so they can eat together. We eat with the captain and the first officers, and are served before the other dining room (our food is the same). So that accounts for my guarding the rum.

Sunday morning I was up at five, and I shall never forget it. We were just raising anchor in the Kirkenes harbor. The sky was tinted with the first pink rays of sunlight. The mountains were gloriously silhouetted against a perfectly clear sky and the water seemed almost as blue as the Pacific. As the sun finally appeared above the tops of the mts, it flooded the harbor with red and gold. In such a glory, our little fleet of four ships and two trawlers put out into the Arctic sea.

Our ship leads. It is not only the fastest, but has the mine sweepers. The other three cargo boats fell behind us, with the trawlers some ways out on both sides of us. On the stern there is mounted a gun, with its ever watchful guards—two men from this navy.

Most of the men in our present crew have been on torpedo boats, we have discussed mines and torpedoes, quite frankly for of course you cannot forget them. But no one is afraid and the trawlers will pick us up of we go down. Only of course, if a torpedo hit this boat with its present cargo, there won't be any gathering up of the strewn.

Sunday, our first day out, was as perfect a fall day as I have ever known. It was quite unbelievable. We sat out on deck the entire day, and without steamer rugs. The air, while bracing, was lovely. The sun warm, we sat and read and wrote and walked all day. Unable ourselves to realize that it could be so lovely so far north. On the other boat, one of the men was quite sea sick. We talked to the other by the signals of the wooden arms [semaphore], of course we were not close enough to talk by voice.

7:30

After lunch we amused the crew considerably by a lively game of cross tag. It has been a grey day. So we have had to take more exercises to keep warm, and to help us take care of the heavy food which we are eating. These three days on this British boat have given me a taste of Anglo Saxan [Saxon] meals. I fairly gasped when I beheld white bread on the Captain's table. We have had real oatmeal for breakfast, and oh such very good things to eat, and all we could eat. Everyone exclaims how fat I am getting. I certainly have not felt so well in several years. But when you realize that for two months I have done very little but loaf and eat, some good ought to come from it. We are all wary, however, of losing so much time, when there is a need of doing so much. I hope we shall find a tremendous amount of work to do to make up for all this long traveling.

This afternoon, we were invited down to have tea with the men. We read the August *Century* aloud and enjoyed it immensely. At Stockholm we were able to pick up a few late American magazines. About four it began raining, and since the wind has grown constantly higher, now our windows are rattling. I fear we are to have a taste of Arctic on the rampage. It is time for the equinoxial storms. Tomorrow morning, we may be scattered more than we were this [morning]. For of course with not a ray of light, it is quite impossible for us to keep perfectly together.

Tonight while I was down in the hole again, while the men were at supper, I had a great visit with one of the stokers. For nine years he has stoked furnaces in seas all over the world. All of these men have great admiration for Lord George, and not much for Askquith. And they certainly are not greatly in favor of women suffrage for English women.

Tonight we girls are reading and writing at the big table in the salon. Fire burns in an open grate fire, and Mike, the Captain's Irish terrier, is sleeping before it. Two Chinese cooks look after our meals and few wants. We have enjoyed their meals so much, that I think they are quite putting themselves to their uttermost to feed us and certainly they have a great variety.

Tomorrow, Tues. morning, we reach the entrance of the White Sea and there our real danger from mines and submarines begins. Only, of course, we do not expect anything to happen to us. We shall get to the entrance where we shall anchor for the night. Then the next morning with our river pilot and the tide with us, we shall go the twenty miles up the [Dvina] River to Arkangel.

How we wish we could know what awaited us there. Whether the way is open down into Russia, or if we shall be busy with war work in Arkangel all winter. We are so eager to arrive, and learn all that may await us there. The first party were fortunate in getting a Russian steamer at Vardo straight for Arkangel. So they have been there about ten days, and doubtlessly have found a place for us to live. It will be good to see American troops there and also get to where we can receive news. Every day now is filled with such giant thrillers, but almost no news reaches us. Everyone up here is very hopeful that the war will be over by Xmas.

Tuesday evening, Oct. 15th, 7 o'clock

When we got up this morning we were in the White Sea. The sea was lovely. The waves were broken and white capped. The water a deep dull gray, while the sky was covered with heavy fluffy but broken clouds, so we had the promise of a fair day. The sailors do not like a clear bright sunshine. By nine o'clock we were out on deck for exercise. We played hopscotch and later a game of cards. Just to get our hand in, for tonight we are to play with the captain. We were glad to cross the neck of water and come into sight of the other side of our coast. About four we raised our mine sweepers and it is good to see the mast lights on the boats in our little fleet. It is not comfortable to travel the seas with absolutely no light. All danger seems to be passed us for now.

We will anchor within the hour and await for our pilot who we take on at a light house tomorrow morning. So we ought to reach Arkangel about twelve o'clock, or there about.

Tonight when I was guarding the rum, I had another long talk with my stoker friend. Fourteen of these poor fellows are terribly worried as to what is to be done with them, for the thirty six gallons of rum which they got away with.

The officers are great admirers of Roosevelt, and now of Wilson. They thought that Hughes and Bryan were in favor of the Germans. They are eager to have Sir Edward Gray one of the representatives at the Peace Conference. The bitterness of the seamen against Germany is very real and deep. They would gladly see five years discrimination made against Germany, commercially. The British had lost fifteen thousand men from the merchant marine alone. Last night at High Tea they were telling us of one of their friends who had been torpedoed seventeen times. He was on the *Lusitania*.

We are going to have a real lark tonight. At midnight the eight of us, and the captain, if he will join us, are going down to have a spread in the hole where the men are guarding the rum. We are going to have George Washington coffee, fruit, Swedish knackebrod, jam and perhaps sardines. All of us have lived so much on cheese and sardines that we are awfully tired of it.

Captain Chevim has just come in and reports that we are anchored near a light boat, so that all our little fleet are near together, and at six a.m. the pilot will come aboard and take us up the final lap. By light signals, the first mate, Mr. Wats, has talked with the Captain of the *Meadosly* where the other four of our party are housed. We invited him and the others to come over but they have decided that it is too much trouble to lower their boat and come over to see us.

Tomorrow we shall have a happy reunion with all our friends. There are about fifteen in the first party [that arrived].

We are all counting on finding lots of mail up there. Undoubtedly February and all our summer mail, unless sent by Vladivostok, will be there. Three months ago we learned that there were two tons of mail held up at Murmansk and Arkangel.

Tonight the first mate told me that the average temperature for this trip has been 37°. So you see how really comfortable it has been.

You boys must write me the latest political news, for we know so little here. Of course if I am in Arkangel all winter, we shall be where we can get world news. How we long to know what is actually taking place in Soviet territory, especially in Moscow and Petrograd. What little we saw in the Swedish papers we didn't believe. We have so many, many friends about whom we are concerned.

This will probably reach you about Thanksgiving time. How I wish I could be at home. It would be such a joy to talk over with you all the exciting events of the past year. My! When I stop to think of it, it doesn't seem possible, that so much could have happened in so short a time. What this second year holds in store for us, there is no telling, but certainly it doesn't mean peace for Russia. It may witness one or two more important Revolutions.

Am struggling with Carlyle's *French Revolution*, but it is difficult reading. I do hope to get some good reading done this winter, I did so little last year. And now five months have gone by since I have had a language lesson. It has been quite impossible to accomplish much during various journeys.

Thursday, Oct. 17th

Well, here I am at my destination, we had our spread in the petti officer's dining room. The captain enjoyed it very much. He said it was his first spread.

We arrived at noon, but did not get off with our baggage until four.

We had a joyous meeting and oh, family dear, the trunk from Am. was here. The rose sweater is lovely, beautiful, and the candy, well it is too good to be true. It will give pleasure to so many. I have put away a 3 lb. box for Xmas and 2 lbs. for Holiday, and the bars for use along as needed. The rubbers are too small—5½ needed. I will sell and buy a pair here. One pair will cost 140 rubles. I will sell these for enough to buy the others. Thanks so very much for your loving thoughtfulness. Will write about things here, in my next. Probably, I shall be here all winter.

A heart full of love from your happy and grateful sister,

Teke   Clara I. Taylor

Sat. Oct. 19, 1918
Where is Genieve?

My dear Mary:

This has to be just business. On receipt of this, please send my white lace waist to Miss M. Sandum 417 So. 10th Street, Minneapolis to be made into pretty waist, if she thinks it is usable. She is not to use it, if she thinks it too heavy. In that case I want two Georgette waists, white, size 40, as they shrink.

I wish Miss Sandum to make me a very pretty dark blue Georgette crepe dress. Sleeves lined with net or something, "V" shaped neck rather than square. Skirt length 36½ in front. A dress I shall wear for informal teas, etc., a practical dress, but not too plain.

It will need to be made at once and sent to New York. If the other secretaries come, they can bring. We have cabled for supplies, so I think things will get here, and if you have not sent, send one more union suit, silk and wool.

Tell Miss Sandum, my pongee[22] was too severe, a dress much like the Alice blue she made is more becoming. Lace waist, V-front also.

Be sure to include the black meline [fabric] which I wrote for, 4 yds for evening dress. (Miss Sandum would buy. It is for scarf.)

Have *New Republic, Digest Colliers,* or *America,* or some other magazine sent here. I will be here all winter, and mail will reach us here regularly, and I can send out one letter a week also. Do not send mail via Vladivostok. We shall be doing war work here all this winter. We receive army rations, and are now laying in a supply of vegetables that keep during winter. There is no cause for anxiety about any of us. It is

---

22 Pongee is a light tan colored, thin, soft clothing fabric woven from uneven threads of raw silk.

not too cold, we are nicely located. Will open our own hostess house for American soldiers soon, as well as working with YMCA in canteen work and hospital visitations.

Attending the regular Sat. ambassadorial tea this p.m. There are a lot of fine interesting people here. So far about 9 Am. women, two of whom are fine Red Cross nurses.

Sweater is lovely. The things that came to me were:

Rose sweater

Passport pictures and ribbon

2 pair glasses

4 pair rubbers

Hylers candy. Oh, so good.

Will write next week of how we are living and all about us. You should see how fat I am. My two months loafing certainly did wonders for me.

There was no mail here for me. Sorry we shall not be in Moscow again this winter, but since I cannot, am awfully glad to be here. It will be a wonderful year.

Please send me financial statement of cost of things. You can buy practically nothing here. Include five spools of cotton thread and assorted needles.

Love to you all from your affectionate sister,

Clara I. Taylor

Did my things and list of distribution reach you?

Diary
September 12 – October 16, 1918

September 12, 1918, Uppsala

Thurs. Wild scramble getting reports done and cake for luncheon. 33 of us sat down for dinner at hotel as farewell to Mr. Cotton. Christy & Fellows attended reception at palatial home of the Arch Bishop and visited some of the Uni. buildings. Learned about the servants school.

September 13, 1918, Stockholm

Fri. Nearly all went in on early train. Tended to shopping, had lovely dinner in the evening. All of us took Murial & Katchia to hear *Carmen*. Stockholm lovely. Good news on Western front, but discouraging in Russia.

September 14, 1918, Stockholm

Visited Gallery, got new passport. Long interview with Mr. Jenkins about report. News that probably it will be some time before we shall leave Sweden. Several sailing for home.

September 15, 1918, Uppsala

Spent entire day resting up. Cold & gray day. In evening all of us went to supper together. Word came that we would leave for the North on the 23rd.

September 16, 1918, Uppsala

Mon. Spent day shopping & mending & re-packing for week in Stockholm. Very cold gray day. In evening went to Uni to hear Prof. Caryle [?] lecture. Austria offers peace terms.

September 17, 1918, Stockholm

Came into city. Spent morning getting Room and getting news at Legation. Had lunch with Bess & Marcia. Met Read at 6 for dinner. Spent entire evening until 11 in Café visiting.

September 18, 1918, Stockholm

Spent morning at Legation getting news. Met R. L. went to Grand Hotel for dinner, to Northern Museum in afternoon; after supper we went to station to get off home mail. Good news on Western Front.

September 19, 1918, Stockholm
Thurs. Eliz & I did old port city. Met R. L. for luncheon & took Interurban [light rail road] into resort district for long walk, attended two new operas in evening. Still no cable news from home or N.Y. to any of people. ["Paradid Foyer" inserted between lines.]

September 20, 1918
Fri. Helen & I went shopping for her, buying things for Arkangel trip. Muriel called home. R. L., Helen & I went to Hotel Grand for dinner, then to see the Publicity offices. Still no cable news

September 21, 1918, Stockholm
Sat. Shopped at a.m. Met R. L. at — took Interurban to Saltojbodum [?] Wonderful climb over rocks & glorious sunset. Had dinner at hotel, walked home thru narrow streets of the Inner city. Saw two acts of *Hamlet* & then home.

September 22, 1918, Stockholm
Sun. Helen & I worked madly on her acct's. Met Jerome & Read at Legation, went to Vaxholen at 1:00—climbed rocks. Ate 2 desserts at hotel. Took wrong boat and went to military island, saw concealed fortress. Ate dinner on boat coming home. Glorious day.

September 23, 1918, Stockholm
Mon. Spent a.m. doing accounts. All lunched at Nordiska. Decided on Narvck route. Read discouraging news about Russia. Read L. & I shopped for books, then went to the theatre cafe for dinner & home at 9. Everybody getting anxious to move on.

September 24, 1918, Stockholm
Tues. Engaged passages home for Marcia & me. All ate at Nordiska at noon. Marcia & Bess left for Uppsala. J. D. Hel O., J. Cran, F. Leza, Rays, Read & I had dinner Opera Cafe. Encouraging Russian news. *Lohengrin* in evening, not very good.

September 25, 1918

Wed. Met Nina—arranged passport matters, got her home to Uppsala at 5:05! First party left for Narvarik. Moved into Excelior [Hotel]. Dinner with Jerome. 20,000 Amer. troops reported by Mr. Poole in Arkangel.[23]

September 26, 1918, Stockholm

Thurs. Glorious day; visited bath & shampoo'd. Did errands with Marcia. Had afternoon tea with Mr. Foster & Russian woman. Marcia, Read & I had dinner at the Strand Hotel. Made out R. shopping list.

September 27, 1918, Stockholm

Friday Spent morning shopping with Marcia, ate lunch R. L. and shopped in afternoon. Marcia & I read aloud *New Republic* in the evening. A glorious day. Everybody eager to go north.

September 28, 1918, Stockholm

Sat. Called on Factory Inspector, Mr. Lamb at YWCA in afternoon. at 4 R. L., Marcia, Ralph, Rhe & Brasket & I went Saltjoboden for tramps [a family word for a short hike or walk, e.g."tramping around"] & dinner. Walked thru Inner City, had ice cream at Opera cafe. Bulgarians suing for peace. Everything seems to favor Allies.

September 29, 1918, Stockholm

Sun. Attended Eng Church, visited city missions. Rec'd cables at Legation. Met Read for dinner at Roseboden Hotel. Wrote letters & cards in evening. R. and I had supper at Excelsior. Wrote home mail.

September 30, 1918, Stockholm

Mon. Shopped with Marcia. Lunched with Read. He left for Norway—In evening Ralph, Muriel, Marcia & I went to hotel for big feed. Worked & packed until 2 a.m. Last day in Stockholm. sent cable home.

MEMORANDA [signature of the captain of the mine sweeper ship]
October 1918
J. T. Cheavms
10 Western Hill Sunderland
S.S. "Clydesdale"

---

23 In fact, only 5,500 US troops were sent to serve in the North Russian Expeditionary Force.

October 1, 1918, left for boat, Uppsala

Tues. Wed. Left on early train for Uppsala. Repacked. Had lunch at 4 with Miss Shorler. At 6:20 ten of us left for Narvick. Murial gave us lovely basket of fruit & Miss Tennagstrin flowers. All were in gay spirits. Tea with The Friezes.

October 2, 1918, traveling to Narvick, Stockholm

Tues. [Wed.] Cold rainey day. Busy doing last minute things in shopping.

October 3, 1918, Sweden traveling

Thurs. All day traveling thru beautiful rolling country. But rather gray & somber. Plenty white bread. Splendid news from Western Front & So. West. Crossed arctic circle.

October 4, 1918, Northern Sweden & Norway, Narvick

In early morning ran thru swamps boggy land. By nine oclock the Mts. snow capped were in sight. Not so very cold. Arrived in Narcisk 1:00 oc. Glorious Mts. MOD & I did the town. Too rainey for walking. Saw 1st Laplanders—Slept under feather beds. Sent out mail.

October 5, 1918, Narvick, Norway, Letter 37—Fritz

Sat. All morning Marcia & I wrote & mended. It rained so we could not Mt. climb. At 4:30 we took the boat to Lodingen.[24] All tho there was much rain, we were able to see something of the beauty of the Fjords & Mts. Everybody was in gay spirits. not very cold.

October 6, 1918, Arctic Ocean

Sun. All day we were thrilled by the beautiful scenery. Many Mts. snow capped. Most covered with glorious rich Brown trees and yellows.—at Harstad we spent 3 hrs, climbed to a beautiful look out. We reached Tromso at 9. The scenery all day was glorious. We took boat at Lodengen at 6:30. Gorgeous northern lights. Wonderful sun set.

October 7, 1918, Hammerfest, Norway

Mon. This a.m. we stopped at Skjevro [Skjervoy] where we saw our first glacier, until 10 a.m. scenery glorious. Then we struck open sea. R. L., Dan

---

24 A town on the island of Hinnoya off the Norway coast opposite Narvik.

& I sat up at the Bow for 1 hr, where Don & I were ill. Wonderful filmy mist coming over Mts. At noon all felt better. R. L. and I climbed Mts, took wonderful walk at Hammerfest. Not very cold. Saw Laps again.

October 8, 1918, Arctic Circle

Tues. Nearly every one ill most of day. Spent all day on deck. Don, R. & I stood out on the Bow while going around North Cape 71° [latitude]. [dove?] gray water steel color—Rocks baren—Every body went to bed at 6 o'clock—While we tossed about on our small *Kaaron Jarl*. Hyllefyard at noon. Did not go up to dock but loaded barges.

October 9, 1918, Kirkenes, Arctic Circle

Wed. Arrived at Vardo about 5:30. Read, Marcia & I explored the town in a misty rain. Fish racks were everywhere. 2 Eng. Cargo boats camouflaged came in from Arkangel. We played cards to while away the gray hours. at 4 o'clock we arrived at Kirkenes. Marcia & all the rest of us explored the town and went to movies. Bought cookies at Vadso.

October 10, 1918. Kirkenes, Arctic Region

Thurs. Letter 38 Mary Breakfast 9:45, sardines, cheese, coffee. At 12:30 R & I walked 5½ kilometers to iron ore mines. Explored lovely low Mts. Ate boiled eggs & bread & butter, took train back. Met Captain of freighter. Had dinner with 5 men at their hotel—wrote letters & cards. Mild and balmy. 10 of us had reindeer meat supper.

October 11, 1918, Arctic Region, Embark on Freighter at Kirkyres for Arkangel

Friday Read & I took walk over Mts. & took few pictures. All read, played games, got off post cards during rainy afternoon & evening. Rumors that Kaiser willing to abdicate. Everybody hopeful over war news.

October 12, 1918, On board Clysdale, Kirkenes

Sat. Morning glorious, R, Marcia & I took lovely walk near Sea, climbed high hills. Went on Board British freighter *Clysdale*. Us four women, R, Ralph, Bra [?], Don. In evening we were taken by boat to *Meadowdale* where other 4 men were. sang, had spread, returned at one o'clock to our boat.

October 13, 1918, Arctic Ocean

Sun. Left Kirkenes at 4:30. Four ships & 2 convoys. Sunrise glorious. warm & balmy all day. We sat on deck all day long. Boys taking 3 hr. turns guarding rum. Meals wonderfully good & excellent variety. Watched mine sweepers dropped. very closely covered and canvassed at night. A perfect day. Jerome on way to States.

October 14, 1914 , Arctic Ocean

Mon. Gray, little cooler, but calm, visited chart room again. guarded rum, while men ate breakfast, played cross tag for exercise. Played cards. In evening all sat & read & wrote in dining salon before the grate fire until eleven o'clock. Had visit with Stoker in hole [ship's hold where the supplies including rum were kept].

October 15, 1918, Arctic Ocean. White Sea

Tues. Morning glorious, Waves covered with white caps, sky lovely with clouds. All play hop scotch on deck. Ralph, Mar, Read & I played cards in morning. Read H. G. Wells in afternoon & slept. We dropped anchor at 7:30 near light boat, after raising the mine sleepers at 5 o'clock. All spent evening writing, reading & having a good time. The average temperature has been 37 degrees.

October 16, 1918, Arkangel, Letter 39 John

Arrived at 12 o'clock. Officers came aboard & stamped passports. At 4 o'clock all came off. After supper opened trunk. Lovely sweater, twelve pounds of candy—rubbers & glasses from home. Very damp & penetrating. All glad to be together again.

Chapter Two
"Last night we danced again until midnight."

Diary
October 17 – October 25, 1918

October 17, 1918, Arkangel

Thurs. Did shopping of vegetables & struggled on the room problem. Marcia & I moved over to No. 8. Spent afternoon doing errands. Had dinner at Paris Restaurant R. came in evening. Went to Bath.

October 18, 1918, Arkangel

Fri. Decided all shall do war work—part time—Spent morning in Market trying to get furniture for rooms, gave dress to dress maker to do.

October 19, 1918, Letter 40 Sis

Shopped. Wrote for dress, skirt 2 waists & underwear. went with Bracket to see Smolony Hut, attended Ambassadors Tea, 5–7. Captain Webster, Lesa, Helen & I play bridge in evening.

October 20, 1918, Arkangel

Sun. Marcia, Helen & I spent morning in ware house going over *Wrexon* Cargo. Read & I took walk along river in our first snow storm. R. & Broc L. came for supper & evening. Everybody in fine spirits.

October 21, 1918, Archangel
Mon. Glorious winter day. Shopped in a.m. In afternoon visited Hospital 53. Made call to interest teacher in work for girls. Cap't Henry & Leut Gross. Hospital 53.

October 22, 1918, letter 41—Eliz. by sailor
Tues. Spent afternoon & evening helping to arrange supplies in YMCA Secretarial Stores. Read & I took walk in evening 'till supper. Bracket decided to open temporary quarters.

October 23, 1918
Wed. Spent afternoon & evening at Smolony helping Bracket getting hut ready for club purposes. Girls entertained Embassador for tea. Also Mr. Simmons.

October 24, 1918
Thurs. Made calls. Went to Hospital and out to Smolony. In evening R., Crawford & Mr. Rily came in. We read President Wilson's speech. Worked on Δ [delta written here; perhaps Clara meant "change"]. Everybody is condemning the English for their attitude towards local & our people.

Letters

Oct. 25, 1918
Arkangel

Dearest Sis:

Well what do you think? On the 23rd of Oct. two days ago, your 1st letter to Petrograd written Oct 11, 1917 reached me! It read just as good as if it were written this year. My how my mouth watered for the "Grimes Goldens" peaches and tomatoes that you wrote about. Where this mail bag has been all these months no one knows. I hope eventually to receive all the mail that has been so thoughtfully sent. Did you send anything on the *Wrexton* ship which left America last Dec (1917) and which was lost on the rocks in the White Sea? I hope not. Oh it was such a dreadful pity, that all those things were lost. All our supplies both food and other equipment which we needed were all lost.

Nov. 1

There is scarcely a day that passes that I don't wish that I could cable home so you would know something immediately of what my life is here.

Yesterday, Halloween, will be a red letter day for us. The gov't requisitioned a building for us. The downstairs for the Soldier's Hostess house, and the upstairs for our living quarters.

This means that we will all get busy getting equipment and making the necessary arrangements for our work and living. We are not satisfactorily located now for living, and today we engaged a fine maid who has worked in an American family in Moscow. We will have another maid and cook who will look after the household arrangements. We need so many because of difficulties in laundry, and because there is so much coming and going until eleven and twelve at night. And this year is going to be very strenuous.

Last Saturday night we attended a dance at the British club, meeting many of the prominent officers. Last night two of us assisted the military mission in a big party and dance. I have spent most of the last two days there, helping to make raisin and pumpkin pies, fudge, and cats, witches and other decorations. Colonel Rugles and others kept visiting the kitchen all day and finally about two thirty yesterday they closed up shop, and

Captains, Lieutenants and others busied themselves in putting up flags, orange and black trimmings for the chandeliers, and arranging for the party in general. One of the funniest stunts was to see the dignitaries lined up in two lines, then relay-race eating a dry cracker and whistling. Everybody entered into the spirit of the occasion so we had a really very happy time. The orchestra from the band was fine.

The general staff have asked us to assist them when they give their party. Tonight is a party and dance at the opening of the new convalescence hospital. Instead of Arkangel being the worst place in earth it bids fare to be interesting and very strenuous. The official circle of Americans alone now is something over a hundred. We are hoping other of our workers will get over, to help meet the many demands which we are constantly being called on to meet. The Red Cross want help from us, the YMCA, and our own work.

It looks now as tho we would do some work at the front. One of the commanding officers has sent a most urgent request for our assistance. They have a fine steel postal car, fitted up for canteen work which they want our help on. We will take turns going for two weeks at a time. It's only a ten hour journey and two trains a day. We all will enjoy helping Mr. Omstead who has charge of the work there. He was one of the men in our party coming over. He is a Michigan man and most of these men here are from Michigan, tho most of the officers are Wisconsin men. There are about 20 alumni here. We soon will have a reunion. Practically all the Petrograd and Moscow officials are here now.

Until our work is established it will be difficult to say just what I shall be doing this winter. Besides helping four nights a week in one of the YMCA clubs, one night in ours, I am representing our Assoc. on a committee that is just being organized for general information and propaganda work with intensive work in the Hospitals.

For the hospitals we are putting up maps with strings so the men can see the progress of things. Sending daily typewritten cable communications of important news, lectures on Russia, entertainments 2 or 3 times a week, and libraries. I am to go over 5,000 books in the next few days, making up libraries both for the hospitals and the various club houses here and at the front.

So far, I have been the only person doing hospital work and it is by far too much for one. So we are organizing this committee.

Today I got out about fifty small packages of Bull Durham [tobacco] to the men, and the news about the Dardannells.[25] I dread to have the short days coming so fast now, as it is especially hard on those in the hospitals. Next Tuesday the first entertainment is to be given at No. 53. I have two professional vaudeville actors, a quartet, Charlie Chaplin, a mandolin and guitar, and one of the consul men who sings very well. I shall be eager to see how it comes off. There is lots of talent to be found among the soldiers and they are mighty responsive to it.

Read Lewis' department is soon to start an "American Weekly" newspaper which will be a Godsend to us all. You can't realize how hard it is to live in these stirring times, without papers. Of course some are coming thru now, and magazines ought to come fairly regularly now. We will have mail all winter, from time to time, not weekly, of course, but often.

Our first snow has come and gone. The past week has been typically middle-west early damp, sloppy winter. We are all hoping for freezing weather to nip the influenza and freeze these awful swamps where our men are fighting.

Oh how we all devoutly hope that peace in Europe will mean the withdrawal of our troops from Russia. Surely Russia presents a most difficult problem to all the world. It has seemed difficult to get at the whole understanding of the present situation. You have no idea how we long for real authentic news of what is going on in Moscow and Petrograd. We know that much that is in the papers is greatly exaggerated. How we wish that we could know what is happening to our friends in both cities. Poor old Russia. She seems to have so few friends.

Tonight we had oatmeal for supper, and it was good. In Moscow we couldn't get it and even if we could, we wouldn't have had sugar or milk enough to have with it. Thru the gov't supplies we are getting things which are a real luxury to us. The variety is limited but it makes a difference in our diet. We long for dried fruits, dates, etc., but I think still we may get some before winter is over. We have a few precious prunes and raisins which we use with rice and for sauce. The pies at the party were the first

---

25 Clara may mean the release of the official report concerning the disastrous allied campaign also known as Gallipoli. Or, perhaps she means to tell them about the Armistice of Mudros (signed October 30, 1918) which gave the Allies control of the Straights of the Dardanelles, among other concessions by the Ottoman Empire.

real pies that I have had since I left home. And they were good. We are really wonderfully well off for food this year. We won't crave sweets as we did, for our sugar and jam supply is sufficient to meet that need. Besides, we get two big bars apiece of sweetened chocolate every week from the YMCA. My candy which came from Hylers will last until after Xmas. And the other we are eating a little of every day as our desert, or when guests come. In Stockholm we all ate quite a little of sweets, so we do not eat so ravenously the sweets which we have now.

Sunday afternoon we are invited to a British Club for afternoon tea where we will meet some more officers and the few women here in the British colony. Then Sunday night two officers from the *Olympic* warship, Captain Lively of the Red Cross mission, Lieutenant Bricker of the staff, and one or two others are coming in for the evening. The *Olympic* has been in Murmansk for months, and how these people hate to return there, for everyone says life is absolutely deadly there. These men did so enjoy the Halloween party. For their sakes, I am sorry that the Ambassador's Sat. afternoon tea had to be omitted this week, because of the illness of the Ambassador. His teas are a great place for everyone to congregate, and to see everyone else. He loves to dance, and is a very good dancer himself, dancing all the new dances.

I am looking forward eagerly to hearing from home. Hope Thanksgiving will be lovely at home. I shall think of you. I shall probably be attending some big function here that night as I fancy every holiday will be made an occasion for get-togethers here.

With a great deal of love from your ever affectionate

Clara

Sunday, Nov. 3, 1918—Personal

Dear Sis and Geney:

I am dependent on you girls to help me solve the clothes proposition. This living where the social side of life is so prominent had been difficult for us. I am a bit better off than many of the others, but none of us have enough. We have all kinds of occasions, teas, dinners, informal and formal dances and our own "at homes." Couldn't you write Penelope Bond of

Pansy Burch in NY to get what you direct. I want material for an evening [gown], not pink or rose. The lining of the net dress is good. Send thread and trimmings, picture of suggestions as to making, Georgette or silk, plain or fancy. Perhaps you better send lining also. Or if you decide on the style have Miss Sandum make. Perhaps it would be better to have her send you a diagram of style and have her make. Then send dress to you, Geney, to try on. We are about the same size. The rose dress is a lovely dress, but not my style. We are having a little alteration made. If you could have tried it on, Genieve, you could have had the necessary alternations. Here nothing can be bought. The dark blue which I wrote for I need to take the place of the Alice blue, which I am hanging onto for dear life, but which is giving evidence of going into little holes. Then I will need something for summer, only one new dress. I wish I could have another like the blue you gave me Geney. Everyone likes it and it was so becoming. The summers are short, so if you can send dress, or material in the spring please keep me in mind.

I am asking NY to deposit in Taylorville both my December and January salaries in full. As there is very little here one can possibly spend money for, I shall hope to have March and April's salaries also. Which will help to defray these expenses.

The latest excitement is that Catherine Childs of our staff is to be married on Thursday night of this week to Mr. Ryle of the YMCA. The wedding will be in the little English chapel. She will continue to work on our staff until spring, when they expect to return to the states for five months, coming back here for the fall work in Russia.

My supplies are all holding out beautifully. Be sure and write me if the two month's salaries are deposited at the Bank. You might suggest to NY that the things be sent via Stockholm, for if they get there, they will be forwarded to us in the Legation Pouch. Of course the packages ought to be made small as possible if they come that way. It is expected that there will be currier service between here and Stockholm all winter. Mail sent via Europe is the safest and surest now. I firmly believe that we will be back in Moscow in April or May. With peace dawning on the French line, it cannot help but effect the Russian situation. If there is any power in the dominant desire, surely our warfare with Russia must soon stop.

Tomorrow night, Col. Stewart, Head of the General Staff, Mr. Cole, Head of the Consular Staff, Read Lewis, Crawford Wheeler, Head of the

YMCA work, and a few others are coming in to play cards. This afternoon, after visiting the men in the hospital I was invited over to have tea with the officers, and there met the Physician who doctored C. Hughes and Vice Pres. Stephens (associated with Cleveland [hospital], I believe). I despair of ever learning the names and proper ranks of all these officials. Almost everybody has some rank or title, about which he is very particular. When in doubt, I always address them by what I know is a higher rank.

It is a crime to put you girls to work on this clothes problem. When you both are so busy at home yourselves. But here there is absolutely no way of providing and we did not foresee what a social whirl we were so soon to drop in the midst of, and become the very centre. When our names were posted up in the office of the General Staff, one of the men remarked, "Are they really all honest to God American Women!" At the hospital the other day, one man followed me thru four wards just to hear an American woman talk. It would make you both smile and weep to hear what the soldiers say to us, when for the first time they hear us talk and recognize a country woman. They don't wait for introductions, but want to know if its true that we really are Am. and from what states we come from.

This is really all now, this goes by one of the returning YMCA men who sails from here on the 9th.

Lovingly,

Clara I. Taylor

Nov. 8, 1918
Arkangel

Dear Father:

How I wish that I might be at home to celebrate your birthday. I surely will be thinking of you and perhaps some of my many good thoughts for you will come as wave messages.[26]

Since the cables are all under military service, it is hard not to be able to cable home freely and often. But surely you are getting the mail and what few cables we have been able to send thru to New York. If we could

---

26 Spiritualism was in vogue in the late 1800s, and here Clara is joking that she hopes her father can receive her thought messages telepathically.

only know how often and how long a time it takes mail to reach home, it would be a great satisfaction to us here. While we are not yet receiving, I do hope you are hearing from me. Xmas will surely bring me a direct word from home. The things in the trunk which came made me realize that you were getting some of my mail. When you realize that the latest letter I have rec'd was written last March you can imagine the longing I have to hear what you are all doing. I don't mean this as a complaint, for I am dead sure that the family is writing me, and occasionally cabling. Someday, I may receive some of them. But all must write me often now, for there is no reason why the mail shouldn't come to me with every pouch.

We are having "unusual" weather. It remains quite mild and even balmy. I am not yet wearing my heavy winter clothing or coat and am feeling fine. I am one of the few people who has distinguished herself in not having Spanish influenza. "Flu" as they call it here. Marcia Dunham and I both have been the only members of our household to be free from it and that probably is because we do not live in the same house with the others. All are well now.

We are waiting for the people to move out of our building so we can move in and start our work. We are so eager to get the hostess house going. I am so enthusiastic over the hospital work. Yesterday, I got Lt. Cleoforth of the Military Mission to take over the general chairmanship. We have five dept's—1st is war maps and daily typewritten communiqués from Allied Bureau of Information; 2d is library books, magazines and papers; 3rd, weekly concerts, with the orchestra from the American band always assisting; 4th, weekly lectures, or educational moving pictures from the American Publicity Bureau; and 5th, visitation.

Last night we had our first concert at the big receiving hospital. We have a big ward which is to be kept for a recreation room. Iron beds were put in, with three boards across for seats. The men hobbled in, dressed in their funny bright blue hospital uniforms, and had one good hour of fun and music.

The YMCA will let us have moving picture machines for both the Receiving and Am. Convalescent Hospitals. We may include the Hospital ship, too, later in the season, after we get things to going along in these two places. The Doctors and military officers in charge of these hospitals are delightful people to work with. The soldiers surely are very appreciative. Never did my citizenship count so much as now. The very fact of just being an American helps much.

Yesterday at noon occurred the wedding of Catherine Childs of our staff, to Mr. Ryle. It was a very simple wedding. We could not buy a single flower. Flags composed the decorations. There were seventeen of us which included Mr. Cole, Consul. For in Russia a consular representative is required by law and consular papers must be filled out. The marriage could not be held at the Episcopal Church, because the marriage banns had not been announced the three previous Sundays. So an Am. Episcopal Clergyman performed the ceremonies at our own rooms. The wedding breakfast was the most curious that an Am. bride ever had. But necessity, not choice was the deciding matter. Irish stew, escalloped potatoes, home made rolls, strawberry tarts, fruit cake, some of my candy and coffee. Really, throwing rice on them when they left for Barkerreetsa, where Catherine is helping in the canteen, was the only wedding feature of the whole affair.

Wednesday night two of us were at Lt. Cleoforth's for dinner, where we enjoyed meeting the French consul. Mrs. Cleoforth was a lady in waiting at the [Russian] court, before the overthrow of the Czar. Her husband is a Wisconsin graduate, and was for a while secretary to Miss Jane Addams.

We are all interested in hearing of Mr. Bullard's and Graham Taylor Jr.'s marriages since their return to the states. Only a few days ago [the news] came to us. Mr. Bullard, I believe, is back in Siberia. We all wondered if Mr. Taylor got home before his mother's death.

Tomorrow I am hoping to finish up the work of going over the library books, making up libraries for the various huts at the different fronts. We will be so glad when it freezes up, for this swampy country is dreadful for the soldiers. Also, communications will be easier. I am looking forward to helping in one of the traveling huts which we have been asked to help in. We need more workers, but if they don't come very soon, we will be frozen up for the winter excepting for mail service.

Ambassador Francis left yesterday for England. He is very far from well. Is to undergo an operation. We do not expect him back, but he thinks that he is going to return.

The Wisconsin alumni are having a get-together, as you see from the enclosed invitation. There will be about 18 of us, besides ten others who have been invited in because of their affiliations. Also including all the American women of the colony. I am to plan the refreshments. We are going to have ice cream, and chocolate cake and fudge. The consulate furnishing all the materials. It is being held at the home of the Consul. It so happens that 3 of the men there are University of Wisconsin men. We will have the orchestra from the Band.

Tuesday we are having an afternoon tea for several Arkangel women who have been very thoughtful of us. Some of them are English and some Russian. I am not studying any Russian these days, but hope soon to have a teacher three times a week. The days are so full that language work gets crowded out. Then Arkangel doesn't seem like Russia. It is not like any other place in the world. English and Am. seem to predominate.

We, like everyone, are speculating as to how peace is going to affect the Russian situation, and us personally. Whether it is going to be possible for us to go south before the winter is really over. The western war news truly is wonderful. Oh how I want this awful war to stop. My work in the hospital makes me realize the truth of Grant's description of war.

I am sorry not to write you about the things here that would be most interesting to you all, but I am sure that you realize that it is quite impossible. We will have it all to talk about when I get home, or when the war is over and we can all write quite freely. The letter about Mirback's [German Ambassador assassinated in Moscow] death and the events that followed, I never dared mail, as I knew it probably would never reach you, and as a diary I value it. So will send home after the war. I do hope you are saving my letters for they will form something of a diary. Most of us decided it was unwise to keep war diaries.

Now be sure to write and send clippings about suffrage, the Duy vote and other interesting political events. What is Teddy doing these days. Over here we are all wonderfully proud and loyal to President Wilson. I wish that he could be the first president of the League of Nations. He would be great for it.

Now, my dearest Father, this brings a heart full of love to you, and may this be one of the very happiest birthdays that you have ever had. Every day I give thanks that I have had so wonderful a father. I hope and pray that I may live loyally and truly to the highest and best ideals as you have. All that I am, and the ability and equipment that I have for this work, I owe to your generous thoughtfulness and sacrifices. The fact that you too, suffered a great loss in the civil war and rose triumphantly above it, gives me now the courage and conviction which I need, to help encourage some of those who now lie in the hospital, with an awful dread of the future, as they face life maimed and crippled.[27]

Oh what a lot we will have to talk about when I come home. The time will fly quickly for the hours, days and weeks are so full that one is scarcely conscious of how fast the time is slipping by. A year from this spring, I will complete my circling of the big globe, and come home for a nice long visit when we shall drive and talk and live over together these wonderful years that we are living so far apart.

With love and deepest gratitude for all that you have been to me as Father and companion from your affectionate daughter,

Clara I. Taylor

Nov. 11, 1918

My dear John,

It is five thirty, I have just returned home from the hospital, and found all members of our family writing madly. A ship is about to sail, and only a few minutes in which to write.

This has been a glorious balmy day, with a beautiful sunset over the river at three o'clock. The days are getting noticeably shorter with every day. We are not dressing yet by lamplight, but soon will. The afternoons seem so very short.

I spent the afternoon out at one of the hospitals giving the men the latest war news from the Bulletins. It's lots of fun to visit with the men. There are a group of Britishers who have been thinking a lot about the whole social situation throughout the world, whose views interest me very much. In one ward in the hospital, I feel as tho the corners of the world meet. There are men there from various British Colonies, and Americans mostly from Michigan. It is really quite difficult to understand some of the English. It is so broad. I wonder if they find my accent as bad as theirs.

---

27 Clara's father lost his right arm during service in the American Civil War.

Yesterday three of the men came in for dinner, then we took a long walk along the river for miles. It is quite like one continuous city, as one village sort of overlaps another along the banks, especially on the Arkangel side. On the way home, I stopped in with Read Lewis to see a box of new books which his dep't has just received from Washington. Among them was *Wilson's Foreign Policy* by Robinson and West, which I sat up until midnight to read. It certainly gave me a clear understanding of his Mexican policy. So many of his speeches seem so pertinent to the present world situation. Another book which I brought home was John Spargo's last book on socialism in America, published in 1918. These are the first of the latest books any of us have seen. There are about forty of these books all on civic and political questions. I hope to read one a month if not more while they are available.

With peace on the western front it makes us again live in constant uncertainty. It seems to me a move has constantly threatened me ever since last February. But I imagine that we will be here until spring, for even if peace should come, the Russian problem is going to be a very serious one to consider and decide. Of course we shall be glad to see the withdrawal of troops from Russia, and a different kind of intervention undertaken. Somehow I can't see anything very settled in Russia for several years to come.

It really looks as tho the Bolsheviks were stronger now than when we left Moscow. None of us think of Arkangel as being Russian. There seems to be so little of real Russia about it. But if Bolshevism spreads thru Germany, and creeps into all the countries on the globe, the Russian situation may be viewed differently than it now is.

From the evening Communique it looks as tho Wilson's dream of an overthrow of German Militarism had really come true. I feel sure that the Russian Bolsheviks feel that they have had a very real share in that overthrow.

If Jerome Davis should be speaking in any of the cities near home, be sure to hear him, and be sure to meet him. He is one of my very good friends and he, more than any other American, has had unusual opportunities of understanding and knowing the Bolsheviks. I certainly would like to know what he is saying about Russia and what America thinks. You boys must write me and send me clippings. We long so to know what is happening in Siberia, and what our country is doing there. [28]

---

28 Jerome Davis was an American scholar and activist who spent a year in Russia and published articles about the political situation. He was supportive of the Bolshevik cause.

We feel just a little jealous of all those who are at home getting every latest news items and enjoying the wonderful thrills which come with the news each day now. The cable is still broken, but what little wireless news we get we are so grateful for. Tomorrow we are entertaining several ladies mostly Russians at afternoon tea. Friday night we go to a dance at the American Convalescent hospital for enlisted men only, Saturday afternoon the Embassy tea at five, and Saturday night is our Wisconsin Alumni reunion. The days are full and interesting. So time fairly flies by. I shall look forward eagerly to mail from home. Hope everyone had a happy Thanksgiving, and will be together for Xmas. I shall start my Xmas letter to the Family within a few days so as to have it ready when news comes that a ship is sailing.

Just loads of love to all from your affectionate sister,

Clara

Nov. 17, 1918
Arkangel, Russia

Dearest Ones at Home:

A very merry Xmas to you all. And the Happiest New Year that we all have enjoyed for four weary years.

My how happy the world is going to be this year, with fighting ended in Europe. It seems too good to be true. I hope next year will see some of the tangled knots solved here in this big troubled country. The problems to be faced at the Peace table seems to me no greater than how best to help Russia solve her fate of future gov't. It is so complex. The country is so huge, and made of so many people, of such different nationalities, traditions, and temperaments. There is scarcely a day goes by that we do not find ourselves speculating on how long it will be until a stable gov't will be established.

Well, this has been a busy week. I am enjoying getting down to the hospital so often to visit with the men. Tues. night we are to have our second concert. The Band will go, and five professional entertainers will help end the evening with a good sing. Many of the men have requested the good times at singing such as they used to have at Camp Custer, Michigan.

We hope to make a lot of Thanksgiving Day. We will try to give pumpkin pie to the men in hospital if we can obtain the materials. Then in the evening we will have an entertainment of some sort for all about seven o'clock. The plan of the day in general is: a Thanksgiving service at 11 o'clock at the YMCA auditorium. All the various messes having their own dinners. The officials calling on [Consul General] Mr. Poole at Main YMCA with a patriotic gathering for officials at the headquarters of the General Staff at 9 o'clock p.m. I am on the decorating committee. There will be speeches, music and dancing. I suppose it will be a strenuous day for us all. It will be very thrilling one in America, I am sure, and in France.

Thursday night we attended a dance at the Convalescent Hospital. We got there a little early. In the big room, around the wall, sat a row of men, and the hallway leading into the hall was crowded. It seems to be that there were a million men there. There were just six of us Americans, but later about twenty Russian girls came. Officers were not permitted to come. After a few dances, we got the band to play Turkey in the Straw, and had two lively lines of Virginia reel. The men all clapped and entered into the spirit of it and seemed to enjoy immensely. Then we had a circle two step, with robber dancing. That is stealing partners. In this way, we danced with a great many different men, and gave a larger number an opportunity to share in the fun. The Russian girls are fast learning the American dances, so by midwinter there will be many more dancers.

It was interesting to see couples go off together, each teaching the other a few words in the different languages. Our small amount of knowledge goes a long way here.

Tomorrow I begin lessons again. Hope to have one a day to begin with, may have to content myself with every other day if I don't find time for study.

That night, Sat., we had a most happy and successful Wisconsin alumni Reunion. There were fifteen of us present who were graduates. About thirty-five in all attending.

During the evening, a newsboy came in calling, "Daily Cardinal." All the men eagerly bought. One of the men read it out. It told who's who in Arkangel and local bits on Alumni members, old class yells and campus notes. We had an orchestra from the band who played "On Wisconsin" to which we danced and danced and sang. We had a most charming song fest, led by a man who has studied for Grand Opera. Then the fellows began doing stunts. It was altogether one of the happiest occasions that I have enjoyed since coming to Russia. Dignitaries ceased being dignitaries and all went in for a very jolly time. We gave them chocolate cake, chocolate ice cream and tea. I made the ice cream, and it was a proposition, when it was necessary to use canned milk and powdered eggs. Both taste so strong. I shall hardly know how to cook where there are conveniences, proper utensils and good ingredients. You should have seen me making double boilers out of wash basins, My labors were compensated for by the tastiness of the cream, and the delight of the men in getting real ice cream. We came home at two a.m., the whole consular staff coming with us. The Consulate building was an altogether ideal place for such a gathering. When our Hostess House is complete, I hope to invite the crowd in some night for another informal gathering. Probably during the Holidays.

Wednesday night I stopped in at the Consulate about eight-thirty to see about dishes, service, arrangements; and when I came to leave, they all insisted that I take off my sweater and play cards with them. We had such fun. At 11:30 the maid called us to tea and when we went out to the dining room the men were so amazed to see a fresh table cloth, pie and cookies, all in my honor. We drank tea and visited until long after midnight. Mr. Cole, Head Consul, is very charming. His wife is waiting in Harbin until she can join him. Pete Pierce is also a Wisconsin man whom I knew when I was in Madison. Read Lewis takes his meals there also and Mr. Strother, a jolly Harvard man, who was a heap of fun at the party. Helen Ogden and I will go over some night this week if we have any free time and play bridge with them again.[29]

This afternoon, one of the British officers, a monolog-ist, entertained us and several of our callers at tea. He certainly is one Britisher with a very keen sense of humor. We had a Colonel, Major, Captain and Lt. and several civilians who came in at four. Our friends know that we are "at home"[30] at tea every Sunday from four to seven.

---

29 Clara graduated from University of Wisconsin, Madison, in 1910 with a BA in economics. Peter Pierce was later to be a great help in getting Clara a visa out of Murmansk when her passport was questioned due to Strother's attempts to detain her as a Bolshevik spy (see Diary entries for August 23–26, 1919, and notes introducing Chapter Five, below.)

30 Being "at home" meant that the women were prepared to receive visitors during those hours.

How I wish you could see the room in which we have to entertain all our guests. Almost everyone here is doing more or less camping. We have a settee which looks like an old fashioned church pew. Two medium sized tables, five taberet stools, two hard bottom straight-back chairs. There is in the room a large wardrobe and bed. On the floor three rugs belonging to one of the YMCA sec'ys. Across one side of the room is a beautiful big flag, and the Russian stove opens, giving us a sort of open fire. Which is the delight of all. The ceiling is low. It is surprising how the open fire and singing Samovar gives a distinctly homey atmosphere to the place, so everyone at once feels it is homelike. All the men live in such barn-y places that anything cozy seems a relief to them.

The cable is fixed again after being broken for two weeks, so more news is pouring thru. We are expecting several from NY this week. A mail pouch bringing lots of papers came on Friday, so we have been catching up a bit. Some are as late as early October. But no letters. Surely some will be coming for us very soon. Do rush letters thru without fail while I am here and the boats are still coming. So the long delays by currier service won't make us impatient. Surely something will come for me soon. Don't fail to send me a cable at Xmas time, for I shall look for one, and it will make up for these long weeks and months without any news directly from home.

Did the things which I sent from Russia ever get thru to you. I shall be eager to hear. I hope to have some pictures to put in this letter of our trip to here from Norway.

The maid has just brought in my steaming Samovar and I am drinking a cup of cocoa while writing and just before going to bed. I am going to bed now as I am truly dead tired, for I have been up until twelve, one, and two almost every night this week. I am still husky, happy and well. And can usually stay up until one with great pleasure and breakfast at nine. The mornings will be somewhat shorter. Think of sunset at 2:30, what will it be like in Dec. and Jan. It continues to be very mild, we had a light snow fall today. We all devoutly wish it would freeze up, as it is so damp now.

I want you all to know that I am enjoying my lovely sweater, rubbers and candy. Please don't ever send so much at one time again, and include nut goodies and dried fruits. We are getting regular chocolate rations now. So we are not craving sweets so much. The lemon drops have been wonderful. There were three tins of drops, one box of caramels, 1 box of 12 or 24 bars of chocolate and a 3 lb. box of chocolates. The later will be opened Xmas day. It all came packed in tin boxes so will keep. Everybody has enjoyed it immensely. You must not for one minute have concern for my food, living or clothing. We are wonderfully well off. If the muff gets thru it will add greatly to my comfort. But you remember, I have wonderful fur lined gloves which I will wear over nice wool mittens which I bought in Stockholm, along with a white wool scarf and cap which pulls down over my ears. We are not wearing our heavy winter clothing yet. The weather is most unusual, as mild as in Illinois at this time of year. They say we have missed a whole month of snow already. Now it is ten o'clock, and I am off to bed.

Nov. 19th

Yesterday the men were delighted with the newspapers and magazines which I took out, and today the communiqués are interesting, I think now that the excitement is over regarding the signing of the Armistice, that the men here will settle more quietly in their own minds. Of course at first everybody wanted to go home at once, but now they realize that there is still work to be done.

Nov. 20

Just thirty minutes until this must be in the mail.

Last night our concert at the hospital was fine. The men enjoyed it immensely. We now think that our Hostess House for American soldiers will be ready to open on Thanksgiving. So we are busy with plans for it. At present I am arranging programs for Thanksgiving at two YMCA huts, one hospital, and find myself chairman of the decorating committee for the big party at Headquarters Staff. Tonight the committee meets with me to discuss plans.

Last night after the hospital concert, I attended a farewell party for one of the YMCA men who is returning to America and will soon return to Russia via Siberia. He will write you all before leaving the States, so you can send a letter by him, if the censorship is raised.

The ground is covered with snow, so winter has at last come, and we are truly glad for there has been a dreadful amount of illness due to the dampness. We are expecting Miss Dunham back from the front Sat. or Sunday.

I am hoping to go there after Thanksgiving and have charge of the canteen car for a couple of weeks. The men were so delighted to see one of their countrymen there after her arrival.

Tuesday night we are invited over to the Consul's for a Thanksgiving dinner and to play cards in the evening. It will be our only Thanksgiving dinner as we shall be too busy on that day for a special dinner ourselves.

Well dear ones, this must go into the pouch. This brings a heart full of love and greetings to all of you and may the New Year be the happiest that our family has ever known. You are in my mind constantly, and I am wishing for you happiness and good health.

With ever and ever so much love from your affectionate daughter and sister,

Clara I. Taylor

EXTRA

My stationary got mixed up. So this side doesn't belong to the regular letter.

John, I am having my Dec., Jan. and Feb. salaries sent to Taylorville, as I have never rec'd any letters, I don't know how my finances stand.

Girls, if you haven't had a chance to have the blue dress made that I sent for, be sure and ask Miss Sanden to send to Geney to try on before sending here, so as to see if all is satisfactory and pretty. Also have evening dress—practical sleeves ought to be elbow length.

I had a little alteration made on my net evening [gown], so think it will see me thru several more parties before it goes quite to pieces. I am so thankful for every dress I have for this life calls for much. But on the other hand, I don't want any more than is needed for it is hard to take care of them living in baggage as we do most of the time. My velvet dress is a great joy and is just right.

Nov. 25, 1918
Arkangel, Russia

My dear Fritzie:

It has been a long time since a letter was written to you. I always feel about you, George and Genieve, that there is a bit uncertainty of receiving the letters, so usually send them all directly home. It has been so many months since I have known anything definite about the family plans. I could very easily allow myself to get truly desperate over the mail situation if there were not many others who are not hearing. It is the few that are now getting Oct. mail that make the rest of us unpatient, to put it mildly. All Arkangel will know it, when I receive word from home. This year all of us will have to send our Xmas cables thru NY because we are living in a military centre.

Yesterday morning three of us took a glorious walk along the river. A fluffy snow covers everything and much fell all day yesterday. After walking about five verts,[31] we persuaded a Russian to drive us home in his sleigh, not the kind that you have ever seen. In the afternoon, three captains, two of whom are Doctors, and two Lt. Wisconsin engineers, came in for afternoon tea. We had a jolly time. The engineers are an especially fine group of men. Several in the Headquarters office have built themselves a charming little house and are having the furniture made for it.

This morning I had a great surprise. I had many appointments so started out early. At nine thirty when I went up the street (I was dressed as usual) noticed everybody's eyebrows were frosted and their hair, and their coats (all covered with frost). When I reached the Red Cross Headquarters, I learned that it was 4° below zero. A drop of about 44°. Before the day was over, I came to realize that it was cold, but certainly, I have not been uncomfortable. I put on my fur coat and hat this afternoon and will be careful how I dress from now on. Winter, I imagine, has come now in dead earnest.

You will be interested in knowing that our Thanksgiving all the men in the hospitals are to have game bird, potatoes and pie. Helen and I are

---

31 Clara means *verst* which is a now obsolete Russian linear measurement. 1 verst = 1.067 km = 0.67 miles

making 50 for one hospital. How the men are counting on it. The attendants told me this evening that the days of the week are now being counted as to the time for receiving their long wished-for pie. They will be made from dried apricot.

In the evening at the hospital whose interest I am chiefly concerned in we will have two vocal solos, cornet solo, saxophone trio, band, and talk by Consular Cole, ending with a fine sing of all the men, and perhaps a moving picture show. While the entertainment is going on downstairs, I am going to give candy (some of which you folks sent) to the men who are unable to leave their beds. Our entertainment is from 5:15–6:15. From 6:30–8 at the Arkangel YMCA Hut, there is a very big party to be given to the enlisted men. I regret that I have to miss it, but I will have to go to Headquarters to decorate the tables for the evening party for officers and dignitaries which begins at 8:30.

Nov. 30

Thanksgiving is over, and somewhat weary we all are after the strenuous preparations. The hospital plans carried beautifully. Everybody had a big dinner and very happy time. There was some criticism because the few Bolshevik prisoners had the same big dinner in the hospital as everyone else, but all the Am. were glad they could have it. I was responsible for the order going in and the Colonel in charge gave the order to be carried out.

I was able to get to the YMCA for an hour. There were many men there, the room being filled. There were appropriate speeches, songs, and a splendid time. Everyone had to fairly pinch themselves to realize that they were out of America.

Our party at the General Staff headquarters was very interesting. We had moving pictures, and later dancing until 1:30. The big Red Cross ambulance brought us home.

Last night we danced again until midnight with the men at the Convalescent Hospital. I think the men are all getting more settled in their minds as to their winter plans. Of course every one wanted to go home after the Armistice was signed. But they realize that the problem of this country is not yet settled and they must stick by until it is.

Mr. Hallick is up here, but I have not met him yet, as he is at the front. I shall probably see him when I go down to the canteen car. Marcia returned with many interesting accounts, and Helen went back in her place. On Helen's return, I imagine that I will be the next to go as each is to stay two weeks, it will bring me back during the holidays. The family can cable me direct to Arkangel in care of either the Embassy or Consul. They do not have to go thru the State Dep't.

I looked and looked in vain for a cable both in Stockholm and since I have been here. If the boat Sunday does not bring me a letter I shall wire for immediate answer, as 8 months with no direct word from home is becoming unbearable. And cables are coming thru regularly now. Your postcard telling of your father's death was the last received from home. Yesterday when every one of our staff got letters but me, I did weep. Oct. mail is being received from the States now. Of course I am a victim of circumstance but I do hope the family is using every ingenuity to seeing that somehow mail gets thru. One of the YMCA men has rec'd mail regularly from his father. I want the family to draw on my bank acc't for cables for Jan., Feb. and March. Don't fail to do it. For I shall expect them. And there is no reason why they shouldn't get thru.

Tonight four of us are going to the Consulate's for dinner after which we probably shall play cards. We are all invited to the Red Cross Missions for dinner Monday night, but I cannot go as I begin at one of the new canteens on Sunday, so shall be busy from 3–9 every day now. Besides helping to plan for some vocational lecture work at the Convalescent Hospital.

I must go down and make up packets of magazines for two hospitals. We are wiring again today to NY to send more sec'ys for work in Russia when the way opens. NY does not wire often so we get terribly used up both as individuals and as an organization, and we are so helpless to do so many things for ourselves because of the isolation and conditions which we have found ourselves in ever since coming to Russia.

I long, Fritzie dear, to hear all about your work. I suppose you have written about it, but your letters have never gotten thru. I try to picture what you all are doing and how thrilled everyone must have been with the Armistices and am wondering how its going to effect [YW] Assoc. work. There is still lots to be done yet, I am sure. I keep saying to myself it isn't the family's fault, I am dead sure that you all are writing and cabling and someday maybe they will come thru. But I trust not a year and two weeks late as Sis's 1st Petrograd letter. I suppose it has been lying around up here somewhere for a year. The mail that came in yesterday was forwarded from Stockholm.

It is mild here again, but the ground is covered with snow. It is quite like Wisconsin and Michigan weather. So our winter can't be so terribly cold.

Now good bye dear ones at home. Don't mind this out burst about mail if your conscious is clear, but if they are not, do some wiring at once.

With a great deal of love for each and all from your very affectionate sister,

Clara

Clara I Taylor

"Elope," which you used to see on corner of envelope, was a required address which now is not necessary. Names which may be signed, besides mine, to any cables, will be either a consul or Ambassador, if sent thru State Dep't

Dec. 3, 1918
Arkangel, Russia
Tues. 11. p.m.

Dearest ones at home:

You should see me. Everyone says I look ten pounds heavier and ten years younger. I have just gulped down two cups of hot chocolate and was perfectly oblivious to what I was doing. And all the excitement over my mail from home. Sis's letter of Sept 18th written to Stockholm was brought to the house at 10 o'clock just as I was returning from Solombola where I have been at the YMCA hut. I have read it thru four times, and shall doubtless read it thru as many more in the next few days. Now I know how the missionaries feel when they receive a barrel at Xmas time. Now I can picture you all in the various cities, and oh family you can't possibly know what the news in that letter means. Eight months was a dreadfully long time to wait for news of you. The past week was the worst. And the first time that I have given away to tears. And now I feel ashamed, if my faith could have carried me a couple of days longer. Well now letters must come with every boat and how eagerly we shall look for them. The long silence is broken and letters will come, I know. Don't take any chances, write often so there can be no chance of a boat sailing without mail. Put in newspaper clippings also. Send mail and you can cable directly to me, Arkangel. Don't do it thru the [YWCA] National Board. They are delayed. In any country where fate may take me, c/o of either Embassy or Consulate will always reach me, so do your own cabling.

I am having the most interesting time at the Sombola YMCA Hut, where I spend eight hours each day. Tonight one of the sailors came up and said, "Do you know, you could do something for me," and when I asked what it was he replied, "I want a hairpin." So I produced a small wire one with which he cleaned his pipe. There was a chap there from Springfield [Illinois] who came near coming right over the counter tonight when he learned that I came from Taylorville. That was almost like coming from home. There are such a lot of fine chaps here, I do hope that they get back home safely.

Yesterday afternoon, one of the Captains from the British Officers mess came over to invite me over to have tea with the officers at four. It was very nice to go and meet them, as they will be dropping in occasionally to the hut, and I shall be seeing them on the street cars going and returning. I have talked with some of the Britishers who have served in the war all four years, and on several different fronts. They surely have been thru much. And how they long to go home.

11:30 p.m., Wed.

This a.m. I spent at the American Convalescent Hospital arranging with the Sergeants for some instructive and vocational talks to be given to the men there. Then had dinner at the Hospital with one of the Red Cross nurses. At 2:45 I was out at the hut where we have had lots of men in. The Sombola Hut is smaller, so much more informal and the men seem to love coming up to the counter to visit. Today one solider asked me for magazines to take with him, as he is going away with a squad of Russians to be gone three weeks. Another wanted a History of Russia, so I am taking out my personal copy of Kornilov for him. The Band came out at 7:30 for a concert, so we had an unusually large crowd. Tomorrow night the physical director goes out for wrestling, etc. Each night has its own specialty.

Since I have been doing so much canteen work, I do not get out to the Hospital as much as usual. And I do miss it. For I enjoy visiting with the "shut-ins" and the nights are so long. It is dark now at four, the sun setting about 1:30.

Tomorrow morning I go to the Red Cross Headquarters to help about the Christmas stockings which they are planning for the men. And then to the Arkangel canteen to take the place of Elizabeth Dickerson, who is ill with a bad cold. I have been so well and so fortunate about illnesses. Miss Dunham and I are the only ones of our group that escaped the Influenza.

Miss Boies is sailing for America via England on Saturday with several members of the Red Cross Mission people. It is necessary that she go home to see that we get more assistance here. We feel that NY is very neglectful about cabling and keeping us informed. We have sent and sent cables. They don't even cable us that the assistance asked for is impossible. If only they knew how much we needed to hear every month. Bess needs very much to go home, and we feel that it is absolutely necessary that someone of us does go. NY needs to know firsthand what we need. And we must have ten or twelve more sec'ys come over in the spring to prepare for the fall work.

I am terribly afraid that my flag was lost, so please send me another. I am still hoping that it will be found. It was borrowed for the Officer's Thanksgiving party. I have phoned about it and still hope it may be found.

I am so glad that Father had the western trip, and has sold the farm. Oh to think there is a stop to all that interest that he has been paying. I am so thankful Father dear, for the relief it must bring to you. Do spend the winter down at the new farm. Both you and Sis dislike the cold weather. I am glad for both John and Fritz that the Abstract business is better and that John could buy Fritz out. For I know that Fritzie ought to have her money invested so it can bring in a steady and sure income regularly. How things are changing. I feel surely I shall be quite a stranger when I return home, and feel just like Muirison.[32] The children will be quite grown up.

Did you ever receive the things I send from Stockholm. They should have been sent to you in October. Surely you have received them. I do hope so. It was such a pleasure to send them.

---

32 Clara's nephew, who was about 13 years old at this time.

There is no opportunity of buying things here, or I should be sending home things by Miss Boies. You can write her when she reaches NY and she can write you all the questions which may fill your minds, and of things which I cannot possibly write about. But which she in America could. I feel as tho my letters must be very disappointing. There is such a lot of things that I would like to fill my letters with, but of course cannot. How much we shall have to talk about when I come home. Just think half the time is gone. It won't be long until my joyful homecoming.

I imagine Helen Ogden will be following Bess home in the late spring or early summer as she does not wish to return down into Russia. And Eliz. Dickerson is getting very restless. If the girls knew poor Eliz's state of mind, I am sure that Marcia would be quite desperate. It really looks as tho Marcia and I were the only sure ones for next year's work, out of this first group. Of course this is confidential information.

It is nearly twelve thirty and time that I was getting into the Land of Nod. It is still mild here. I am not wearing either woolens or furs yet. I wish I knew if you were going to be able to send my muff as I don't know whether to tell Miss Boise to send me one from London. Which would reach me in January.

Here is some more confidential information. If Miss Boies gets sec'ys here to do the war work from France, Marcia and I will sail for Odessa about the middle of January. I think, however, the chances are very slim of our getting out of here this winter. I am not counting on it. But it is a possibility. Five or six of the experienced YMCA men will probably leave here the last of Dec. for there. This is strictly confidential.

Please drop cards to all the friends to whom you have been sending mail, and tell them to write me, for there is no reason why I shouldn't get lots of mail now. Oh, home seems so much nearer now since Sis' letter came.

If you were unable to get the clothes over to me, don't worry, I am getting along famously, and shall be glad of the blue [dress] when it comes, and the waists. The evening dress doesn't matter much. I have asked to have my Feb. salary deposited too, at home, so there will be money to cover the expenses. I hope John has written me of how I stand financially. I must get out of debt soon.

12:15 Thurs. night [Dec. 5, 1918]

This has been a busy day. The morning and afternoon I spent at the Red Cross helping to plan out the Xmas stockings for the Am. soldiers. Each soldier is to have a dandy warm pair of socks. One sock will be put in the toe of the other. Then there will be 20 dates, 25 pieces of hard fruit candy, cup of raisins, and a box of cigarettes and a cup and ½ of assorted nuts. It will take ten days to get the job done, with eight or ten working on the job, mornings and afternoons. We have some high school girls who are helping with it. The Red Cross is giving coco and crackers to the school children of these small towns, so the children are very glad to help.

This evening I spent at the Arkangel canteen taking Eliz. Dickerson's place. It isn't half so much fun, for the crowd is so much greater. I had a jolly visit with some soldiers from Indiana who had just come from the front and hadn't seen an American woman here. They were so delightfully astonished. One of the men showed me a big knife sheathed in a reindeer's foot that he had taken from a dead Bolshevik. The men love to tell of their experiences and especially of their battles and hardships. I have seen pictures of their wives or sweethearts and have really awfully good times if not amusing times talking with them. Most of them are like children in many respects.

Captain Pile, one of the doctors, walked home with us, where we had callers to bid Bess a farewell and wish her safe voyage. Her decision to go on two days' notice has meant lots of extra. We hate to see her go, but all realize it is for the best in all respects.

We have had many irritating delays about the Hostess House. But hope to be in it for the Holidays at least. The men are looking forward eagerly to our opening it. We bought a piano for it today.

Now I must to bed for I am weary, and getting Bess off will be very strenuous tomorrow morning.

Give my love to Mrs. Hogan, I certainly shall send a letter to her on the next boat. Meredith's death is surely a tragedy. It doesn't seem possible that it could be true.

Please tell me about what percentage of my letters have got thru. I shall be eager to know if those that were mailed in Moscow at the Post Office got through or not.

Your asking if I knew of Mr. White's death makes me think that my letter to Fritz did not get thru. A postcard from Fritz rec'd in May telling of her Father's death was the last news I rec'd.

Bess will probably be going to Chicago. She will notify the family so some of you can see her, if you should be there. We hear there are 150 bags of mail on the boat due from London next week. I hope it has something in the way of family letters to me.

With a world of love to each and all, and deep gratitude for the mail, affectionately,

Teke

Clara I. Taylor

Diary
October 25–December 28, 1918

October 25, 1918
Fri. Staff meeting a.m. Made 2 calls on towns women & went to Bath. Girls went to Ralph's for tea. I unpacked & settled things in my room. Rec'd letter written Oct. 11, '17 from home.

October 26, 1918
Sat. Marcia & I busy at Hospital all afternoon. Went to Embassador Tea. Then to Canteen & Dance at British Club.

October 27, 1918
Sun. Read & Ralph came in for tea. Helen laid up with Spanish Infl.

October 28, 1918
Mon. Visited Hospital; need for entertainment there. Am going to help on recreation & Ed & moving pictures

October 29, 1918
Tues. Eng. Chaplain called & invited us to Officers Tea Sunday. Helped in

canteen. Frank returned from front, told of bad swamp conditions under which men fighting. Neva ill.

October 30, 1918
Wed. Spent day helping at Military Mission helping Eliz. with pies & plans for party. Had lunch with the mission. Spent evening at canteen & saw new films. Ralph & R. came down with us.

October 31, 1918 Ark—
Thurs, Spent most of day at Military Mission preparing for Halloween party about 60 people there. Stunts & dancing. Am. feeling more & more resentful at our being in Russia. Permission for Requisition of Hostess House given.

November 1, 1918
Sat Fri. Opening of Red Cross Convalescent Hospital. Darnells open and all fronts turned over to Allies. Spent afternoon at Hospital 53 & evening at home reading & writing. One of the very few quiet evenings at home.

November 2, 1918 Letter 41—Sis
Sat. Spent most of day in bed. Went to the canteen in the evening.

November 3, 1918
Sun. Glorious spring-like day. Attended church. R. L. & I visited Hospital & took walk over target ground bullet went whizzing over head. Attended tea & Central club. British officers Cap't Lively, Lewis, Barr, Bracket came in the evening. Katchia decided to be married at once.

November 4, 1918
Mon. Spent afternoon at Hospital 53. Had tea with officers at their Mess. Spent evening going thru R. publicity material. Talk of peace in Europe continues to grow more prominent every day.

November 5, 1918
Tues. Called on Dr. Langley, went with him thru Olga barracks. Had dinner at General Staff where we had great talk on Bol. Tea at Mrs. Carr's

at 5. Mr. Cook, Consul, Read, Crawford came to play cards in the evening. Definitely arranged 1st concert at Hospital.

November 6, 1918

Wed. Spent day helping to get ready for Catherine Child's wedding—Eliz & I went to the Cleoforths for 8 o'c. dinner. Planned Wisconsin alumni.

November 7, 1918

Thurs. Catherine Childs married at 12. In afternoon had first entertainment at Hospital. Spent evening at YMCA doing Lib. books & films. Delegation left Berlin to plan Armistice.

November 8, 1918, Letter 42—Father, Archangel

Fri. Mrs. Carr & I made calls about rooms for girls work. in a.m. helped Helen with stenciling curtains for YMCA. Wrote letters & did acc't in evening. Germ. is said to accept terms of Armistice. Snowing.

November 9, 1918

Sat. Afternoon at Hospital. Evening helping about books at YMCA. Weather mild. Everybody excited & expectant about peace.

November 10, 1918

Sun. Attended church in a.m. Called with Mrs. Carr on about club rooms. Read, Crawford & Barr came for dinner. R. & I walked to Solombola. Spent evening reading.

November 11, 1918

Mon. Called Embassy, Military Mission & spent afternoon at Hospital 53 & evening marking at YMCA. The Armistice was signed. The French jubilant.

November 12, 1918

Tues. Mrs. Carr, Mrs. Hilder, Mrs. Cleoforth, Col. Stewart came in to afternoon tea. Pete Pierce & I went to Cleoforths in evening. There met Brazilian Argentine Consul, Cap't Carrier & Dr. Langley. Had wild discussion on Bol.

November 13, 1918

Wed. Marcia went to the Front. Saw Col. Morris about mov. pictures. Spent 2 hrs. at the hospital. Men told how French wanted to go home when news of 1st Armistice. Then were appealed to by their General for sake of Am. to stand by. so they did. R. spent evening.

November 14, 1918

Thurs. Mail left for States Neva's name day. Went to Hospital in afternoon. Spent evening at Consul playing cards with Mr. Cole, Pierce, Read—Had delightful tea at 11:30. Perfect weather. Glorious sunset at 3 and moon light at 7.

November 15, 1918

Made chocolate ice cream for Wiscon. party. Went out to Sombola to talk with Mr. Bonti. Attended dance in evening at Convalescent Depot. Thousands of men present.

November 16, 1918

Embassy tea at five o'c. and Wisconsin reunion at 8:30 at Consul's. 14 Grad. Delightful time about 30. We danced, sang college songs. Did stunts. Had edition of "Daily Cardinal."

November 17, 1918

Sun. Snow. for tea Col. Crawford, Major Longley, Cap't Pile, Luet. Parker, Bracket, Lewis came. Read stopped in at 6 o'c. Spent evening writing Xmas mail.

November 18, 1918

Mon. All up about Hostess House. [?] Big meeting of Armistice [?] at YMCA. Took mags & papers to 53.

November 19, 1918

Tues. Spent entire day doing errands. Had concert at 53. Read & Helen came to supper. Later went to Doris & Brackets for party. Glorious snow & moon light.

November 20, 1918, Letter 43
Wed. Began Russian lessons. Sent letter to Father. Went with Bracket to Smolony & later to Mrs. Carrs. Leut. Faye & Cap't Pile called on committee plans for Thanksgiving party. Announcement Wilson's leaving for France.

November 21, 1918
Thurs. Afternoon at Hospital. Evening canteen. In evening Maj. Williams & Kirkpatrick, Cap't Level & Barr came for apple pie spread. Lovely snowy day.

November 22, 1918
Friday Bess & I called at Embassy & Military Mission in a.m. Took magazines out to Am. Hospital. Learned of election returns. More suffrage & more Dry States. Repub. gaining. Wonderful winter weather.

November 23, 1918
Sat. Planned program with Don & two. 3 com. meeting at Red Cross. 4. Hospital 6. Embassy tea. Dr. Kirkpatrick & Cap't Barr came to supper. Dr. & I planned Thanksgiving dinner for Hospital 53.

November 24, 1918
Sun. Bess, Eliz. & I took glorious walk in country. Leut. White & Johnson called. Cap't Henry, Carrier, Pile, Bracket, Crawford came to supper & spent evening. Read went down to the front for a couple of days.

November 25, 1918
Mon. 4° below. Heavy mist until noon. Went to Staff Headquarters at 10 to place decorations. Arranged for Thanksgiving at Hospital 53. Went out there in the evening. Spent evening at home.

November 26, 1918
Tues. Spent day making apricot pies for Hospital 53. Marcia & Frank returned from front. Read came in for the evening. Very cold.

November 27, 1918
Wed. Finished making 52 pies. Took dinner in evening with Cap't Pile at Headquarters. Helen left for the Front. Mild and lovely.

November 28, 1918, Thanksgiving Day
Thurs. Attended church at 11. Dinner at home at 1:30. Entertainment at Hospital at 5 o'c. YMCA wonderful meeting at 7. Party at Staff Headquarters at 9 o'cl. Danced until one. Everybody very happy. British obj. to Bol. having extra dinner.

November 29, 1918
Fri. Every body dead [tired]. Went to Hospital at 4 to visit men & Convalesce Hospital. dance & party at eight. Mail, but none for me. Mild weather.

November 30, 1918, Letter 44 Fritz
Sat. Stayed in bed all morning. Fixed up magazine packets for two Hospitals. Dinner at the Consuls in the evening. Charming time. Cap't Winslow was one of the guests.

December 1, 1918
Sun. Mr. Poole, Crawford & Mr. Summerville came to dinner. Began work at Sombola Hut with Mr. Bonte. The surprise of the men was delightful.

December 2, 1918
Spent afternoon & evening at Sombola Hut. Had afternoon tea with British officers at Sombola Mess. Girls ate with Red Cross & planned Xmas stockings for men

December 3, 1918
Tues. Sent cable to Father in a.m. and received dandy letter from Sis with enclosures in eve. work at Sombola most gratifying.

December 4, 1918
Wed. Bess decided to go to America on Friday's boat. Band concert at Sombola. Out look for Hostess House more hopeful. Weather very mild.

December 5, 1918, Letter 45—Sis
Thurs. Spent practically all day working on Xmas stockings for Soldiers at Red Cross. Cap't Pile, Dan & Read came in at 9:30 for tea & to say goodbye to Bess.

December 6, 1918
Fri. Everybody head over heels getting Bess packed & off. Helped at Red Cross with stockings for soldiers.

December 7, 1918
Sat. Bess sailed on the *Slephuis* S.S. for London. Danced with the men at the Consul until 2:30 teaching Mr. Cole, Strothers & Read to dance. Sang for two hours.

December 8, 1918
Sun. The Davises & Miss Gosling came for dinner. Mr. Poole & Mr. Doolittle came to tea. Read in late evening. Walked home with Mr. Panafor

December 9, 1918
Mon. Cable re'cd from Father. Marcia & I made several calls having tea with Mrs. Carr. Crawford came for supper. Bracket & R. in evening.

December 10, 1918
Tues. Unpleasant rumor that Co. "M" has mutinied because of Eng. killing Am. with Bom from airplane. Days glorious with frosted trees & pink sky.

December 11, 1918
Wed. Russian soldiers refused to go to front. They fired on Am. troops—3 Russians injured. Every one very much stirred up over situation. Went to Smolony & Hospital 53.

December 12, 1918
Thurs. Lesson

December 13, 1918
Fri. Popularity of Hut increases

December 14, 1918
Sat. Marcia & I attended Embassy Tea. & later went to Reg. Headq. with Mr. Cole & Read to picture show, lect. & dance.

December 15, 1918
Sun. Made 500 Biscuits for men at Sombola Camp. Pete Pierce, Mr. Strother, Leut Reis—Leut. Bricker & Miss Forester & Read in for evening.

December 16, 1918
Mon. Went out to Sombola in evening; at 9:30 we all went to Consuls to dance until 1 a.m.

December 17, 1918
Tues. Spent entire day & evening helping Bracket to fix up the Smolony Hut. Visited men at Hospital & decided on Xmas plan for them.

December 18, 1918
Wed. Opened Smolony Hut. Col. Stewart & self guests at dinner at officers Mess. Mr. Poole spoke. Had splendid evening visiting with the Col. & Maj Young. Mail distributed but none for me.

December 19, 1918
Thurs. Busy day at Canteen. Place greatly crowded—4 platoons just returned from the front. Hostess Houses evacuated

December 20, 1918
Busy with Xmas arrangements & Hostess House plans.

December 21, 1918
Sat. Marcia & I had delightful time at Embassy tea, girls went to Engineer's party. Read & I spent evening at home. Helen returned from front.

December 22, 1918
Sun. Mr. Cole, Capt. Lurley & Major Henry came for dinner. Went to Sombola in the evening taking Miss Knox with me.

December 23, 1918

Mon. Helping arrange program & details for Hostess House afternoon & evening at Smolony. Made final arrangements at Hospital 53.

December 24, 1918

Tues. Happy afternoon decorating house & trees. Solombola in evening. Lovely dinner at 10 p.m. Bracket, Don, Jim, Crawford, Read. all had slaws [shredded vegetables, usually cabbage dressed with oil], Eliz & I had cablegrams from home. fixed stockings for hospital. Went to Red Cross Hospital 3 a.m.

December 25, 1918, Archangel

Wed. Began singing carols at 6:00 a.m. 15 of us. Red Cross, Consul, annex, Olga Barracks & Headquarters. Read & I went to Hospital 53 to take dinner. Evening at Smolony. Helen & Marcia at Bakerste. Gloriously happy day. Cable from Father. Made 30 40 gals. of punch.

December 26, 1918

Thurs. Everybody dead tired. Open afternoon & evening at Solombola. Worked on invitations for Opening of Hostess House until 12:30.

December 27, 1918

Fri. Afternoon at Smolony. Took Bracket over to the Hospital. Attended British entertainment in evening at Hospital. Hostess House is lovely.

December 28, 1918

Sat. Everybody engrossed in Hostess House plans. Attended Embassy tea & later Headquarters dance. Weather wonderful.

PART TWO

December 29, 1918 – February 29, 1919

The beginning of December 1918 found the six American women establishing a very busy schedule of canteen work, entertainments, and planning for the Hostess House. Clara's first letter in this section is full of news about their efforts for the soldiers, and then her sudden reversal of role—from comforting patients to being in a hospital bed herself when appendicitis put her out of commission for eleven days in January 1919.

During the second week in December, a mutiny of sorts occurred that increased tensions among the international troops and the native Russian recruits in Arkhangelsk. The situation was downplayed by the official reports, but had the city pretty well "stirred up," according to Clara. The details are unclear, but it seems that some American soldiers refused to muster for duty on December 10 due to their extreme unhappiness and the rumored killing of an American soldier by British "friendly fire" (see diary entry for December 10). That situation was diffused and the American soldiers returned to their duties. However, unrest was rampant in the Smolny barracks, and the following day Russian soldiers of the Slavo-British Allied Legion[33] refused to go to the front. Their barracks were fired upon (a dirty

---

33 This was a company of 3,000 men recruited and trained by British General Poole in Murmansk during the early months of 1918. The men were a motley group of injured former Red Army soldiers, refugees, and volunteers who were offered food and money to join the intervention forces against the Bolsheviks. They proved to be unreliable and reverted to their original loyalties in the summer of 1919 as the international forces were leaving. Known as "Dyer's Battalion," they were meant to be the core of the Russian White Army to whom the British were to hand over the region after the intervention.

job given to the American gunners), and three Russians were killed. The Russians surrendered and returned to duty. In Moore, et al., 1920 (Chapter XXI, "Icebound Archangel"), there is an account by one of the American gunners who is saddened and disgusted by the behavior of the British command over this incident. It is a prime example of the bad feeling between the British and the American forces during the entire Expedition.

The Red Army had increased over the course of the last months of 1918. By mid-January 1919, Soviet Russian troops in the Arkhangelsk region numbered over 22,000 men. They also had sixty-six field guns, nine heavy guns, and 150 machine guns. As David K. Martin notes, in his 1964 manuscript "Teke's Russian Adventure," the Red Army was a formidable force: "Behind the Bolsheviks were the vast resources of Russia. Behind the Allies was the White Sea" (Martin 1964, IX-2). The Red Army was much better equipped, trained, and prepared than the Allies' initial briefings suggested. This was not a rabble, but a well-disciplined guerrilla fighting force engaging in combat on their native soil. The American troops were game but increasingly disgruntled. Their commanders could not tell the men why they were in this conflict—not because the information was classified, but because they truly did not understand. The chain of command from the British Commander in Chief through each of the international contingents was at best difficult and at worst dangerous. The American's "guard duty" had instead become active duty in offensive skirmishes against a well-ordered enemy. Skirmishes gave way to defending the territory taken, and, within short order, the US troops were retreating back to Arkhangelsk. The expedition was failing, and the men knew it.

A series of disastrous battles for the Allies at Kodish, Kelshevo, Nijni Gora, Shenkurst, and Pinega occurred in January and February 1919. The violence had personal consequences for Clara and her friends. Lieutenant Clifford Ballard, a good friend of the YWCA women, was killed at Kodish on February 7. Clara's diary notes this fact, but her comments many years later to her nephew David K. Martin are more poignant. She said, "Lt. Ballard was one of the finest officers we had. He was loved by his men and admired by everyone. Just two weeks before his death he had thought he was to be sent home, so we gave him a special dinner at our house. Oh, there are so many Lt. Ballards. Each such death hit us with the same shock that unexpected death hits in normal circumstances. The shock never lessens because of quantity." Martin recounts how Clara had planned to help Ballard shop for linens to send home to his fiancée and how she lent Ballard her Kodak camera, just a week before he was killed (Martin 1964, IX-21). There were numerous similar stories of brave men who one day were dancing and laughing at the Y entertainments and the next were killed in action.

There are conflicting records of the number of Americans killed in North Russia. As many as 353 fatalities are listed in the Report to Congress by Newton D. Baker, US Secretary of War, 1919. However, Moore, et al., (1920) notes 236 deaths; Cuhady (1924) lists forty-two; and the *Ludington Michigan Daily News* (1919) lists 244 killed in action. Total US casualties have been reported at 2,485 killed and wounded.[34] The final report by Captain C. A. Greenleaf, the commanding officer of the US Medical Corps, lists 1,180 patients between October 1918 and June 1919 at the American Convalescent Hospital in Arkhangelsk.

Much of the work the YWCA women did was to listen with sympathy to the grumblings of the soldiers. Helen Dickerson wrote to her family, saying, ". . . the men are getting very discouraged and low spirited. We spend most of our time trying to jack then up and give them good reasons for being here and sticking to the job until it is finished" (Martin 1964, IX-4, 5). Clara also recounts how she tries to cheer up the soldiers and how she talks with the men about politics. Later, Clara wrote: "We paid dearly for despising that enemy. The Bolshevik soldier is as well-equipped as our men, and his heavy weapons are incomparably superior to ours. He often is better rationed, and, let it be said, he many times appears to be better led" (ibid., X-4). The only saving grace of that disastrous expedition was its short duration.

The Christmas holiday celebrations for the men took an enormous amount of organization. For each man in the three hospitals, Clara and her friends stuffed stockings with dates, nuts, candy, tobacco, and other special treats that had been sent from America. On Christmas Day Clara, Elizabeth, and Helen, plus the hospital staff and commanding officers,

---

34 It is still difficult to find definitive numbers of casualties for the North Russia Expedition. Some sources combine the Arkhangelsk and Siberian actions together, confusing the issue. Some sources are not verifiable. The decades of suppression of information around the Intervention has muddied the waters considerably. Recently, as many as 10,475 total casualties have been reported (McEwen, Y. 2019).

sang to the men as they lay in their beds in awe. December 26, the British holiday called "Boxing Day," was also full of entertainments organized with the women's help.

Christmas was on a Wednesday. On the following Monday morning, December 30, 1918, Clara "stood up and promptly keeled over."[35] She was rushed to the American Red Cross Hospital where she underwent emergency surgery for appendicitis. She is full of chagrin that she should cause so much bother and consternation among her friends. She is also furious to discover that the Red Cross had cabled her family at home. She planned to let everyone know about it once she was completely well again. In her first letter of 1919, she hastened to assure her family that there would be no financial concerns—her operation and nursing after-care costs were covered by the military.[36] Once the surgeons and nurses were fully confident that she had taken no infection, Clara returned to her rooms and commenced a six-week rest and recovery period.

The world news in the early months of 1919 was dominated by events at the Paris Peace Conference.[37] The gathering was convened January 18, 1919, in order to re-establish the fabric of governments and social structures that had been torn apart in the four years of violence across Europe. The war had ripped open borders, devastated cultures; it saw the murder of officials and royals, and "shook forever the supreme self-confidence that had carried Europe to world dominance" (MacMillan 2001, xxvi). Repair was the work of the Peace Conference. One, perhaps best known, result of the conference was the Treaty of Versailles (signed in June, 1919), which set out the terms of peace with Germany. But there were many other relationships in conflict that required treaties to clarify boundaries and recognize the legitimacy of rulers. The geographic boundaries of the new nations created by the fall of the European and Asian Empires needed to be redrawn. "Most important of all, the international order had to be re-created on a

---

35 See Clara's letter dated December 28, 1918, to January 15, 1919.

36 Both of those sentiments—Clara's concern that her family not worry about her, and her extreme concern about finances—were strong character traits found in the Taylor family, and these are present today in their descendants.

37 Please note this summary is greatly simplified. Much of the information presented is taken from Margaret MacMillan, *Paris 1919* (New York: Random House, 2001).

new and different basis" (ibid.). One conundrum engaging the Conference was the Russian problem.

Previously, Russia had been a valued member of the Allied forces. From 1914 to 1917, the Russian Army had held the Eastern Front, inflicting the serious damage to the German army that contributed to the relief of France. But the fall of the Russian monarchy, the murder of the royal family, and the signing of the Brest-Litovsk Treaty in March 1918[38] effectively removed Russia from partnership in the Allied cause. A heated debate at the Paris Conference centered around whether the Russian Republic of Soviets (declared by the Bolshevik party on January 25, 1918), had, by those actions, negated any mutual agreement with the Allied Powers. To complicate matters, the members of the conference had no reliable information on which to base decisions. In the summer of 1918, the Soviets had expelled all foreign diplomats. By early 1919, foreign news correspondents had also been banned. Information reaching Paris was scanty at best. The delegates of the Peace Conference had contact only with a Bolshevik representative in Stockholm who fed them propaganda created by the Soviet government. As Margaret MacMillan wrote in her book *Paris 1919*: "The new regime was under a virtual blockade. . . . The land routes were cut by fighting. Telegrams took days or weeks, if they got through at all" (MacMillan 2001, 64). Lloyd George, the British Prime Minister, later wrote: "We were, in fact, never dealing with ascertained, or, perhaps, even ascertainable facts. Russia was a jungle in which no one could say what was within a few yards of him" (ibid.). The delegates at Paris disagreed about whether the Russians had a legitimate claim to participation in the Conference at all. Some felt that the betrayal of the Allied cause at Brest-Litovsk was enough to exclude the Russians. But more delegates felt that Russia was technically still fighting the Germans and so deserved a seat at the Peace table. The debate was moot—no representative from the Russian Soviet government was present in Paris.[39] And, although the problem of Russia repeatedly came up,

---

38 The Brest-Litovsk Treaty was repudiated by the Soviet government directly after the General Armistice in November, 1918.

39 There was, however, an organization in Paris of non-Bolshevik Russian exiles calling themselves the Russian Political Conference. This group was led by Sergei Sazonov and Boris Savinkov. It was not recognized by the Soviet government, and was discounted by both the Tsarist General Anton I. Denikin (fighting in southern Russia against the

particularly in regard to the borders of the newly independent regions of Finland, Estonia, Latvia, Lithuania, Poland, Rumania, Turkey, and Persia, nothing was settled.

Other significant international news in early 1919 included the Estonian victory over the Red Army in February. After a prolonged siege, the Red Army captured the city of Kiev. A Ukrainian paramilitary unit murdered 1,500 Jewish villagers. In Rugova, Yugoslavian troops massacred 432 Albanian civilians. In the US, a general strike paralyzed Seattle for five days in February. (The mayor of the city blamed the events on the Russian Revolution and announced any man attempting to take over the government would be shot.) Also in February, the US Senate defeated a bill introducing a Constitutional Amendment that would give women the right to vote.

Meanwhile, as Clara recuperated from her operation, Elizabeth, Helen, Catherine, and Marcia took over all of the duties as "morale officers." The Hostess House was completed, and it opened with a party for the enlisted men on New Year's Day. The housekeeping duties were reassigned, with Helen going to the railroad canteen and Clara's YMCA canteens being staffed by the others in rotation. The feeling was that because Clara had set up strong programs for the hospital patients, those could move forward without help from the American women, so that aspect of her work was left to the management of the staff sergeants.

Clara spent her January convalescence studying, reading, going to musical concerts, resting, and completing some paperwork for Marica Dunham and the YWCA administration. She returned to helping at the Smolny Hut Canteen on February 23, and by the twenty-fifth took up all of the housekeeping duties as before.

The early months of 1919 saw the fiercest battles, the fewest victories, the coldest, rawest weather, and the lowest point of morale for the international troops in Arkhangelsk. For Clara, Helen, Catherine, Marcia, and Elizabeth, it was the hardest time to keep the cheer alive. Years later, Clara wrote: "These boys poured their hearts out to us. I agreed with them. I saw no point to our being there. To tell them they had an obligation to

---

Red Army) and Admiral Aleksandr Kolchak (Commander of the northern Siberian anti-Bolshevik forces) who were busy trying to outmaneuver each other for power in Russia (MacMillan 2001, Chapters 6–7).

democracy and the cause of freedom would have been a sham, an insult to their intelligence and ours" (Martin 1964, X-12). Although the stress and tension are of a different caliber than that which they experienced the previous year in Moscow, the war work in the far frozen Russian north is as taxing to their spirits as was revolution in the streets.

Mentioned in This Section:

Miss Gosling and Miss Forester, Red Cross nurses.

Major Henry, Major Longley, Major Kirkpatrick, American surgeons.

Major J. Brooks Nichols, of the Third Battalion of the 339th Infantry, US commanding officer of Railroad Force (Vologda front).

Frank Omstead, Head of Work for YMCA.

Mr. Harry Inman, colleague of Read Lewis in the Public Information office. He was a motion picture specialist.

Leslie Davis (1876–1960), US Consul, and his wife, good friends to the YWCA women.

Chapter Three
"We made thirty gallons of punch."

Diary
December 29, 1918 – January 13, 1919

December 29, 1918, Letter 46
Sun. Miserable. Taken with indigestion at noon. Went to Solombola in evening. Had wonderful talk with group of Am. about Russia. Suffered acutely all way home & all night.

December 30, 1918, Went to Hospital
Mon. Dr. Kirkpatrick called at 3 p.m. pronounced appendicitis. Miss Gosling came with Ambulance at 4. Consultation by Majors Kirkpatrick, Longley & Henry. Operation at 9:15 P.M. All girls & Read came up to Hospital while operation was on.

December 31, 1918, Hospital Archangel
Tues. Quiet comfortable day. several callers. Letter from Genieve—Everything satisfactory. All friends greatly amazed at news of operation. R. L. in twice—bring milk daily. Hostess House musical dance & reception to officials. Cleoforth baby arrived.

January 1, Archangel, Hospital
Wed. Catherine and Eliz., Read in. Much Suffering from gas, hot

applications are on all day. Card from Mr. Pool. Letters from some of the boys—a number of callers & 3 doctors—Consul received from 4– 6. Hostess House opened to the enlisted men. Many there—boys love it—

January 2, 1919, Hospital
Thurs. Leut. Commons came in for long call. Mrs. Carr, Don & several others. Dr. Kirkpatrick secured eggs from somewhere—Temperature and pulse continue to run above normal. eggs $1.00 a piece.

January 3, 1919, Hospital
Fri. Weather mild—feeling better each day—Doctors and nurses wonderful in their attentions. Major Williams sent cable to Father.

January 4, 1919, Hospital
Sat. Letter from Father. Feeling weary from too many callers. Sent long cable home to family.

January 5, 1919
Sun. Very quiet day. No visitors allowed. Helen, Marcia and Read were only ones permitted to come. Pulse and temperature continuing [?] every night.

January 6, 1919
Mon. Frank Omstead, Miss Knox, Dr. Capt. Hall and girls called. Read coming twice a day. Roosevelt died and word received of President Van Huse death. Mr. Copson, Bedman, Watson brought lime juice and coffee.

January 7, 1919
Tues. Weather continues to be very mild. Leut. Reies came in for a long visit and to give gossip of the front. Last drive not satisfactory should not have been ordered. 80 on casualty list. order did not reach men to delay drive.[40]

---

40 During the week of January, the Bolsheviks held Kodish with 2,700 troops; it was recaptured on the seventh by Americans, Canadians, "the King's Liverpools," Russians "Dyer's Best," and French troops.

January 8, 1919

Wed. Men uneasy again to go home. Feeling runs high again against the English. Party at Olga for Co. I men.

January 9, 1919

Thurs. Sat up in bed for first time. Mrs. Consular Davis called and brought cherries. Marcia & Read. Doctor probed wound a little. Temperature very warm slightly rainy.

January 10, 1919, Arkangel

Fri. 11 day in hospital. Sat up in bed most of day. Miss Knox, Bracket, Helen, Eliz, Capt. Livley, Mr. Pool, Col. Stewart. Col. Rugles, Maj. Williams, Mr. Doolittle. Major Langly & Mr. Chikowsky called. Inspected hospital. Crawford and Read came in evening.

January 11, 1919, Hospital

Sat. weather warm and damp. Dressed for 1st time. Marcia, Eliz, Leut Packard, Kleesforth, Chaplin Watson and Watts called. Read in for short time and brought *New Republics* Rumors of Big drive of Bol.

January 12, 1919, Hospital Arkangel

Sun. Dressed, cable from Father. Read called in for dinner. Mr. & Mrs. Davis called in a.m. Gloriously beautiful on the River with rose sunlight. Leut Bricker, Don, an engineer, Nina & Helen in. Nice visit with Dr. Kirkpatrick. 30 degrees below zero. 19 patients came into Hospital.

January 13, 1919, Hospital

Mon. 30 below, clear & beautiful. Lovely pastel colors on the River. Dressed at noon. Read Nov. 23 *Digest*, wrote letters. Received five letters from home all excepting John. Bol. again talking to allies asking to withdraw by [Mar?] 1 as they didn't want to kill them.

Letters

Weather: Dec 28–20° above/ Jan. 13–20° below
[This letter is undated, but presumably was written on January 13. See diary, above: "wrote letters."]

Dear Ones at Home:

You are wondering, I am sure, how we spent the holidays in the Polar Regions. I longed to send you a fifty-word cable telling you all about it, for it was such a very, very happy and unique one.

In our original plans we had not included anything for ourselves, but Elizabeth Dickerson said it was not fair to go two Christmases without any celebrations. So we all agreed. Xmas eve we were busy at our various Canteens. At Sombola the canteen room was beautifully decorated with pines over the windows, candles on the walls, and a beautiful tree electric-lighted on the auditorium platform. Forty members of one of the best Russian church choirs sang there for an hour. When the men returned from the concert room into the canteen, we had the lights out, with only the candles burning. The program, the decorations, and the spirit of the place gave everyone a sense of the Xmas feeling.

At ten o'clock we were all home, that is the four of us who are now in Arkangel. Our rooms we decorated in pines and on our table was a lovely little tree bedecked with cotton, red ribbon and tinsel thread. Five of the men came in, to enjoy the dinner with us. We had a Russian soup, chicken, potatoes, peas, rolls, chocolate ice cream, oatmeal cookies, coffee and the candy which you sent in Aug. (We kept it packed in the tin box, so it was lovely.) A truly wonderful meal for "starving Northern Russia." On the tree for me was Genieve's cable. Read took our cables there at the Embassy and kept them for the tree. For each guest was a [gift] of some sort, which we bought from the peasants in the market. And for each of us girls, done up in various shape packages, was a yellow pencil with a rubber eraser, from Read. Lead pencils with erasers are not to be had in all Russia, Sweden or Norway. Also a large-sized can of powdered George Washington coffee for family use. We finished our dinner about midnight, then sat about the table, and while several helped me fix up tobacco, chewing gum, chocolate bars and cigarettes, for my special men at the hospital, one of the men read aloud the "Dear Mable" stories.

At three a.m. the boys took us up to the Red Cross Hospital where we found Miss Gosling and Miss Forester, the nurses, tucked in bed. We half undressed and slipped in bed until 5:30, when we were awaked to see a little Xmas tree all lighted in the room (we were all sleeping in the same room) and found tied to the heads of our beds, bulgy stockings. We gaily scrambled into our clothes again, and after a cup of coffee, we began our tour.

There were fifteen of us, several officers and privates with excellent voices, and us six girls. We carried big wax candles, and then tiptoed into the big room of the hospital, where the Xmas tree had already been lighted and all the doors leading into other rooms had been opened. We sang "Joy to the World," "Holy, Holy, Holy," and "Silent Night." The patients were much amazed and while they all said they enjoyed it, I fear we sent many heads under the covers, with lumps in their throats that were too big to swallow. One chap that has been in bed for months and who has lost his fighting spirit, looked so ghastly white and pathetic, that I felt as tho for him it were a swan song. In one hospital, one of the men who was lying in one of the rooms where he could not see us, but could see the flickering candle light, was terribly frightened by the singing. He thought he had died. It took him some minutes to get up courage enough to put his hand out to feel if someone was lying in the adjoining bed. But on the whole the Merry Xmas that followed the singing, helped to make the men realize it was Xmas, and this was really going to be a lovely day for them, if they would enter into it. The big ambulance took us from one hospital to the other to one of the big barracks, ending at staff Headquarters where we sang to the officers.

At nine o'clock we were brought home, as day began to brighten. There, hanging from the top of the Russian stove, were four more bulgy stockings, which had been sent to us from the American Red Cross, which were stuffed with hard fruit candies, currents, dates, soaps and pins.

After breakfast, Marcia and Helen left for Bakeritsa, and I began my preparation for my dinner at Hospital 53 where I had been given permission by the charming English Colonel to do whatever I pleased, in the "badly fractured" ward. A few days before I had made all the necessary preparations with the ward orderlies and superintendent Sergeant.

In this room the men lie flat on their backs in wooden frame beds which have a bar running full length over the top of the bed, to which their badly fractured legs are strapped and held by iron weights. Blankets are draped over, so the general effect is of a little dog tent, with only the patient's head visible.

The room was truly lovely. The orderlies had decorated it with pines, and cotton balls made a "merry Xmas" under which they hung an American flag. One of the Russian sisters made a charming cotton Santa Claus which hung suspended from the chandelier. A big table with white cloth was brought into the room, and tables cleared off between the beds.

At twelve o'clock Read and I arrived there, with our trees and hampers in an *Isvaschick*.[41] I put white covers on the little tables, and then little Xmas trees and candles in brass candle sticks. Read brought three lovely posters, which he had just received from Washington. While he tacked them where the men could see them, two other American patients from other wards helped me. I made the men cover up their heads while we tied socks to their beds from the Red Cross filled with dates, nuts, candy, and cigarettes, and four or five other strings of things which the YMCA had given me, and lovely delicacies which had been sent to Am. boys who had either died or been returned to America. (Two big baskets had been turned over to us, to be used in the hospitals as we thought best.) Then we lighted the candles in the trees before the men uncovered. Of course they were delighted.

For dinner we gave them canned corn which I got from the American embassy, turnips, escalloped potatoes, cottage cheese, pickles, home made bread, chocolate ice cream and fruit cake, coffee and candy. Each man had two helpings of all the vegetables, three of cheese and pickles, and ice cream, and the coffee was the first that they had had since coming into the hospital. As they lay there sipping their coffee, they were the most satisfied happy looking men that I had seen in a long time. For an hour Read read the "Dear Mable" stories to them, which brought forth real laughter. The next day the temperature of two of the men went down to normal for the first time in two months.

When we left at three o'clock, we left two pies for the next day, three cans of fruit for evening suppers, and coffee for a second serving.

---

41 A type of one-horse sled, used like taxi-cabs in the city.

From the hospital, I continued on down to Smolony where I am in charge of the canteen. There, we made thirty gallons of punch, using ten apricots, pears, and lime juice. Not a very good combination, but the best and only things that we had.

In the evening we had movies and a jolly sing, giving the men all the punch and a sort of cake, cigarettes, and hard candies.

The open grate fire, the greens, and Xmas tree helped to create a homey, festive atmosphere which generated a genial spirit.

All the men admitted at having a happier day than they thought possible so far away from home. Each American received a stuffed sock from the Red Cross (which we helped to fill) and had extra rations and cigarettes, and happily, the mail came in only three days before with 136 pouches for the soldiers, so home papers, letters and Xmas packages were in evidence everywhere.

Needless to say, that night I crawled into bed too weary for words. I had promised to go up to the Convalescent Depot to a dance at eleven, but I was too weary. Instead, I went home and was the first to turn in.

Thurs., the 26th, the next day, we celebrated the big British (or English, rather) holiday, "Boxing Day" at all the canteens. I went out to Solombola, my other canteen and one I am most partial to, where we have many British, to be hostess there. We had special movies in the afternoon, with vaudeville and a concert in the evening.

There was no chance to do any resting between times, for at least, after long weeks of impatient waiting, with friction and red tape, our Hostess House for American soldiers was turned over to us, so every minute was spent in getting ready for the opening which took place on New Year's Eve to gov't officials and Army officers, and to the enlisted men on New Year's afternoon and evening.

On Saturday, however, I did not go to the canteen, but after putting in most of the day working on the Hostess House, went to the Embassy tea at six o'clock, and to the Regimental Headquarters dance in the evening. We live about a mile from headquarters and the trams stop running at ten. Because of the embassy tea is from 5–7, most people are careless on Sat. night about their meals. So we girls and our escorts, by the time we arrived home at 12:30, were all ravenously hungry.

We started the Samovar going and got out some bread, jam, and can fruit. It was 2:30 a.m. before the men left and we were able to go to bed.

Sunday immediately after dinner I was taken with indigestion, but before I could do anything for it, one of the sec'ys with whom I was planning some new work came in. I thought he never would go. At 4:30 I dashed to my room with a hot water bottle and lay down until 6 o'clock when I took the car for Solombola. For three solid hours I stood in one spot talking with a big group of Americans who were upset over Bolsheviki ideas. I was so engrossed explaining to them why Russia was not prepared for such ideas yet, that I was perfectly unconscious of time or pain. But when the lights were turned out and I started for my wraps, I nearly died with acute pain in a region hereto unknown for pain with me. That hour's trip home in the cold street car seemed endless. But eventually I reached home and I got into bed where I put in the most painful night of my life. I still had no idea what was wrong. The next morning when I stood up and promptly keeled over, made us think there might be something more than indigestion. Dr. Kirkpatrick, a fine surgeon and physician, was called in at three. At four-thirty the ambulance and nurse were there and, to the horror of the Russian household, lifted me out of bed and carted me off to the American Red Cross Hospital.

All the orderlies and sergeants in the hospital were at the door when I arrived, and nice big Dr. (Major) Henry, who was the Am. doctor at British Hospital 53 when many of our men were there. I was carried up to Miss Gosling's and Miss Foerster's room where Miss Foerster was waiting to receive me.

Then followed the examinations by Major Henry, Major Longley who is head surgeon of the medical forces in the Expeditionary force, and Major Kirkpatrick. They decided it was unwise and unsafe to wait even six hours longer, and as I was in a perfect condition for an immediate operation it ought to be done.

An operation has always seemed as far removed from possibility to me, as coming to Russia, and sailing on the Arctic and White Seas. But Sunday nights' suffering had prepared me for any suggestion, so when the three physicians, at 8:30, asked me what I was going to do about it, I replied that I thought it was a case of my waiting judgment on a jury in whose hands

I had suddenly fallen. They never waited a second longer, but ordered the ambulance sent for Marcia and they retired to the operating room.

The orderlies, who, thirty minutes later carried me down there looked so pathetically concerned, that I had to laugh to cheer them up, and at the same time I was quite like the small boy who whistles in the dark.

I went under the ether very quickly and without a sound, just as my whole family arrived upstairs. At ten o'clock, just one hour from the time I went onto the table, I was returned to my room, regaining consciousness at midnight. Altho my operation was sudden and at night, by midnight all Arkangel knew and was amazed at the suddenness of it all. Letters, messages, and callers poured into the hospital all during the next three days. I have truly been quite overcome with the thoughtfulness which has been showered upon me. In this land where we have been living on canned and powered food, I have had fresh cow's milk every day—three glasses procured and delivered by Read—fresh eggs, which Dr. Kirkpatrick miraculously bought, rusks (a sort of zwieback) from Mr. Cole of the Consular staff, grape juice send in by Lt. Morley, cherries from America from the wife of another consul, coffee and lime juice from British and Am. YMCA; Madison and St. Louis newspapers from some of the soldiers, reading matter, candy and innumerable other things.

My "Major Operation" performed by three Major doctors was quite the joke of the town, and in fact you will see it heads the funny column in the Am. newspaper (which you might pass on to Lou as he will find it interesting). There never was a girl anywhere in the world in more skilled and thoughtful hands than I. Not only did these three busy doctors help in the operation, but have come in once or twice a day and Miss Gosling is another Miss [...?...] Taff. She has been head of a hospital in America, and both she and Miss Foerster are such good friends of ours. From the orderly who brings my tray (the tray being made by one of the men especially for me), down (or up) to the cook who has helped in the preparation of my meals, everyone has done his best to serve me, and are interested in seeing me get along well. And with such loving care, and having been in fine physical condition, I have proven to be a model patient. My case has been true to form, no complications, no infections, and not the usual unpleasantness that comes with operations. The doctors and nurses finally had to shut down entirely on callers as I had from five to fifteen a day and began running a temperature and pulse. All the dignitaries have been in, from Col Stewart head of Am. Forces, Mr. Pool of Embassy, Col. Rugles of Military Mission and many friends among the officers. But best of all were the two long letters. Geney's 2nd to Archangel with pictures, and Father's (this morning). Capt. Livily from the Red Cross mission came up with Father's cable gram. I can't tell you how deeply I regretted that the Red Cross thought it best to cable home. Never would I have done it and it was decided against my wishes, for I had not expected to let you know anything about it until I was entirely well, as I knew you would be anxious and that you could not possibly realize how well cared for I am. And as for expenses, this is where money is absolutely no consideration. Perhaps I can pay part of my indebtedness in pies to the doctors, but some way and somehow I want to express my appreciation in a very substantial way to Miss Gosling. When she returns to America I think it can be arranged. This was a "military operation" so to speak, so no personal expenses are in any way attached. And in America I would not have had so much expert medical attention as I have received so generously and graciously here. The days here in the hospital have been beautifully spent. I have slept ten to twelve hours a day, and am feeling fine.

This is the end of my stationary so will bring this to a close. Will write another letter for this same mail to Genieve which you will have in time.

Up to date I have received Genieve and Father's Xmas cables, Father's cable in answer to Major Williams, a letter from Sis, the one from Father about his trip, and Geney's 2nd letter to Arkangel. There is mail in today but so far no mail for me. Helen Ogden has received 9 thru Embassy pouch.

Father, arrange for a code address with Western Union, and send it to me. Don't worry dear ones, I am not working until middle of Feb., resting 6 wks, am leaving hospital Jan. 14 (tomorrow) the 15th day. Five more sec'ys are on their way here to help in work.

Mail just rec'd. 2 from Sis, ones from George, Leslie, and Fritz. All Stockholm mail. Deeply grateful, with a big heart full of love to all you blessed ones at home, from your affectionate and convalescent,

Clara

(Father's cable came Xmas morning)

Jan. 15, 1919
Weather 10° above
Arkangel Russia

Dearest Geney:

Your first letter in almost a year, written Nov 4 (1918), to Arkangel reached
me my second day in the hospital. You can never know its welcome. A week
later Father's came just exactly a year from the time I rec'd his first letter
in Moscow. On Jan 12th (Sun.), the following letters came: Leslie's, Oct.
11, with Kodak pictures, George's Oct. 15, Mary's, Sept. 24, and Oct. 11,
Fritz's Sept. 23; yours and Father's letters of a later date written directly
here came two weeks earlier.

From Sis' letter of Oct. 11, I arrived at the conclusion that my cable of
Sept. 28, stating, "Sailing Narvik to Arkangel, weather fine spirits high,
plenty food, warm clothing, send mink muff." never reached you. Also I
never rec'd Father's cable sent Oct. 9 as you doubtlessly gathered from my
wails.

After all your lovely letters came, I was filled with contrition for having
doubted for a minute that you all were not doing your best to get letters
thru. Well, you will forgive me, I know, and you all are such comforting
trumps never to breathe the anxiety that I know I caused you during June,
July and Aug. when we were in such constant danger, and could absolutely
get no word out to you. Father, I am sure, can easily understand how in
time, we got so we were perfectly regardless of shooting. It went on daily,
but somehow we, like everyone else, went about our business, with sort of
a fatalistic spirit that the soldiers grow to have—that we won't be hit unless
our time has come. Altho we all felt the strain keenly, and suffered because
of the misery about us, we became, excepting on those days when things
were especially tense or serious, perfectly unconscious of the ever-present
danger of a life and death matter. And while we left Soviet territory with
the deepest regret (a regret of taking comfort away from those who so
needed us in all their distress), from the health stand point, of course, we
are infinitely better off. Here, there is no strain that used to nearly snap
our nerves. All the buoyant joy, which I thought had been entirely crushed
out, is again perfectly natural. So when the opportunity comes again, for
returning into Russia proper, we shall go, fresh, strong, and ready with
enthusiasm to take up our work again in Petrograd and Moscow and other

new centres. And family dear, I am so thankful to be here, doing this army work, doing my bit in war times, and being ready to return to Moscow where the needs are unparalleled.

Your letters were such a comfort because everyone seems so happy and well. The news of the sale of the farm which meant cutting down part of Father's heavy indebtedness was the best of all. How I wish it might all have been wiped out. I hope the new investment is a first class one. And Leslie's having bought a farm, John's business greatly improved, and Fritz loving her work are such comforting facts to make me happy. And oh how thankful, you can not realize how thankful I am, that our men folk are not needed for active army service. I am proud of their desires, enthusiasm and loyalty, it couldn't have been otherwise. As a family we have so much, so very much, to be grateful for.

My hospital experience was very happy, which was fortunate since it seems to have had to be. My room had three large double windows looking out to the southwest over the snow covered Dvina River. At Arkangel, it is about two miles across. At about nine thirty or ten, on clear days, the sky would grow rosy pink. At ten (or so) the big red sun ascends a little above the horizon, sending its slanting rays across the river, covering everything with those exquisite shell pink and lavender colors that are so divinely lovely. By one thirty the sun has run its short course, and the richer deeper colors once more paint the sky. The uncertain daylight of the next hours is so mystic.

My river is more than a great white snowy way. From my bed I could see the frequently passing, fleet-footed reindeers with their horny branches looking a heavy adornment for such trim little beasties. The Laplander drivers are dressed often in brilliantly dyed skin coats of green and yellow with banding of bright red and blue, always wearing the white fuzzy fur cap. There are many roadways to Bakerita and little neighboring villages across the river, which I shall explore during my convalescent period. For I am to loaf for a month from the time I come out of the hospital.

Right opposite the hospital, a short distance out from shore is a clump of pine trees planted in the ice. While it looks like a little green oasis, it is no other than the washing hole for the women of the neighborhood. All during the day women go back and forth, balancing their burdens suspended from the wooden yoke bar across their stout shoulders. Can you imagine what it would be like to dip wet clothes into ice water in temperatures varying from 20° above to thirty below. I have yet to see the big ice breaker ships which ply between here and Murmansk, and which are looked forward to with such expectancy, as they bring our mail. No matter what you hear about our being shut off, rest assured we will not be, and mail will reach us every three or four weeks and even oftener. Some of the things which are being written about our being locked in this ice bound coast are most absurd. Until the 10th or 13th of January we have had wonderful weather, steady at about 20–30 above. A few times going down to zero or a little below. The 12th it went to 30° below, but today, the 15th, it is snowing and milder. We are enjoying one of those exceptional winters. The admiralty forecasts were for our severest weather in Feb., March, and April, and I guess they are true.

Well, I was in bed only eleven days, returning home on the 15th day. I felt quite humiliated to be brought home in an ambulance, but it was 9° below and two flights of stairs down the hospital and one up to my rooms. My return trip was very comfortable and not filled with the strain and pain of two weeks previous. I brought home with me a dandy down comforter which I am to keep until ours comes from England with the five secretaries who are to join us. They are supposed to be leaving England about now. So I suppose it will be about the middle of Feb. when they arrive, as all must go by Murmansk. So if you sent things that I wrote for from Stockholm, you may know about when I will receive them. I am disappointed about the muff, but I may not need it at all. Don't send evening dress, if you haven't arranged for it, but the silk will be gratefully received. Canteen work is very hard on clothes, but I am getting along nicely. I don't want any of these things to hold over when I return home.

Last night I had a great lark. I felt quite like a boarding school girl, breaking rules. Over at our [residence] house, where all but Marcia and I live, and where we have our sitting room and dining room, the girls had a small group in. Two Wisconsin University men, whom I had not met, and several other officers, and the two women (Scotch and American), from the Embassy. Read decided it wasn't quite fair for six Wisconsin alumni to come to our house and for me not to be present. So up to the hospital he trudged to ask my two good nurses what the prospects were of my going. They approved and said it would do me a lot of good, provided I didn't walk up or down stairs. He made them draw up a document and duly sign it, addressed "To whom it may concern," and came down at eight o'clock determined to take me over if I felt equal to it. The girls were busy at the Hostess House until nine o'clock. When Marcia appeared at our room with three of the men, who wanted to see me, I was laying down, as any patient might be expected to do who that day had just returned from the hospital. At ten o'clock, I bundled up, and Read carried me over, which is just next door. The guests, in true Russia fashion, were all sitting around the table at tea, when we tip-toed into their astonished midst. The amazed expressions on the faces of those who had thirty minutes before been in our room, was perfectly delightful. It did seem good to be at home once more and see a little life. Just one hour from the time I went over, I was safely back in my room, no worse for the outing. Today, Miss Gosling, my nurse, came in for a couple of hours, and finding me looking so well, said that, with Helen's help, I might walk downstairs and over for supper. Which thing I did do. Tomorrow I walk a block and a half to see Mrs. Davis, wife of Am. Consul, and so each day lengthen my walks until I can walk four blocks over to the Consulate where Mr. Cole, Head of the Consular Staff, has invited me to come the very first dinner that I am able to take away from home.

Just as soon as I feel like taking longer walks, Miss Gosling and I are going to walk out to the big hospital ship and have tea with the twelve English nurses there, and incidentally see some of our boys who are ill there.

This month will be terribly trying in many respects, but very profitable in others. Miss Boies who was married in Nov. [to Thomas Cotton] is doing canteen and hospital work on the YMCA canteen cars on the R. R. which stops at all points where there are troops, taking supplies of all sorts, and comforts. One car is fitted up with library, writing tables, Victrola, and there also the boys can buy hot coffee and coca, etc. At present Elizabeth Dickerson is at one of the canteens at the front, where we supply a worker. (It was my turn this time.) So with me laid up, it leaves Miss Dunham and Miss Odgen and our Russian sec'y, the responsibility of our own Hostess House and the big central canteen here in Arkangel, and my two places, Smolony and Solombola, and Hospital 53. To say nothing of the innumerable demands which are constantly coming up. It is going to be very hard to loaf and see my colleagues carrying such heavy responsibilities. If only the workers [from NY] could have started in Dec. as we so persistently and insistently cabled, for they would be here now, and what is more, I probably would not have had this attack of appendicitis which came from getting too tired.

By the way two of the five are probably Industrial club workers who will be in my Dep't when we go down into Russia again.

The month will be profitable because I will sleep ten hours a day, have Russian lessons twice a day as soon as I feel like it. A big pile of Nov. and Dec. magazines were sent to me by the Bu. of Public Information to be read while I am getting my strength back. I have also two of H. G. Wells' books, and three Russian books which I hope to read, and so get caught up a bit.

Did I write you that John R. Common's son is here and is a very delightful person, a Lt. in the machine gun company. We exchanged calls on each other while [we were both patients] at the hospital. He was not well and was there just the week before I was taken ill. He is at the front now. Yesterday, I received a note from Mr. Hallick and hope to meet him when he returns to Arkangel, or see him when I go down to the canteen at the front. He happens to be stationed at the field headquarters at the field canteen. Tell Mrs. Chas. Young that I know the Major, with whom he corresponded. You might add that I hope he is no relative.

You all know of course that most of the men are from Michigan, and most of the officers from Wisconsin. Many being University graduates. However, I have met men from Springfield, Virden, Clinton, Carbondale and other central Illinois towns. I would give anything to know what you in America think is going on up here. Well, someday you will know. It would make amazedly good juicy writing. A year from this summer, we will have long talks about the great events which I have been so fortunate to witness. I can't tell you of the many happy memories I have had, of that last Sunday night when we all went out to the farm for our supper and sat about the campfire discussing the war and Russia's part in it. For two weeks now, I have dreamed every night of being at home and, because of your letters, they are very happy times.

A year from this summer we must have one grand time. Already I am looking forward to a year from March or April, when I probably shall sail for home, as the N.B. [National Board of the YWCA] will doubtless expect me to do a lot of conference work. So I will get home early in the spring to ensure a long uninterrupted visit before the conferences begin.

Now just a little about our Hostess House before I go to bed. I will write more about it in my next letter. We have three large rooms filled with small square tables, around which are taberet stools, and on the tables are little earthenware dishes painted blue for ash trays. At the windows are unbleached muslin curtains, stenciled in blue, and heavy linen curtains, also stenciled in blue, hanging as portieres between the doors. In the first big room is a Victrola, which the men keep going constantly while they drink their tea, coffee or coca, which is served to them by attractive Russian girls in peasant costumes. Next is the music room where the piano goes constantly, and where the men sing as the spirit moves them.

Hurrah, a soldier has just brought me you first letter to Arkangel, Geney, written Oct. 26th. Ain't it grand. Another boat has just come in. Maybe tomorrow there will be other letters. Wasn't it nice of the Embassy (not Legation) to send it right down, and it is now ten o'clock at night. (Stockholm has a Legation, but Russia an Embassy, the Embassy will always know my whereabouts.)

To continue, in this room and the one just back of it, the reading and writing room, the men spend much time. We have a very limited library of magazines and books but they are used to the limit. Chess, dominos, and checkers are played a lot. On the walls of all the rooms are candles, and some splendid US posters sent from Washington. The place is supposed to be open from 2:30–9, but as a matter of fact, soldiers are there from 9 a.m. until ten p.m. It is a surprisingly homey, cozy place. Two plants and home made cookies add much to the popularity. The men are quite crazy about it, and have spent more time there than at the big YMCA. Every company that returns for rest quite takes us by storm. We have no special entertainments excepting some informal musical evenings. The officers would love to come there after nine, but the men don't leave, and it makes our days too long.

Now for your questions, Geney. I have all my worldly possessions with me. Half of them were on the Volga boat all summer. To leave them behind was to lose them. My coat was cut short about 7 inches. It's plenty warm. If it isn't, I shall have a trench coat from the YMCA. I can get army equipment if I need it. I am getting a warm helmet. My cap does not come over my ears. We are doing only army work, canteen, hospital, and acting as hostess to the whole Am. forces and officials here. Our very presence counts for a great deal. We have no idea when and how we shall return to Moscow, many rumors are afloat, but it is quite impossible now to forecast. The unexpected and seeming impossible has happened so frequently that I may yet find myself embarked for Odessa before the middle of the summer.

Now, dear ones all, continue to write, all of you, and tell the people who are receiving copies of my letters that I long for newsy letters from them. Fritz's letter was a wonder for news. I was quite breathless after reading it. Ask me questions if I don't tell what you want to know. While I am laid up for repairs, I hope my letters will be better. Most have been written during midnight hours. Lovingly,

Clara

Diary
January 14 – 19, 1919

January 14, 1919, 9 Below, Home from Hospital
Came home in ambulance at 12 o'clock. Marcia sent cable to Am. In evening Read carried me over to the other house to the amazement of all. Leut. Taylor Johnson, McMurry, Crawford, Wisconsin & Ballard. Woodward & Knox. It was a great lark & I was none the worst for it.

January 15, 1919
Wed. Wrote letter #47 Genieve—Read. In evening walked over to other house. Miss G. in for 2hrs. reports 3 companies will go to Murmonsk at once. Much milder weather.

January 16, 1919
Thurs. Not feeling very strong. Did not go out, read & lay down most of the day. Read came in for cards until 10:30.

January 17, 1919

Fri. Went over to other house, twice. read letter from Sis. Miss Gosling came in. Read read aloud H. G. Wells. Had great discussion on Strother poem. Weather clear, crisp and lovely about 10° above.

January 18, 1919

Sat. Went to Hostess House & over to meals. wrote letters. Visited with soldier from the front & wrote Eliz, Mr. Halloch, finished reading *New Waskear* [?]

January 19, 1919, 25° below, clear & beautiful

Sun. (Began Russian tutors) Read, Col. Stewart Maj. Nickolas, Craig came to dinner. Russian Pedg Uni girl Loerstu, Gosling, Let. Bricker called. Read came to supper, took me to Hostess House for 15 min. Terp [?] and Berk came in evening. Read & I began *The Passionate Friend*.

Chapter Four
"Loafing is a strenuous time consuming demon."

Letters

My dear Leslie:

It was good to receive your long newsy letter (of Oct. 11) with the enclosed pictures. You can have no idea of what it means to be for months in total ignorance of all that is happening in the lives of your loved ones. I felt that the war must be making many changes. It was with a joyful relief that I read of the good health and prosperity of the whole family. I am sure that we will feel that we are all much closer together, now that letters and cables can be pretty surely relied upon of getting thru within a reasonable time.

I still feel a protesting regret that the family were informed of my illness. We all regretted it, but since it was done, I hope that it has not caused an undue amount of anxiety.

I have been home from the hospital just a week now, and am steadily regaining my strength. The family may rest assured that I will not return to work until I am fully recovered. I walked four blocks today on the protected side of the street. Almost immediately on going out of doors in this temperature the hair, eyebrows, and eyelashes become frosted. The horses are completely white. The sled drivers are so picturesque in their big white and brown fur coats. These coats barely clear the ground, and the head of the animal forms the cavernous hood in which the man's face is all but hidden. And yet the natives say it is quite mild. We have heard of temperature from 50–70° below. How would you like doing guard duty for four hours at a time in such intense cold.

Our soldiers look very comfortable in their outfits. Beside heavy woolen underwear, most of them wear sweaters under their uniforms, and a sleeveless leather jacket. Topping off with the big over coat, fleeced lined, with high collar. Besides a warm scarf. They each have a heavy woolen helmet which covers the face completely excepting the eyes. Over this is worn the big fur hat, with flaps which button over the chin. On their feet they wear heavy stockings which come up to the knee, two pair of heavy socks, and may, and often do, wear as many as five pairs, inside a big no. 12 white canvas shoe, the top of which comes about half way up the legs. Everybody wears yarn mittens regardless of position. I should say mittens, for the usual number is two pairs. The soldiers of all the allied forces are equipped the same in their midwinter suits, so unless they wear their emblems on their coats or hats, it is often difficult to tell which nationality they are— American, British, French, or Russian. One of the distinguishing marks in the suits of British and American is that our men have dull buttons, and the others' are shiny. While the French wear a grey blue uniform and a sort of tam hat.

How I wish you could see the YWCA Hostess House for American Soldiers. Sunday night I walked over there for fifteen minutes. Every chair was occupied, one of the engineers was playing the piano, and all the fellows in the music room were singing. In the reading room, the table lamp, and the magazines and papers strewn about, and men writing at the writing tables gave the whole place such a homey atmosphere. I went over to take two new December magazines which Read gave us and to say good bye to a group of engineers who were leaving for the front today, and who had told Marcia that they had hoped to see me before they left. Several were U. of Michigan men to whom I had been lending my personal books on Russia. It makes me very eager to get back to work. I am rather planning to loaf until March before resuming very much responsibility. It's hard to get used to lying around and reading. I am getting informed, for one thing. I am reading one magazine a day. I began Russian lessons yesterday so hope to make some real progress in language work. When we are busy with canteen work language work is quite impossible. None of us here will make good language students because we take the shortcut by using interpreters.

Sis asked if we were doing anything with French. No, but we do wish for it. It is quite essential to have it. And in our canteen work, we would find it so useful.

Sunday, Colonel Stewart, Major Nickols and Mr. Craig came for Sunday dinner. Col. Stewart we like very much. He is so informal and chatty. He is head of the American troops here. (My special comment of Col. Stewart is no reflection on the other two men who are among the finest here.)

I have not met Mr. Hallock yet, but will when he comes up here, or I go down to the canteen where he is stationed. I had a note from him the other day asking for some information which I could get for him. By this time you know of Link's death. He died before my arrival at Arkangel. He was taken ill on the boat with influenza, suffered a relapse, and died of pneumonia about Sept. 7.

The men very naturally dread going out and being out at the front during this bitter weather. When they return here, everybody does their best to give them a happy time. Evening with special movies and refreshments are usually exclusively given each returning company. At the Smolony, central huts, and our Hostess House, some of our most important work is inviting nice Russian girls for various small dancing parties. On next Tuesday night, we are using the Hostess House exclusively for a dancing party for the band men. They play for all parties and entertainments and rarely have an opportunity to join the fun. So this party is especially for them.

We feel very discouraged about the arrival of the other secretaries. They haven't left England yet, and probably won't for a couple or three weeks longer, and then it will take them most of a month to get here after they leave England. It isn't likely that we shall see them much before early March. They are bringing us new uniform blue suits. Now that we can have them, we are not so keen about it, as we have come to realize that in this land of uniforms the men are grateful for seeing us dressed like Americans. Our American clothes are one of the things that remind them of home. Canteen work is hard on our clothes, so by spring we may be very glad to have them. And since I need another suit, I am doubly thankful. It will be good to travel in, whenever we shall leave here. A date about which we all do much speculating. My guess is June. We are awaiting, eagerly, the results of the Paris conferences. We all long to hear what the policy is to be here in North Russia. "British North Russia," as it is often ironically spoken of.

One of the sergeants was telling me an interesting incident which truly exemplified the charming relationships here between the French and the Americans. On this particular front a few of our men were killed and it was not possible to send their bodies back here for burial. The French, with all their impulsiveness, insisted on making the wooden boxes for burial. And one Frenchman who thought he was about the size of a particular Am. got into the box to see if it was comfortable. They dug the graves, assisted at what was a very impressive funeral, and later built a fence around the graves. The impulsive, generous, gay Frenchmen not infrequently embarrasses his admiring loyal American friends. The fraternal spirit which exists between them is truly beautiful. As beautiful as some other relationships where understanding is most expected, is deplorable. To put it mildly and discreetly. If it were not for the censorship, what a lot of amazingly juicy bits we all could tell in our letters.

Now, Leslie, I have reread all the last letters and find no questions asked, so guess I must have told all that you particularly desire to know. We have about 10 inches of snow, only. Will probably have severe weather now for two months. Our houses, where we both live and work, are always comfortably warm. Our food is good, and plenty of it, and so far my clothes seem plenty warm. I can at any time have a fleece lining from a trench coat should I need it. So I have no complaints, and you all at home have no cause for worry about me. Any mail, no matter how addressed, if sent to Arkangel, will reach me. There are only seven American women here. So we are well known. All mail better be addressed in care of the Embassy, as in case of change of residence in Europe, it is more likely to reach me thru the Embassies. They would naturally know of our whereabouts.

Tell Dr. Guy I have been grateful many times for the adhesive and other things with which he equipped me before I left. I hadn't known until your letter that Sam Herdman had reached France. I supposed he will be getting home in the late spring or summer. Oh Lelliboy,[42] a year from this summer

---

42 Clara's affectionate nickname for her brother Leslie.

I shall be home. Already I find myself planning about it. I dream of home so much these nights, I suppose it is because of the recent letters and cables and because I have so much more time to think of home.

Genieve's cable came Monday morning the 21st, and brought me lots of joy. What does it cost you a word to cable me. From here to Taylorville (Chicago rates) it is three rubles. By the way, please enclose a small calendar in your next letters. You know Russia uses two dates and the calendars are most confusing. I like the little one page calendars.

Jan 23, zero and snowing
Well my room got cold, so I undressed and went to bed, and read H. G. Wells' *Passionate Friends* until Marcia came home at ten.

This morning I thought that I was getting up early, but it was about ten thirty when Zoa, the maid, brought in my steaming brass samovar. After finishing my breakfast of George Washington coffee, bread and jam, I studied Russian for an hour. Then went over to the other house for dinner. Since then, in spite of the raw disagreeable weather, I walked six blocks on the wind-sheltered side of the street, have lain down for an hour and a half while reading Russian, and will finish this before going out to call on Mrs. Davis, wife of one of the consuls.

On my way home from there I will stop at the Hostess House to walk home with Marcia and Helen. Fortunately for us, the Hostess House is just a short block from where we live.

Last night we received a letter from Colonel Stewart expressing his and the officer's appreciation of the Hostess House and all that it means to our men.

This morning I sent a cable home thru the Red Cross. They informed us the other day that we were eligible to cabling thru them, and thus saving 12c on each word, so I have saved two dollars on this last cable. I will cable often and the truth about my health. Everyone is so amazed to see how well I look. I lost only a few pounds, but fortunately my face doesn't show it and now that I am sleeping and eating so much, I will not only quickly regain, but add a few pounds, I am sure.

Today the Embassy folk called up and offered us "Loot," a roguish little pup which we have coveted for our Hostess House. The girls are turning it over to my tender care for a month's training, before we take him over to the other house. The men will love petting him.

I have been deeply interested in what the *New Republic* is printing about Bolshevism. As well as some other magazines. Leslie, you ought to subscribe to that magazine. It is a very progressive and somewhat daring opinion magazine. You and John and Dr. Guy would all find your sentiments very satisfactorily expressed in its articles.

All of us here regret so exceedingly the deaths of Roosevelt and President Van Hise. I wonder what has been done to fill the vacancy made by Pres. Van Hise's death.[43] Leslie write me (1) about what happened to Raymond Robins as regards to Russia. Was he not allowed to talk. (2) what did you men feel about Wilson's appeal for a democratic congress. (3) What do people think is the policy for northern Russia, what do they think is going on up here anyway. What seems to be the general sentiment in the country of the Russian situation anyway.

I am sending home another *Sentinel* which I would like passed on to Lou when the family is thru with it. Also please give the enclosed letter to John. I am hoping to get my business, or finances, rather, in a better condition during the next six months.

I am so glad that you have been able to buy a farm, Leslie, and John the abstract stock, it certainly spells prosperity. I have wondered if Geo wouldn't like to get into some of the foreign work. His legal education would certainly count a lot. He might work in the Bureau of Public Information. Propaganda work in the various countries, or in Consular service. Hundreds of consular positions are opening up as a result of this war.

Now must close. This leaves on a boat going from here on the 24th. I wonder when it will reach you. My guess is about the last of Feb. as the service between here and England is very slow during the winter months.

With a very great deal of love to all of you dear thoughtful people at home, and best regards to a host of friends from your affectionate sister,

Teke

Clara I. Taylor

---

43 Charles Van Hise (1857–1918) was an American geologist and progressive academic who served as president of the University of Wisconsin from 1903 to 1918.

Feb. 1, 1919
Arkangel

Dearest Family:

Tomorrow the mail closes, and a boat will soon be leaving for home. For one whose chief duty in life is loafing, you naturally would think that I would have a diary letter begun. But no such thing. Loafing is a strenuous time consuming demon, which leaves no time for worth-while accomplishments. This fall I got into the habit of going to sleep about two a.m. and haven't been able, altogether, to break it up. So I usually sleep until ten. Shortly after my breakfast is finished, my language teacher comes for a lesson. Then it is time for one o'clock dinner. That is followed by a nap, a walk, stopping in at the Hostess House for a few minutes, and home for supper. In the evening I usually prepare my lesson for an hour and a half and then either read, or usually there are guests.

I am looking so rested, and having lost no flesh, it is hard for people to realize that I have been ill. There is no question but that I am looking fine, better than in Dec. when I was so dreadfully tired. I am taking long daily walks now, which will put me in trim very shortly. This morning was glorious. When I awoke, I saw a deep blue clear sky, and the snow fairly red in the brightest warmest sunlight that we have had. When my teacher came, I suggested that we have a very practical lesson and walk for an hour. Perhaps it was twenty or twenty five degrees above zero. The air was dry and bracing, and life seemed altogether worthwhile. We strolled up the main street until we came opposite the reube (market) where we turned off and wandered through the stalls, enjoying the sights of the heavily furred drivers, the sleds, and the bargaining of the shoppers. For one always bargains in the market.

This afternoon I had promised to go at three o'clock with one of the machine gun officers to buy, or pass judgment on, Russian handiwork. But a note arrived just a few minutes ago saying that at midnight last night he had received orders to go early this morning to the front. So the time, you see, is to be spent visiting with you loved ones at home.

Wednesday evening we gave a party to the members of the Band. They are such trumps in always playing for all the parties and entertainments which are given here, that we feel it was only fair that one night they should be free to enjoy themselves. So we requisitioned the entire Band of forty members, and closed the Hostess House to all others. Besides dancing, we arranged a short, but very beautiful, musical program. A Russian violin-cello and singer came in for an hour. Their music was truly lovely. The best that I have heard since leaving Moscow. The accompanist for these two artists has composed a very stirring new national hymn for Russia. He presented each one of us with a copy.

On Thursday afternoon, Miss Gosling, my nurse, took me to call on the nurses on the big hospital ship. This enormous freighter, which used to ply between England and South Africa, was converted into a wonderful hospital. All the comforts, luxuries and conveniences of a modern hospital are to be found there. After having tea with the nurses, the matron took us all around so we could visit our men, who look so comfortable and well cared for. Before we left, I promised to arrange some band concerts to be given there in the afternoons. Our men were delighted, and will go there for an hour next week, and each week after, if everything is satisfactory. There has been very little in the way of entertainment at Hospital 53, since my illness. So I am anxious to get back on my job again.

Tomorrow (Sunday) Col. Richmond, Head of Hospital 85 (just opened in Solomobala), Col. Orward , Head of "53," Mr. Poole, Charge d'Affaires, Mr. Lee, of Embassy, and Read Lewis are coming in for afternoon tea with me. These three English officers I have enjoyed knowing so much, as I have met them in my work, and socially, at teas at their officer's mess. They all have the welfare of all the men very much at heart.

Friday night I had a real coming out party together with Mrs. Kliefoth, wife of one of our military mission Lieutenants. Miss Foerster, who assisted in my operation and stayed until I came out from under the effects of the ether at midnight, was called at 5 a.m. that same day, to the Kliefoth home to assist master Kliefoth's arrival into the world. So last night at the consul-ate, Mr. Cole, Mr. Strother, and Read gave a "patients-nurse" party for us. There were twelve guests, a delicious dinner and a really very jolly time. Our nurses gave us permission, from henceforth, to accept invitations in moderation. It was Helen Ogden's birthday, so Read surprised her with a beautiful big chocolate layer cake. With candles. I happen to know that that cake contained twenty eggs at fifty cents an egg. Needless to say, we do not eat eggs often at that price. This a.m. the people where I live sent in a fresh egg for me to have with my breakfast. For the most part we struggle with the various kinds of powdered eggs.

Yesterday being Helen's birthday, we celebrated it by taking a delightful reindeer ride across the river. First, we crossed the river, then changed teams to return and go up the river for some distance. Our little wooden sleigh was scarcely big enough for us to sit on. The Laplander driver, in his pretty white fur coat, stood on the runner. Our four little reindeers were driven, or rather, guided, by one line, and prodded on by a long pole. These large-hoofed little animals are very fleet. The brown ones being prettier than the white. I still associate them with fairy tale land. But you know, in some ways this is a veritable fairy land.

Last night at eight, when we went over to the consulate for dinner, the sky was brilliant with scintillating stars, and suddenly off to the northeast, the exquisite filmy, mystical fairy-tinted northern lights swept across the heavens. In places it played like a soft moving curtain, and in other places, deep, thick shafts of light would come suddenly into being, to remain for a few minutes vividly, and then to separate into myriads of little shafts. At midnight when we returned they were even more beautiful than earlier. I had supposed that we should see them often here, but it has been only occasionally and those times not very brilliantly. They were much more brilliant and colorful in Norway.

We are so happy to have the daylight longer. At four-thirty tonight, there was a really quite a little light in the sky. In another month I supposed the length of our days will be quite the same as yours, and then grow constantly longer.

It is unbelievably mild and comfortable here. We have had so very little really severe weather and now that January is gone, we feel that we cannot have very much, or long periods of bitter cold weather.

Well it is now ten o'clock, and numerous have been the interruptions in this letter. Read came in for supper and tried to persuade the family to go up to headquarters for the movies and the dance. I didn't attempt to go again this week, as I found it was too tiring to sit through so long a program. And having been out last night, and expecting company for both afternoon and evening tomorrow, I decided it was the wiser thing to stay home tonight. However, I did walk over to the Hostess House with the evening official communiqué and visited for an hour and a half with some of the men. The boys love the Hostess House and hate to leave it for the front. We have so many fine men in the army. Oh, why can't this

Russian question be settled quickly. How we long for definite news of a definite policy. We are so fed up on rumors. It is quite like the days in Moscow when we were always expecting to hear that either the Germans were coming, or that the Bolsheviki gov't had fallen.

You probably know from New York that our seven secretaries from France are still waiting in England for passage here. If they don't leave London within two weeks I doubt if they get here before April. But two YMCA secretaries have passage on a boat leaving England soon, and will bring the trunks that contain supplies and things for us. It looks as tho it would be some time before you can send the dress that I wrote for. I guess that I wrote you that we are eventually to have uniforms.

A letter went out on the last boat to New York instructing [the YWCA office in] New York about my salary, so John will want to ask at the bank if the full amount is being sent for all months beginning with Dec., to and including April. After that just half.

I certainly have appreciated the enclosed letters from Loraine and Harriet Cunningham. I wish all these friends would write me, as they are getting all the news that I am free to write about in the only letters that I am writing.

A mail boat is reported to be coming in on Monday Feb. 3, the first in two weeks. One mail boat with Dec. mail was officially reported lost in the White Sea. If this Monday boat does come in, we can send out mail again next week. How long does it take my letters to come? I fancy this will reach you early in March. Long after I am husky and fine. I have no pain, my back aches considerably, but my side is fine, tender of course, but well. Even my secretarial family here think I am awfully sensible and they have had no complaints to register about my wanting to go to work too soon. But loafing after you are feeling well is mighty trying, and I ought to be this very minute at the canteen at the Railroad Headquarters at the Front. It is my turn to go and no one else is free to go, so no one is there, and such urgent request come in from there for a YW sec'y.

Now I must go to bed, this is an awfully stupid, news-less letter, but perhaps next time I can do better.

With dearest love to each and all, and best regards to the friends, from your affectionate,

Clara

Tell Guy I wish to goodness that he was up here and Sam H. also. When does Sam return from France?

Clara I. Taylor

Arkangel, Russia

Below is a letter fragment that was probably written February 8 or 9, 1919, in Arkangel:

. . . and the shining white walls of a monastery. Far away, we could see the low sleds pulled either by the stolid little Russian horses or the fleet quartet of reindeers. Some times these lines of teams would be a block long. It was just at the hour when the peasants were returning to their villages across the river from our market here. From the river Arkangel is the most lovely with its numerous towering church steeples of blue and gold, and the fascinating looking masts of the ships frozen in along the shore. It is so monotonously level all about here, that often I long to climb a church steeple to get a view of the country. When I come home, I hope I can have a few days in the mountains somewhere. In the evening we went up to Regimental headquarters to see the movies and dance. But the news of Lt. Ballard's death took the joy out of our evening, so we were glad to come home early in the ambulance that was thoughtfully provided by Dr. Langely for Mrs. Kleifoth and me.

And now I must run to dinner for we are having three guests.

This last week we took onto our staff a Russian School teacher who was teaching at Skenkurk, and who was helped here by the army. She not only speaks English, French and other languages, but plays and sings. Since we are unable to get permissions for the seven secretaries in London to come here, having Miss Dmitrievsky will help. She was in one of only three cellars for protection against the firing when she was told to come at once. She has only the things which she was wearing. We are helping her out and will do everything we can to accumulate sufficient clothing.

The two YMCA sec'ys who left American with things for us will eventually land here, along with others, from England. We shall probably have them by March 10th at the latest. The men probably left England last week (Feb. 1st). I shall be very grateful for the waists which you sent, Sis.

Marcia is at the canteen at the Front for a couple or three weeks. When she returns I hope to go. There the work is easier than anywhere else and perfectly safe. It is miles back of the outposts. I have gone over to the Hostess House a few evenings for a couple of hours a day, but have taken no real responsibilities altho I am feeling equal to it. I shall visit the hospitals several times this week as they come in the paths of my walks. On Friday of this week, I saw thirty-four reindeers in a small caravan on the main street here. It is very unusual for them to come into the town, as they are afraid of the train cars, and the city horses are afraid of them. I wished that I had my Kodak with me.

Last Wednesday evening Helen and I had dinner at the American engineer headquarters with two Wisconsin men. The engineers have built their own charming living quarters, and artistic it truly is. Little narrow gage rails are the andirons for the logs in the grate, and all the electric lights fixtures are made out of brass shells hammered and tooled.

On Thursday evening Elizabeth Dickerson and I, with several others, played cards at Consular Davis' home. Just before we began playing, Mr. Davis announced that we were playing for prizes, especially the ladies. The wonderful prizes being no less than home mail. Part of mine came thru the Embassy, and part in the Consular pouches. The latest date was Dec. 18th. Now family, once a week address a letter to me, "care of State Dep't Washington DC" Then, left- hand side, "care of American Embassy, Arkangel Russia," and family name on corner. Have address typewritten. If they don't send the letter back, it will come to me. Helen's family send all her mail that way. Her latest was Dec. 29. Send thru open mail as well. All mail ought to reach us now. If my friends wrote to me at Stockholm, the letters never came thru. Tell them to try Arkangel. I certainly shall be here until early summer.

We are all so sorry to have Read leave. He, as well as all other Bureau of Public Information men in other countries and in Siberia have been recalled to Washington. So it looks as tho the gov't was closing up that part of their work as a war measure. He regrets going while the Russian situation is still so far from being settled, and needless to say, we are dreading his going. He, with three or four other men have been such good friends to us all. He probably will leave before or by the first of March, stopping in England and France before going to America. I really look with dread on the coming of summer, for Helen, Elizabeth and Catherine are all expecting to leave for the States, leaving Marcia and me as the only ones left who have come over for the Russian work. I fancy that practically all the YMCA men and many of the gov't officials will go for several months, coming back in the early fall. Only of course many will not return. I feel sure that our sec'ys [wont return] but they are planning to. Of course there will be new ones, but you never can tell if they will be congenial.

Feb. 10, 10° above

Well, I have just returned from a short walk. The day is glorious. It quite defies description, clear, sunny, and bracing. The days are getting longer so fast now. It is fascinating to watch the change. At five o'clock it is quite light. By May we shall be having much longer days than you. Perhaps yet I shall be in the land of the midnight sun. The time goes so quickly, especially when the days are so full and eventful.

Last night Read and I attended a lovely Russian concert at the City Duma. A small orchestra of thirty pieces, and beautiful pianists. But there is no audience quite like the Russian audiences. From the smallest child present, they seem enrapt and they are so demonstrative in their appreciation. I can imagine how amazed our artists would be to hear husky and shrill voices calling out their names.

Today noon, they telegraphed from Headquarters that the mail would close at ten tomorrow, so this will get off sooner than I had thought. A second mail is promised for departure next week, so may get several letters written by that time.

I am feeling OK and will soon be as good as before. Am loafing, or rather not doing much canteen work. I can't say that I am really idle most of the time, but study, lay down and read. Read is instructing the mail clerk that all magazines coming to him after his departure are to be turned over to me. So I shall get the benefit of quite a number different kinds until June at least. I have just finished reading *New Republics*, *Digests*, and the *World's Work*. So I am not so far behind the times. Do send me clippings of home news.

Now I must get at my Russian lesson and also write a business letter to Marcia for the "Evening Messenger." Don't have any anxieties about me, even tho the papers may have alarming headlines. We are not in danger.

Don't forget that we are only nine American women here, and being under military orders, all of us would be sent out long before there was any occasion for it. Some of the things which the boys are writing home are greatly exaggerated. I am sure that it must be hard to know what to believe and what not to, from all that you read in the papers.

With very best regards to my friends and loads of love to the family, from your affectionate sister,

Teke

Clara I. Taylor

Sis, I don't know what has become of letter 34. Letter 36, I have, and will not send. What other letters are lacking? No. 36 was written July 7.

Feb. 21, 1919
Arkangel, Russia

Dearest ones at home:

It isn't often that one can be home so early. It is just eight-thirty. I have just returned from the Hostess House where I have planned, with the cook, the cookies for tomorrow. Being Washington's birthday, we are having a little specialty in the cookie line. It is very much milder today, about 20°, and snowing some most of the day. The northern lights are trying hard to shine and probably shall by midnight, if it clears off. Helen left for the front yesterday morning, and Marcia returned this morning. Marcia looks fine after her two weeks down there. Everyone comes back looking rested and well. I shall go about March 7 and stay, I hope, for the rest of the month. There I shall see Neil Hallock. He is stationed there.

Tuesday night we had a really very charming time at our dance. There were only about thirty, but a very congenial crowd. All the people from the Embassy, from the consulate, several from the various missions, and army officers. The orchestra from the band played. Our guests were invited to come at ten, the "Home Sweet Home" being played at one-thirty. We chose a favorable week because the soldiers have to be in at ten o'clock now, so they had to leave the Hostess House by nine. We served coffee, cocoa, sandwiches and little cakes. On Wednesday night after canteen we went to

Crawford Wheeler's for a spread, when all the guests gave Read their family address, so he could write them on his arrival in the States. I think probably our letters will reach our families long before he arrives home, for he must drive overland to the Murmansk railroad which may take a week or ten days, then getting boats from there to Bergen or England is uncertain. He will go to London or France before leaving for the States, so I doubt if he gets home much before the middle or last of April.

I think the conditions are pointing favorably all the time to all of us getting home in the summer. I really think I may get home by July for a couple or three months, then return to Siberia. Do not pass this on, especially to NY. If we could only talk instead of having to write, and because of the strict censorship, it is necessary to be careful about letters. Bess Boies in London talked with one of our friends who did not come out of Soviet Russia until the last of October. He doesn't think that any of us will return there for some time to come and I feel very sure that Marcia and I will not remain here all summer, if we are going to try to return to Russia next fall. If canteen work is going to be necessary here all summer and into the fall. I am sure that we shall return to Siberia via the States. This is for family consumption only. Helen Ogden and Elizabeth Dickerson probably would remain here as long as canteen work is needed.

Wednesday I went up to Regimental Headquarters to have dinner and a long talk with Colonel Stewart. He has been very much interested in our work here. Saturday afternoon Mr. Poole is receiving from five until seven in honor of Washington's birthday. We shall probably dance a part of the time. Then at Regimental Headquarters we shall have movies and dancing until one. We girls usually do not go until nine-thirty, that is after the canteens close.

A few days ago two letters came which had been relayed thru the Russian Post office. One was Sis' letter dated Dec. 13, and Maud Hunter's. I certainly did appreciate Maud's letter with Hazelmere's enclosed Xmas greetings. Please telephone to Maud my appreciation, and tell her when it isn't so difficult to get out letters, I shall write her.

At last the frozen-in period has come to a limited extent. The ice probably will prevent further navigation for six weeks or two months. However mail will be sent by sleds to Murmansk.

I certainly appreciate all that the family have done in getting clothes for me, and in sending the chain and lavaliere [pendant]. They are all quite safe in London, sometime in April they will reach us. And great will be the excitement when those things arrive. I take it, you received the cable about the muff. Don't send magazines if you haven't already done so. Read is turning all his over to me, and if we leave here in the summer, it will not be possible to receive them. I appreciate the desire of you all to do for me. If you have subscribed, ask the publishers, if they can't suspend the subscription until next year. It was a splendid of you to send the chain and lavaliere. I should love it and do appreciate all that you have done for me. Don't worry about the fruit, we are faring splendidly on food. And I still have some Hylers bars which came in Father's gift. That was a wonderful candy gift, Father, you must have sent New York fifteen dollars or more. It has given pleasure to many different people and on many different occasions.

Sunday, Feb. 23 25° above
Well Family, this is one of the most glorious days imaginable. Clear and bracing, and not very cold. At the Hostess House the army chaplain held his first service this morning for officers and officials. Altho there were not many there, the service was truly lovely, and I am sure will grow in attendance as time goes on. Three of the men came to dinner, after which Read and I went out to take pictures. We walked out on the River where we get some of the loveliest views as well as some of the most typical and interesting. The sun did not set until nearly five, so you see our days are getting longer rapidly and we are having more sunlight and clearer days.

Yesterday we had a delightful time at the Embassy's Washington tea where we saw people from the various foreign offices, as well as our own officials and officers. In the evening we went up to Regimental Headquarters and danced until twelve-thirty. All of us were thinking back to just a year ago, when word came to Petrograd and Moscow that we must evacuate to Samara. How little we dreamed of Arkangel then. Two years ago I had a wonderful climb in the Rockies out of Colorado Springs. I wonder where I shall be next year.

Read and Mr. Inman leave early Wednesday morning. They probably shall not reach England until the middle of March. Read will not go to America, I imagine, until early May. If he goes to Wisconsin for this class reunion in June, he will drop George a note when he reaches Chicago, so he can give much information which will be more satisfactory than writing. Since letter 52 got cut up by the censor, I find it hard to write. I suppose there is much that I could write about that I don't, just because I don't want my letters hacked up.

Today, or rather, yesterday, Sis' cable came to gladden my day. It is such a comfort to know that all at home are well. How very much we have to be thankful for. Some way, I feel sure that we shall be together this summer. For the official announcement from the Embassy a few days ago said all these American troops were to be withdrawn, probably in June. Of course others may be sent in their place, but if they are not, that will mean that we too will leave in June, and would get home early in July. Oh wouldn't it be a grand and glorious feeling to be with you all again.

Now I must run and take the car to Somolony to help there at the Hut until ten o'clock.

Feb. 24 clear, a perfect day, about 25° above
I had a good time with the men at the canteen last night. We had a good sing around the piano of some of the old songs. We are hoping to get a good cook out there this week so we can have canteen specialties. How would you like to make rice pudding for several hundred.

I have taken over our housekeeping for the next two weeks or until I go to the front. So I am getting a kitchen vocabulary. Fortunately, the cook and maid are so well trained that the directing and planning of meals is not very difficult now.

Tonight three British and one Am. secretary are coming in at nine o'clock for a Samovar. Tomorrow Read comes for a last meal. The cook wishes to give him a pure Russian dinner. He will come again late in the evening for a Samovar and leave Wed. at nine o'clock. He and Mr. Inman, with an interpreter. They will have three sleds, taking a hamper of food to last ten days. They take the northern route to Saroko, so will skirt [the coast] near the White Sea. The equipment for such a trip is really tremendous. Driving for fifteen hours a day in cold weather is exhausting. They stop about every three or four hours for hot drinks and rest. Will sleep in sleeping bags, on the floor in peasant's huts. It will probably take them a month to reach England. So Read hardly expects to reach NY before middle of May.

This week I am visiting three different hospitals and taking up my regular work at Smolny, for four nights a week. We also plan to have a party of

Russian girls in one evening this week. So far, our work has been entirely in connection with the army. We hope this spring to really do something for the girls. There are a host of them here. When I learn that Dr. Kirkpatrick has reached the US I want you to write him, Father. He was the one who performed my operation and took such good care of me. He is still in England. It has been quite definitely decided that our sec'ys who were waiting in England should not attempt to come here now until navigation opens again, which means the last of April. All those lovely things which you sent will come in May, probably with the YMCA men. If by May we have definite knowledge of the military situation, so far as American troops are concerned, we shall know better how to plan our summer. Please be sure to write me what you have sent because your letters will get thru before the trunks do. Also don't send any more clothes unless I wire, I may have given Bess Boies a list, but disregard it. By the way, she reaches the States about March first. Write her at 600 Lexington Ave. [New York City] for any information about me that you wish. She left here about the twentieth of Nov. and has been in London most of the time since.

Feb. 25, "brite & fare"
Since breakfast, I have been interviewing cooks for the Smolony Hut. I rather dread starting in with the housekeeping on so large a scale. It isn't bad after the work has been well initiated. But when supplies are so precious, experiments are a real risk. We are now using powdered eggs, powdered milk, and powdered custard. Surprisingly good things can be made from these things. But the Russians have to be taught and we must do the experimenting.

Don't for a minute think that we are shriveling up with intense cold, for we are thoroughly enjoying the winter, except for our rare extreme cold snaps, which have come only four times, and have not lasted more than six days at a time. It has been glorious. When I go to the front I shall learn to use the skis, walking with spiked poles. We have no hills here.

Tell me the dates when my letters get through, and if they are coming fairly regular now.

With a world of love to all you dear ones at home, and regards to the host of friends. From your ever affectionate

Teke   Clare I. Taylor

Arkangel

Diary
January 20 – February 29, 1919

January 20, 1919
(Mon.) 25° below, clear & wonderful. Cable from Genieve reached me.

January 21, 1919, 17° below
Tues. Studied, read H. G. Wells *Passionate Friends*. We received letter of appreciation from Col. Stewart on behalf of the officers, for the Hostess House.

January 22, 1919
Wed. Letter 48 to Leslie and cable to Genieve. Zero, cloudy, snowy and raw. Walked six blocks. Helen and I called on Mrs Davis. Went to Hostess House to help arrange Band party.

January 23, 1919
Thur. Miss Foerster and Gosling came to dinner. We went by auto to Solombola. Spent evening sewing, reading, & studying Russian.

January 24, 1919, weather mild
Fri. Cable came with news all de facto govt. would be represented at Russian conf. Feb. 17. Triumph for democracy. Read came in late evening. Visits. went to engineers dance at Solombola. Weather mild. Walked 12 blocks.

January 25, 1919
Sat. Leut Ballard came to dinner. Miss Gosling for two hrs. in afternoon. Newa and I arranged with musicians. Read, Helen and I went to Headquarters to pictures [film] It was so good to be there again and see every body.

January 26, 1919
Sunday. Read and Crawford came to dinner. H & M living at Embassy. Re. finished *The Passionate Friends* while I sewed. In evening Leut. Jeffries, Rulbeuof, Johnson & Crawford came in. Weather quite lovely about 20°

above. Retreat of Shanherst [Shenkurst]. Funeral of Lubtkesk & 32 social-ists in Germany.

January 27, 1919
Mon. In bed most of day. Finished reading *American and Social Democracy.* John Spargo. Read came in late to say he was giving dinner for me at consulate on Friday night.

January 28, 1919
Tues. Miss Gosling in for afternoon. Took short walk. Read and I walked over to Hostess House in evening about nine o'clock.

January 29, 1919
Wed. Walked up to Embassy. Attended party for Band at the Hostess House in evening Beautiful Russian music. very mild weather.

January 30, 1919
Thurs. Mild weather, lighter days. Two mail boats lost in White Sea. Miss Gosling and I had tea on Red Cross boat. Many ill from hospitals rec'd. Paris conference in full swing.

January 31, 1919
Fri. Very mild. Snowy. Helen's birthday. Had visit with Frank at Hostess House, then Helen and I went for reindeer ride to Bokerits and up river—4 little reindeers, 3 brown & one white. In evening Read dinner party. Miss Gosling, Foerester, Knox, Helen & I. Lt. Bricker, Wheeler, Cole, Strouther, Kelleforth & R. Wonderful northern Lights.

February 1, 1919, Letter 49 John, 24 above
Sat. Glorious day. Teacher and I took walk thru the market. Gloriously beautiful. Read came for supper and took Eliz. to Headquarters. All men ordered to the front. Conditions serious. Spent evening at the Hostess House.

February 2, 1919, mild snowing
Sun. Took car up to Headquarters with mail. Visited nurses in Hospital.

Miss Foerster & I had dinner with Leut. Bricker. Col. Richmond Poal, Lee Lewis, Gosling afternoon tea. Helen had guests in the evening. Situation at Front very serious. All reserves out.

February 3, 1919
Mon. Staff meeting in A.M. Helped Marcia in afternoon. Was at the Hostess House for evening. Stop in at allied Sargents dance for a while. Unrest again because of talk of evacuation.

February 4, 1919
Tues. Marcia left for the Front. Spent afternoon at Hostess House. Read & Crawford came in for Samovar for the evening. Weather about zero, but glorious. Read rec'd news to report to Washington.

February 5, 1919
Wed. Took Neva to Dr. Langley. Hostess House in afternoon. Helen and I went to Engineers with Mr. Johnson for dinner. Taught Major Henry to dance—late in the evening. British troops arriving.

February 6, 1919, All trees covered with frost.
Thurs. Everybody engrossed in mail. Eliz. and I went to Davis to small card party. Mr. D. had lots of mail for us all. Sent cable to Genieve, Tommy A. & Rose Henry. Read mail until 1:30.

February 7, 1919
Fri. Leut. Ballard killed at Kodish. Miss Domitrievsky came to us from Shenkurst. Read and girls came up to my room in evening for Samovar. Local popul. terribly worried over Bol. situation. Much fighting on front. Saw a caravan of 34 reindeers in city.

February 8, 1919
Sat. In afternoon Read & I went to the *Kaylon* Hospital ship to Band concert & distribute papers. Many A company men there from Shenkursk. Went to Headquarters with Read in evening. Came home in ambulance. British refuse permission to our Secy's.

February 9, 1919
Sun. Glorious day. clear—20° above
Lt. Klesforth & wife Maj. Longley came to dinner. Spent afternoon read-
ing & lying down as side ached after too strenuous a day on Sat. Helen
& Lt. Johnson went skating. Read & I went to a Russian concert at the
Duma.

February 10, 1919, Letter 50 Sis very mild
Mon. Took walk after dinner. At Hostess all evening. Studied Russian
lesson until 11:30.

February 11, 1919, 0 degrees
Tues. Clear, cold. Marcia called up from the front at 8 o'clock. Conference
with Col. Stewart. Eliz & I attended Girl Scout meeting in evening. Read
& Crawford came in for Samovar.

February 12, 1919, 12° below
Wed. Went up to Red Cross Hospital in afternoon. Eliz., Neva & Cole,
Strother, Bricker, Dudley & Read at dinner at Red Cross Headq. Glorious
moonlight night. At 10:30 we walked half way across the river. Perfectly
wonderful night.

February 13, 1919, Trees covered with frost.
Thurs. Went out to Smolony until ten. Then up to Crawfords where met
the nurses. R. L., Lt. Dricher and Jim Summer were invited. Sat around
grate fire and had homey visit & victuals. music. Most of men at front.

February 14, 1919
Fri. Nurses from Hospital ship came to tea, with Mrs. Carr, Davis, Klieforth
and nurses. Evening at Hostess House 9:30 Read came up for an hour. All
quiet both on front and Arkangel.

February 15, 1919
Sat. Read letter from Mr. Poole regarding report to Washington. framed
up letters of facts for period of work. All went up to Headquarters to the
dance after [. . . ? . . .] Had a very happy time. Met Col. Thurston.

February 16, 1919, 10° below

Sun. Mr. Inman & Read came for dinner. Read & I took Kodak pictures in Market. Went to Smolony to "K" program. Lt. Dudley, Dricker, Packard, Jim Summerville, Blaufelt, Crawford, Read, Gosling came in at nine.

February 17, 1919, 35° below

Mon. Air charged with frost. Sent cable to Bess & report to Mr. Poole. Went out to Smolony in evening. Eliz. & Helen went to Olga Barracks dance. Sent letter 57 to Genieve.

February 18, 1919, 42° below zero Arkangel

Tues. Farewell dance to R. L. Guests, Poole, Lee, Inman, Capt. Lewis, Cole, Strother, Mr. & Mrs. Davis, Crawford W., J. Blaufelt, Lt. Johnson, Maj. Henry, Lt. Bridges. Lt & Mr Cleoforth, Gosling, Foerster, Knox— Hourwich, Saucout, Rainon, HO. & Eliz D. Dandy music & very happy time. very few men at Hostess House all day.

February 19, 1919, 10° below zero

Wed. Had dinner with Col. Stewart at Headquarters. Talked of YWCA work. Went to Red Cross Hospital to visit with men. Hostess House in evening. Crawford & Don entertained nurses, Eliz. H. O. & I—Jim Summerville

February 20, 1919, 14° above zero

Thurs. Helen left for 455. R. L., Lt. Watts, Miss Gosling came for dinner. Read official news: troops were to be withdrawn from Northern Russia. Spent afternoon & eve at Hostess House. Read came at 9:30. We got his diary up to date. At 12:00 Bess sailed to Am from Eng.

February 21, 1919, gray, windy day

Marcia arrived from 455. Spent afternoon at Hostess House and evening at home. All are wondering how the withdrawal of troops is going to effect us.

February 22, 1919

Sat. got night passes—attended Geo. Washington tea at Embassy and dance at Regimental Headquarters until 12:30. Had specially good time dancing almost every dance. Col. Thurston very interesting. Had all waltzes with R. L.

February 23, 1919, 10° above
Sun. Church services 11:30 at Hostess House. Read, Frank O. Don came to dinner. Read & I spent afternoon on River taking pictures, a glorious day. Went to Smolney in evening til 10. Read came in for Samovor from 10–12 & we planned food supplies for his trip.

February 24, 1919, 25° Perfect day
Mon. Went out to Smolny Barracks. Entertained at tea. Copson [Kom..?. Beckett, Coffee, Craig. Read came in at ten thirty for an hour.

February 25, 1919, 5° above Perfect day
Tuesday Wrote letter 52 to Father by Read. R. L. came to dinner & breakfast. Helped him make final arrangements. Hospital 53 in afternoon

February 26, 1919
Wed. Read left 10. Came at 9 for breakfast. Snow falling & not pleasant day for trip. All felt sled arrangements not very adequate. Visit Hospital 53.

February 27, 1919
Thurs. Rather disagreeable day. All wondering how R. L. and Mr. Iman are getting along. Went to Hospital Ship with Marcia & to Central Canteen in the evening.

February 28, 1919
Thur. Went out to Hospital 53—Had tea with Mr. Staul and Maj. Young at YMCA hut & Smolny. Preparations for return of 500 troops from R. R. front.

February 29, 1919
Fri. Marcia and I both spent day in bed. Took dose of oil. Marcia getting very tired & homesick also.

PART THREE

March 1 – May 6, 1919

In February, Clara and her colleagues learned that all international troops would be withdrawn from North Russia as soon as was feasible. A communication from the YWCA National Board in New York announced that once the evacuation of US troops from Northern Russia was complete, no American YWCA workers would be sent to Russia—Clara and her friends would not be replaced. At this point, the women were still expecting to return to the interior of Russia or the Ukraine in the fall of 1919, in order to do their own work with Russian women. Clara set plans in place to visit relatives in Britain, to get home to Illinois for the summer, then to return to Russia. Her letters now were more free in tone, and she was able to post missives every Friday. She told her family about the entertainments and her duties at the canteens, described the mystical wonder of the northern lights, and was cheerfully upbeat. She seemed to be having a great time staffing the railroad car canteen. Her tasks included making fruit compote, loaning out library books, serving donuts and hot drinks, and talking with the soldiers about the actions on the fronts and the prospects for world peace. The fighting on five of the six fronts continued with skirmishes, battles, advances, and retreats; the Red Army proved to be well supplied. March and April saw major offensives by the Bolsheviks, and the Allied command began the orderly retreat from each front which would end the Intervention.

On March 18, British Major General Ironside arrived in Arkhangelsk. His charge was to oversee the withdrawal of all international forces, leaving the "White" Russians of the North Russian Army to carry on the fight against the Red Army. The Expedition's strategy shifted to prioritizing offensive maneuvers that were designed to increase the morale and experience of the Russian troops. During March and April, the Allies launched attacks along the western edges of the fronts snaking down from Arkhangelsk. The idea was to beat back the enemy, but the take-lose-retake pattern of the prior few months was repeated. Finally, Allied command decided to abandon the attempt to connect the Arkhangelsk forces with Russian General Kolchak at Kotlas, a city located at the confluence of the North Dvina, Sukhona, and Vychedgda Rivers, 300 miles southeast of Arkhangelsk. Kotlas was an important rail head. That connection had been a major element of the overall mission goal, and one that had legitimized the presence of foreign troops on Russian soil due to Kolchak's request for international help.[44]

Meanwhile, news from the world outside of northern Russia included the first US Post Office airmail delivery from New York City to Philadelphia, Pennsylvania, and the first international air mail service trip from Seattle, Washington, to Vancouver, Canada. Korea declared independence and resisted the Japanese occupation. In Moscow, the Founding Congress of the *Cominterm* was opened. This was the first time Marxists from various countries met together. The Spring offensive by the Siberian White Russian Army began and had some success pushing the Fifth Red Army back to Samara; the Red Army occupied and annexed the Crimea. In the US, there was labor unrest around the country. In Boston, a telephone operators' strike was concluded with an agreement to raise women's wages. In Ireland, Éamon de Valera was elected president by the first Parliament of the Irish Free State. The Paris Peace Conference continued with debate on various resolutions, including the "racial equality clause" presented by the Japanese delegates to the Commission on the League of Nations.

The military news from the Arkhangelsk fronts in March and April made the American women very anxious. Clara recorded her worry in her diary and noted in passing the Smolny barracks were burned on the night of March 26, 1919. As she was taking the train down to Verst 455, for her stint at the railroad car canteen, she noted "heavy firing all day." But,

---

44 For a detailed summary of the actions along each of the six fronts, see Appendix III of this volume.

seemingly unfazed, she served cocoa and watched movies with the soldiers, stocked the canteen in preparation for its departure down the line, made curtains for the car, visited the Block houses along the line, and for the rest of April, brought cheer to the men fighting on the front lines. Clara returned to Arkhangelsk on April 28, just beating ice-out on the Dvina river.

Mentioned in This Section:

Father Roach, Catholic priest captured, then released by Bolsheviks, reported the safety of Ryall, Hall, and Arnold, imprisoned in Moscow.

US Lieutenant Colonel Edward Thurston, the Advocate General.

US Major William H. Henry, one of the American surgeons who operated on Clara in January.

US Brigadier General Wilds P. Richardson (1861–1929), arrived to take command of the US troops in April 1919, charged to organize and effect the withdrawal of American troops.

US Major Jesse Brooks Nichols, Commander, Third Battalion 339th Infantry. A frequent guest of the American women in Arkhangelsk and a good friend.

US Major Charles G. Young, Commander Second Battalion 339th Infantry.

Sgt. Grier M. Shotwell, Signal Corps Photographic Unit (promoted to Master Signal Electrician c. June 1919). Clara notes that he showed her some of the "official photos."

US Consul Shelby Strother (sometimes spelled "Strouthers"), diplomat in Arkhangelsk. Strother was an interesting character. In November 1918, he was noted among Clara's friends as "a jolly Harvard man" and was included in many card parties. However, he was later barred from social events by Clara due to his ungentlemanly behavior (Martin, 1964). In her diary entry of January 17, 1919, Clara mentions a "great discussion of Strother poem." Martin believed that this was an "off color" (that is, obscene) story Strother wrote and asked to have published in the American *Sentinel* newspaper in Arkhangelsk. We think that Clara had a leading role in banning his writings as well as his presence at social events (Martin, personal communication, 2013). Strother took revenge by denouncing Clara as a Bolshevik sympathizer and made trouble about her visas and passport when she tried to leave Russia in August 1919 (see footnote 59). Clara was detained in London for six weeks when she arrived later in 1919 and also was questioned when she finally landed in New York City in October (Diary, Oct. 17, 1919).

Strother was a problem for others, as well. In the summer of 1919, he and Vice Consul Felix Cole had a "violent personality clash," resulting in several uncomplimentary letters from Strother to the US State Department and directly to Ambassador Francis. Strother accused Cole of being a Bolshevik, of undermining Francis, and of giving passports to known Bolsheviks. Strother also complained that Cole expelled him from the Embassy living quarters "without cooking utensils." Cole counterclaimed that Strother had offered the landlord double the rent if he would evict Cole (Allison 1997, 144; Rhodes 1984, 404). In Moore's 1920 book, Strother is a "certain sympathetic American Consul" lauded for helping eight Russian brides of US servicemen escape with their husbands (Moore, et al. 1920, 272). It seems that Strother had a violent, unpredictable temperament to some, but was helpful to others. He was posted to Amsterdam after the Arkhangelsk Embassy closed in September 1919.

View of Archangel in Summer, 1918
(Primm, found in Moore, 1924)

A typical sight in Arkhanglesk, these one horse drawn carts called *isvachicks* were used for the transportation of people and goods around the city.
(YWCA papers, Sophia Smith Collection, Smith College archives)

Helen Ogden and Clara Taylor in Arkhanglesk, 1919.
(Clara I. Taylor Papers, Sophia Smith Collection, Smith College Archives)

Chapter Five
"Very few letters are now being censored."

Letters

March 1, 1919

My dear Genieve & Sis:

I have such a very strong conviction that I shall be at home this summer, that I thought that it was high time I wrote some suggestions. It is possible that it will seem wiser and quicker for us if we go to Vardo or Kirkeness and take Norwegian steamer to Trouyou, thence to Christiania.[45] Then sail from Bergen to England or straight home from Bergen.

Now if I should take a couple of weeks for England & Scotland, Sis, please send me names and addresses of the two or three relatives, that you think I better go to see, and you might drop them a note to ask if it would be convenient for them if I came for two or three days in June or early July. I should like to spend four or five days in London. I truly do not want to delay long in Europe, if we are to return again in the Fall.

Strange to say, I have no desire to do any traveling or sight seeing, we all have a keen desire to get home! For many reasons, I fancy it will seem wise to go to England, and of course we may go straight to England from here.

---

45 Christiania, Sweden, was renamed Oslo in 1924.

Of course, I shall send a wire just as soon as we have any definite plans or facts. This is only for family, don't pass it on to NY. You in America may know what are to be the military plans for this northern expeditionary force, before we will. We know that the YWCA will not continue here after the withdrawal of the troops, and if more come in, we shall expect other canteen workers to take our place, who shall be under the direction of the YMCA instead of YW. None of us who are here now want to be here next winter. We have been tremendously glad to be here, and to have had an opportunity to do our bit with the forces, but we don't want another year of it. I would be willing to return in the Fall if it were necessary, provided I came home for three months first. I have enjoyed the weather here, all of us have. The last two or three weeks have been just wonderful. Sometimes it is 5–10° below, but usually it is 5–15 above. But dry, and now such clear, beautiful days. Tonight the sunset was glorious. The days are lengthening so rapidly by the end of this month our days will be longer than yours.

Now when I wire that I am leaving for home, if I do this summer, send mail in care of the American Consuls in Christiania, if we go that way, and in London, and to the relatives in Scotland if I should go see them. And I probably would go there before going to London.

Then, if, there are so many ifs, we come home, what about the family getting together. I would suggest that you write NY, Sis, if you get word that we are coming home, asking if they plan to schedule me for conference work, and if so to send you the schedule so the family can make plans accordingly. Of course, I should expect to do conference work, and as much as needed for we who have been here are the best fitted to present the work, and our finances depend on the local associates being very much interested. Furthermore I don't think Helen or Elizabeth or Katherine can be counted on for conference work. I can't see any of them making speeches, and Eliz hopes to enter gymnastic school if possible. Marcia and I are the only ones planning to return. I also need some conference work myself, very very much. I imagine that Miss Boies will do a lot of the speech making so not much will be asked of Marcia and me. I wish they would send me to one of the conferences held in the mountains. The monotony of this country is appalling at times.

We know so little about the Siberian situation, I have no idea when they would expect us to return. But you may depend on it, I shall have two months at home, and more if possible.

If it is a hot summer, I wish we could plan to go to some nice resort in Michigan or Wisconsin. But don't let's camp. I have had enough of irregular living to last a long time, and I know how you girls dislike that kind of summering also. Some place where the bathing would be good. Of course I don't know what the family plans may be, or New York's. I am just writing down what comes into my head now, but I do feel certain that we shall come home. Without saying much about it, we are all counting on it. And we probably won't know definitely until May. I can't think of any greater thrill as compared to coming home.

The truth of the matter is, everybody is desperately homesick. The soldiers talk of nothing else, our hardest work now is trying to dispel homesickness among them. You can't hold a conversation with anyone who doesn't ask you, before it is over, when you are planning to go home. None of us think or expect to start before sometime in June.

Since I started this an awfully funny thing has happened. It would be funnier still if the distress of my old landlord was not so genuinely real. In fact, the whole household is quite upset.

Several days ago I took cold, and when I couldn't get the better of it, I decided to go to bed for a couple of days. Well, today Marcia and I became absolutely desperate over the window situation. All winter we have slept in this absolutely sealed up room. We decided that by some hook or crook we had to have one of the inner windows taken off. So this afternoon, Major (Dr.) Hewy came out with Miss Gosling, my former nurse, and in great seriousness, said my ultimate recovery depended on the window coming out, that all Americans just had to have fresh air. So tonight the window was taken out, and the whole family knows that Miss Dunham and I shall probably die at once. My only fear is, that some of this family may take cold, and blame it on to the fact that one of the double windows is off! Its worth having a cold to get ventilation into our room. You have no idea how we have suffered from lack of air, and the man of the house has consistently refused to let us have it done. If Marcia or I are not out tomorrow early, I know the family will think that the night air has killed us. I haven't had the least bit of fever with my cold, it seemed settled in my head and eyes so made me too miserable to try to do canteen work. I shall be out again tomorrow. There has been no mail in now for some time.

We have had no word from Read and Mr. Inman so do not know how they are getting along. They will wire us from Sarkoko on their arrival there which probably will be Tuesday or Wednesday. It would be a great trip. I should love to take a few days sled trip, so many here have had to do it.

I am hoping to send this letter out by one of the YMCA men, who is taking the same trip going to Murmansk.

Read took numerous pictures of all of us before he left, and addresses of our families. If they are good he will send to each of you girls. I doubt if he arrives in the States before May. I have asked Mr. Inman who lives in Chicago, to drop Father a line giving his Chicago address, so if any of the family are in the city, they could call on him and get first hand information. Have you talked with anyone who have seen me here. The families who live in the east, have seen quite a few of our friends. I wish you could know Jerome Davis. He is in NY I think.

This is "blinny" week in Russia, which is the last week before the seven weeks of Lent. And during this week Russians eat lots of blennies, which are a sort of pancake made with yeast, served with drawn butter, sour cream, and cold fish. Today and tomorrow are festival days when the last parties before Lent are given. We ought to see *troikas* tomorrow, that is, the sleighs driven by three horses.

March 2
Well, I am feeling fine today, Marcia and I had our wonderful night's sleep with good fresh air in our room. I came over here for dinner about twelve. Col. Thurston and Crawford had just returned from the front. We sat in front of the grate fire and had a dandy good visit until time for Elizabeth and Marcia to go to their canteens. I go over to the Hostess House at seven for the evening. I have been lazy this entire day.

March 4 very mild
Well we have had two strenuous days with lots of our men visiting the Hostess House. I had some good visits with a group of machine gun men last night. Helen came in from the front on the early train. All of us will be here for at least two weeks, and then I am at last to have my turn at the Front for three weeks.

This afternoon, Marcia and I are visiting the Hospital ship, and tonight seven engineers are coming in for an informal supper. They are men who have done special things for us at one time or another at the Hostess House. If anybody wants anything, they turn to the engineers. And if it can be done, they are the ones to do it.

It has been quite mild the past few days, so we feel surely that spring is on the way. As there is no drainage here, we look forward to the melting of the snow with somewhat dread. But usually things are not as bad as painted. Lots of the Wisconsin University people are here now. We may plan to have a get-together. We are trying to get material out for the *Liberty Badger*,[46] but I doubt if it gets through in time.

Two of the nine bags of mail which came across country have arrived but most of it seems to be for the soldiers. If the ice boats don't get thru, I doubt if we shall have much mail for the next six weeks. But just think what a nice lot of it there is going to be when it does come, and what fun opening the trunks. So far we know all the things which are families sent are still in London.

I will be able to get out mail every week, but it will take it two weeks to get to Murmansk, if overland. I hope by the middle of April, we shall know more definitely here what our summer plans are.

With a very great deal of love to all the dear ones at home, from your affectionate,

Clara

March 18, 1919
Arkangel, Russia

My dear Fritz:

It has been a long time since I have written directly to you, I have sent most of the letters directly home. We are all frozen up today, the weather dropped from 16° above to 30° below in little more than twelve hours. Since this is the first very cold weather in three weeks, we are cold and shivery today.

---

46 A note about the various University of Wisconsin publications: *The Badger* is the student-written yearbook; *The Liberty Badger* was a special edition of the yearbook written by the class of 1920, published in 1919; the student newspaper for the University of Wisconsin is the *Daily Cardinal*, published since 1892.

This afternoon, I visited the men on the Hospital Ship. Some of them had just arrived here after long sledge drives. They were so tired, but glad to be where they are now comfortable and will be well cared for. Altho some were badly wounded, they were awfully good sports. Tomorrow I am taking some books and magazines to one of the officers, a Michigan Uni. man, who has been a practicing lawyer in Detroit.

Last evening I had such a good visit with the men at our Hostess House. Several were machine gun men who have become very much interested in Russia, and hope sometime to return here for business. After we finished serving we had a delightful sing around the piano until I fear some were quite homesick. All are always a little homesick after the mail comes. It was distributed Sat. For some reason, I received very little, only two letters after a period of six weeks. They were Dec. 17 and Jan. 11. In three weeks more there ought to be another mail. I ought to get about twenty letters. Very few letters are being censored now from the States. So write frequently and long. Our letters are censored here or in Washington now, as ours go thru the Embassy pouch for the next two months. I am wondering if you are getting mail at all regularly. My letter leaves here every Friday. The mail is about ten days reaching Murmansk from here and is held there for boat service to England. I delayed cabling from day to day hoping to report receipt of a lot of mail, but the arrival of mail is so uncertain as to times. We spend much time in anticipation. We have all been envious of Elizabeth with her eighteen [letters]. Next time we shall all be fortunate.

I have a new army cook now at Smoley so our canteen work will be lighter and easier, and he's one good cook. His twelve hundred doughnuts were delicious Mon. night as was his rice pudding last. Tonight we have sponge cake with a chocolate custard filling. Using the powdered custard and the chocolate to kill the taste of the custard. We are serving pancakes, french fried toast, oatmeal cookies, chocolate cookies and rice fritters during the next few days. When you have to figure on one or two thousand services, it means some figuring on preparations.

So much of our cow milk which has been frozen is now turning bad. But the powdered milk is really better.

We regret so much to have Miss Gosling and Miss Foerster, the two Red Cross nurses, leave for home. They are to go on the next boat which may mean next week. We will give them a farewell party on my birthday.

For refreshments we will serve the cakes and sweet bread which are always served on birthdays in the Russian households. They are very good and very unlike anything that we ever make.

When the nurses go, there will be but six American women here. We five sec'ys and Mrs. Davis, wife of one of the consuls. We shall not be leaving until we know definitely whether American troops are to be sent here to relieve this regiment. If other American troops are sent, then we will undoubtedly turn over our part of this work to the YMCA so that the new folk who come in will be under their direction. If more are needed, I am going to make application for Genieve to come. If we don't get into Siberia next winter, I will come back here after coming home for two or three months. We all must get away for rest before next year's work. I feel certain that I shall get home in July or August. Let's all hope for it, anyway.

Last Saturday night we all went to the Headquarters Engineer's dance. The room was artistically decorated in green to remind us of St. Patrick's Day. I couldn't help but wish that the families of these men could know what good times the men have, along with the hard work, dangers and hardships.

This week one of the companies is putting on a play at all the various YMCAs in this vicinity. Since so many of the men have been in during the past three weeks, much interest has been taken in inter-company basket-ball games. On the whole the men are in better spirits than they were some time ago.

I am leaving for the canteen at the front on the 28th. There will be more soldiers out so the need for one of us there is greater. I hope to be gone about three or four weeks. Everyone who goes to this particular front are crazy about it.

You should have seen me washing my old blue broadcloth skirt in soap and water, preparatory to going to the front. If that trunk from London doesn't come soon, I think we shall all be disgraced, for working in the canteens is dreadful on clothes.

This morning Helen and I have been making French dressing, so we can have our first salad. This rare occasion is due to having successfully bartered twenty-two glasses of rice and two cans of sweetened milk for twenty precious eggs. We each had a soft boiled egg for breakfast this morning.

The event is worthy of recording in our diary. Friday we shall have creamed eggs on toast. They are too precious to use for cooking.

March 19, 15° below zero

Last night we had a charming evening at the Embassy. Mr. Poole entertained the Norwegian family, representatives from the English and French embassies, Mr. Cole, of American consular staff, and several officers from the military mission. It was a very small select crowd. A pianist and banjo player furnished the music. We danced from ten till one. All the people were in full evening dress, it was a relief to see them after seeing so much uniform. Of course the military people were in uniform. I am going to the front on Wed. the 25th to remain three weeks or possibly four. I am so glad to be going before the thaw. These cold clear days are wonderful and the nights are mystical with northern lights.

Today Geney's thoughtful cable of birthday greetings came. You all are most thoughtful. I will be so glad when the letters come thru more regularly, and more of them. It is reported that a sledge convoy of fifty sledges with overland mail was captured. It's a rumor which none of us wish to believe.

If you are given permission to send mail by pouch, be sure that weekly letters are sent thru the open mail also. For pouch mail is sent from England by currier and that is not very frequent.

Fritzie, dear, I have thought of you so much and wondered how the Assoc. work was coming along. I know that you are making a great success of your work, and that you will be appreciated. Do write me a good general assoc. newsletter.

I am at the Hostess House now and it is jammed, so must go into the other room and get busy. Tomorrow Helen and I are taking a trip across the river for supplies and will return by reindeers. Wish you could be along.

With heaps and heaps of love to you, and all the family, from your affectionate sister,

Clara

Arkangel, Russia
March 24, 1919

My dearest Father:

No better way to celebrate my birthday than writing home. It is a glorious sunny morning with a temperature about 10° above. This afternoon I visit two hospitals and reach Smolony about five o'clock for the evening. My work is so much easier now that we have Mr. Czech (one of the soldiers) for a cook. We have been able to procure some apricots, so will serve apricot pie for the first time on Thursday night, at the close of a charming entertainment which will be given by a group of soldiers from the Durham Light Infantry. One of the men is a very fine pianist.

Last Saturday night we had a concert given by six Russians all of whom were first class musicians. I am afraid it was a bit too classical for the particular group who heard it. After the concert we served them quite an elaborate dinner. As only one of them talked much English, it was quite a strain on my Russian. I feel ashamed that I am not doing more with my language work, but somehow it's just hard to discipline myself to the work. I seem never to carry out my good resolutions to study.

Yesterday for Sunday dinner, we had three boys come. One, an Iowa boy who is serving in the English army having been too young for ours, and two Sergeants. The Iowa boy is nearly dying from loneliness. So we wanted to help him get acquainted with other Americans. When I came home at nine from the Hostess House I found Colonel Stewart and Colonel Thurston at our house. Later two Lieutenants and Miss Foerster came. So we had quite a tea party around the Samovar. This happened to be one of those Sundays when we thought we would have a quiet time, so did not invite guests as we usually do. Altho our friends know that after eight thirty we are supposed to be at home on Sunday nights. Fortunately, I had planned oatmeal cookies and other sweets in case callers should come, and ordered the samovar ready at nine, as usual.

Yesterday we received a cable from Miss Boies stating that probably two groups of people will go into Siberia this summer. One to establish an Association at Vladivostok, and the other to cooperate with the YMCA in an agricultural and educational train thru Siberia. The work will be similar to the boat on the Volga River of last summer. Our plans are no more definite then they were a week ago. I imagine we will not know any more than we do now for the next six weeks.

We are tremendously interested in the visit of these three Americans who are now in Moscow, consulting with the Bolsheviki, and are returning to Paris to report. Who knows but we shall return to Moscow this summer after all. If the way opened for us. We should go, that is Marcia and I should and wait until spring to return. Yesterday Marcia cabled NY urging that I be sent to Washington in October to attend this great world's conference of labours. The convention will last about three weeks. If we can't go into European Russia I surely will get home during this summer.

There is some uncertainty about my going to the canteen at the front for a couple of weeks. It isn't just the most opportune time to ask for a movement order for a YWCA sec'y. I am all ready to go when the opportunity comes, and am crazy to go.

Well Father dear your cable with birthday greeting has just this minute arrived. Thanks so much all of you, for your thoughtfulness on my behalf. Geney's cable came on the 21st. If it is terribly expensive don't wire anymore as mail is getting thru. There is no sign of any coming for some time, but when it does I know there will be lots of it. For only two came on the last mail. Altho my letter goes out with the pouch from the embassy every Thursday, I am sure now that these letters will be long in reaching you, for mail service is exceedingly difficult at present, and will be for six weeks longer. I imagine I will cable every three weeks. There is no cause for worry and I am entirely over the effects of the operation. Of course I am still very careful not to life heavy things or do any thing which means a strain.

We have ten days of very cold weather again. It went down to between thirty and forty below and hasn't warmed up very fast. We all feel that this is the last violent kick of winter. From now on we expect much mild weather with lots of snow. In the country, snow is about waist deep now. Here it is so packed it doesn't seem more than eighteen inches.

Our trunks we heard had left London, but they haven't gotten thru to us, and won't for another month. Helen and I today said that when that trunk arrived, we should take some of our old duds to the market and sell them. I expect we could get quite a few rubles that way. Oh that I had some good American money. Next time, I shall always hold some in reserve. This trip to Europe has taught me many things worth knowing for future use.

Tomorrow we four are invited to have dinner with Miss Gosling and Miss Foester at the Red Cross Hospital. These nurses will likely leave by ice boat April 5th for Murmansk. I am glad that I don't have to either come or leave here at this season. It is delightful here now. All of us dread the spring but it may not be so bad as we fear.

March 27, clear, sunny but very cold
Late last night my heart was gladdened with two letters from Geney and one from Sis with Fritz's enclosed. Genieve's letters were dated Jan 14 & 21. Sis 10th and John's the 16th. I fear the letters between Dec. 14 and Jan. 11 went to the bottom of the sea. Letters addressed like John's care of the Expeditionary Force is fine, but I may be here after they leave. So don't do it after June. Not that they will be gone in June, but like you in America, we are hoping that these boys can return home.

I am so glad that John has things coming his way. May the good work keep up. All the family seem to have prospered since my departure.

I know you are distressed in the long delay of the trunk getting here with our clothes, but never mind they will be just that much more welcome when they come. By cable we learned that uniform suits and hats would be sent us or are in the trunks. Three apiece. NY sent winter and summer, and Miss Boise had ordered made for us in Paris, uniforms like the French. The French have the capes which I adore. Miss Boise also had a lot of books sent to us from London. I shall surely cable when all come thru. Don't send any more summer clothes than are in the trunk. I will make what I have do. Oh you all have been to so much trouble, and have done so much for me, I surely do appreciate it more than I can say.

No, Geney, dear, our clothes are not washed by fish oil soap, but many of the soldiers have it to contend with. We still have soap, ivory, salvaged from the *Dora* or *Wexom* which we are using and will use for some months to come. You asked about Arkangel. In many respects it reminds me of a far western town which is not a commercial centre. The town stretches along the river. One big main business street. On this street are the big three story gov't buildings and city hall. Which are big modern brick buildings. There are numerous churches, schools and orphanages, monastery, a few little factories, and many big two storey frame houses. Solombola, where we have a canteen would be like the paper mill district in its nearness, like a suburb, and Smolny like Henville [?] Mine. There is street car service for all three, just one long line. Of course Arkangel is now quite a metropolis, and life because of the troops and official offices is very interesting and not monotonous. It often is too strenuous for our pleasure and strength, along with our work. I can't imagine a quieter or deader place in normal times. We have been wonderfully glad to be here, but oh we shall be happy when affairs here are satisfactorily settled and we may return home or to Moscow.

The ice in the River and the White Sea are at the worst during these next six weeks, but some mail will come and go. This last mail was overland. Read has found his trip very slow. He had only reached Christian, Norway on the 27th. We are afraid that Miss Gosling and Miss Foerster will find it very slow getting from here to England.

My teacher is due in ten minutes, so must get this ready for the pouch as there is no time after dinner.

With a world of love to each and all, and sincere appreciate for all that you have done for me, from your affectionate daughter,

Clara

I forgot to tell you, that my birthday was royally celebrated by a dance, after which we sat about an open fire, and sang to the mandolin accompaniment of Capt. Boyd. There were sixteen of us. We had potato salad, coffee and Russian birthday cake for refreshments.

Also my Kodak is back. But I may have trouble getting films for it, as they have all been purchased.

P.S. Father dear, your registered letter written Jan. 15th from Louisiana has just been delivered. I am crazy to see those plantations. I hope they prove to be a fine investment, and it will make a comfortable income for you.

March 30. Eliz's letter of Jan 22 delivered today, more mail due next week, am leaving for the canteen at the front Sat.

At the front
[after March 28, 1919]

My Dear Ones at Home:

I came down from Verst 455 where I have been since Saturday night to help for a month in the canteen work. Last night while we were looking at pictures in the recreation hall word was brought in that Mr. Ryall, the second YMCA man was captured. I hopped a troop train and came down to Oberzerskaya to be with Catherine. Mr. Ryall is the second YMCA man captured at the same front. Dear old Catherine is calm, brave and carrying on work here at the Base. I will return to 453 tonight or tomorrow, it is only forty minute ride.

I am so happy to be at the front. The last two days have been giant thrillers. I will be here all of April.

I have a cunning room in the big canteen car. My room is about ten ft. long and four or five wide. My bed lets down like an upper berth, is most comfortable. A Russian lad looks after my fires and my room and any needs which I may have. Back of the canteen car is the Library car and back of that the YMCA office and sleeping quarters. A little rope from my room back to theirs is fixed, in case I want to signal to them. But never was a person safer than I. I am the only woman with the exception of a few Russian women, wives of the Railroad workmen, for miles around. We have a mess hall made from a box car. Which is next to mine at the other end of the canteen. In the evening we serve cocoa or coffee to the men in the hall, following it by movies or some kind of entertainment.

Twice a week our canteen car goes to two other places where we serve coffee, cocoa and sell the men candles, cigarettes and canned stuffs, etc.

I am so thankful to be here. Now I must help Catherine. I am well. Will get a good letter off next week.

Lovingly,

Clara

The evening messenger from Arkangel came in at 6 o'clock with a letter from Sis written Jan. 28. Catherine Ryall is leaving for Arkangel on the night train. I return to 455 in the morning. A cable from London say that two of our trunks are on the way. They will probably be here by the time I arrive from 455.

Write longer letters now. Your letters are not censored. Mine probably still are.

Diary
March 1 – April 2, 1919

March 1, 1919
Sat. Spent day in bed. Major Henry & Miss Gosling came down to see Eliz. Mrs. Dmt & self—glorious sunset. Everybody desperately homesick. Days getting much longer.

March 2, 1919, Letter ?3
Sun. Miss Gosling in the morning. Col. Thurston & Crawford for dinner. Wrote family letters & to Read. Spent evening at the Hostess House.

March 3, 1919
Mon. Eliz. sick. Did errands in the afternoon & went to Hostess House in evening.

March 4, 1919
Tues. very mild. Maria and I went to Hospital ship in afternoon. 6 engineers came to supper. Helen returned from front. French & Eng. have refused to fight. Very mild and spring-like.

March 5, 1919
Wed. Found letter from Read at Breakfast written from Onega. Blustery & wind, not very cold. Went to 53 and Smolny, later for tea with the English Sec'ys at Mr. Copson's.

March 6, 1919
Thur. Shopped in market with Mr. Stone who came home to dinner afterwards. At Hostess House early. Marcia & I called on Mrs. Klieforth's. Later went to Hospital 53 and Smolney. Lovely moonlight & northern lights.

March 7, 1919, 25° above
Fri. Perfect winter day, clear & beautiful. Spent entire afternoon and evening at Hostess House. Marcia and called on Mrs. Davis at 5. Mr. Shotwell showed me the official army pictures.

March 8, 1919, Much snow & wind
Sat. Visited 53 and Smolny. Serving 120 rice puddings.

March 9, 1919
Sun. Lt. Commons, Hallock, Johnson & Crawford came to dinner. Lt. Brecker and Miss Forester for tea. Spent afternoon and evening at Hostess House. Mild weather.

March 10, 1919
Mon. Served 3,000 pancakes at Smolny hut. Men crazy about them. Mild and much snowing. Bolo. using gas in last attack on Co. A at Kitza.

March 11, 1919
Tues. M.D. HO. ED & I went with two machine gun men for dinner. Then visited torpedo boat & air-ice plane in machine shop. Spent evening at Hostess House. Had afternoon tea at Smolny with officers. Received two letters by overland mail.

March 12, 1919, Sent letter 54 to Sis
Wed. Mr. Hall and I visited Hospital Ship. Spent evening at Hostess House. Finished letters to Sis and Read. Mild and snowing.

March 13, 1919
Thurs. Strenuous afternoon & evening at Smolny. tried to serve 900 Washington pie & doughnuts. Had tea with officers. Got promise for additional help from Maj. Young. 12 came in at 11 for Samovar after skating.

March 14, 1919, Snowing, but delightful
Fri. Free afternoon. Evening at Hostess House. Co. I & M in their splendid frame of mind doing much to help spirit. Hostess House until 10. Men had had beautiful sing. Mr. Strother brought Read's telegram from Murmansk and 2 letters from home. One envelope 12 and 16 months old. Beautiful northern lights at 10.

March 15, 1919, 15° above
Sat. Spent a.m. on clothes and at Bath. Afternoon at Hostess House. Eve all four of us went to the Hdqt. Engineers St. Patrick's Day Dance. Rec'd 2 letters from home, Dec. 28 and Jan. 11. Crawford came for supper.

March 16, 1919, Big holiday 3rd Sunday in Lent
Sun. Miss Gosling & Corp. Stafford came to dinner. Went to Central Canteen in evening. Lt. Beach, Johnson and several others came in for tea at 8:30. Windy & blustery, but late clear and beautiful

March 17, 1919, 20° below
Mon. Very busy day at Smolny with new cook. Served doughnuts. Drove home in *Isvaschick* in evening—very cold but beautiful. Still no more mail from home. Tom C. [Cotton] came up from Bereznik.

March 18, 1919, 35 below
Tues. Tom & I called at Hospital Ship. Spent evening at Hostess House. Sent cable to John. Bartered 22 glasses of rice & 2 cans of milk for 20 eggs. Saw a chickadee.

March 19, 1919, 20° below
Wed. Spent afternoon at 53. Sent cable for a boy. Big crowd at Smolny at 9:30. all four of us went to Embassy to the Dance. Norwegian Consulate, English Embassador, French & Am. Consuls, Reps. of Military Mission. Beautiful time.

March 20, 1919, Letter no. 3. R. L. 25 ° below zero, Letter no. 55 Fritz
Thurs. Rec'd cable from Geny. Visited Hospital 53. In evening Tom & Crawford came in. Report of fighting on the R. R. front. All men required to remain in barricks. Arnold YM. missing.

March 21, 1919, 10° below
Fri. Spent after mending clothes. Evening in the Hostess House. Played for the boys to sing. Co. A Engineers. Many of them came in for the first time. Tom came to dance. Maj. Nicklas returned 455.

March 22, 1919
Sat. Cable from Geney. Stopped at Hospital 53. Russian concert at Smolny followed by dinner. All feeling anxious over military situation and activity along R. R. and Onega fronts. Enjoying A Co. Engineers who are in Arkangel for 1st time.

March 23, 1919
Sun. Sargt. Shotwell, Sargt. Wright and Mr. Chamberlain came to dinner. Spent afternoon & evening at Hostess House. Col. Stewart & Col. Thurston called for tea at eight-thirty. H. O. & Lt. Johnson went skating. Miss F. & Lt. Bricker came in for tea.

March 24, 1919, glorious sunny day
Mon. Went to hospital Ship in afternoon, 53 and Smolny. Tom came in for dinner. Mail has arrived.

March 25, 1919, 10° below
Tuesday. Hostess House in afternoon. Birthday party at Crawfords—Capt. Boyd, Lt. Johnson, Dricher, Packard, Blauwett, Summerville, & Tom C. Two nurses & ourselves danced, sang to Mandolin accompaniment. Letter came from John & R. L.

March 26, 1919
Wed. All four of us went to Red Cross Hospital for dinner. Smolny in afternoon and evening. Rec'd two letters from Gen. & 1 Sis. Sent telegram to R. L. to Christiana.

March 27, 1919, cold & clear
Thurs. Sent letters 56 Father. No. 4 R. L. Smolny Barricks burned in night. Visited hospitals—spent evening at Hostess House.

March 28, 1919, cold & gray
Friday Miss Gosling came to dinner. Packed and got ready for 455. Went to Co. 1 Minstrel [Show] in evening & dance at military mission in the late evening. Finished letters at 2 a.m. Rec'd Eliz's letter.

March 29, 1919
Sat. Left at 9 o'clock for 455. shared coupe with British officer Country for most part. covered with pine timber, white with snow. Mr. Hall and Don both met me and seemed very glad to have me here.

March 30, 1919, 455
Sun. Heavy shelling began at 11:30. Mar(?) guns used. 300 shells dropped in 6 hrs. Bolos sent up observation balloon. Aeroplane circled us, Finally sailing straight down track over us. Firing continued all night. Co. M at Malo O. being badly shelled

March 31, 1919
Monday Heavy firing all day. "L" Co. & Engineers & machine guns. We arrived at 455 for Canteen. While at movies, Major Nickolas sent word Ryall captured. Don and I hopped [on] fresh troop train and went to Katya [Catherine Childs Ryal] at Oberzerskya.

April 1, 1919, Oberzerskya
Tuesday Wrote letters for America. Katya and I visited Hospital in P.M. Katya went into Arkangel on evening train. Bolos made 7 attacks during night at Malo Oberska.

April 2, 1919, 455
Wed. R. L. 5, Sis 57 Returned from Oberzerskya at 11. Helped in Canteen all morning. and served coco in Recreation Hall before movies. Received letter from Fritz.

Chapter Six
"The Russian situation is about as bad a muddle as it could be."

Letters

Verst 455 Arkangel
Apr. 3, 1919

My Dear Elizabeth:

These have been wonderful days when letters keep straggling in. You see my mail comes in the open mail, so it takes the Russians as much as a week to distribute the contents of their few bags. Letters from you (your first rec'd), Fritz and Genieve came in during the past four days. Now I fully expect that each messenger out here will have home mail.

I am adoring the experiences that I am enjoying here at the front. I shall be here the entire month of April.

My first three days we could hear the constant roar of battle, but since then, all has been quiet on this front. Mr. Hall who is one of the YM men has been out at the front since early morning making the rounds visiting the men, and supplying them with a few luxuries like gum.

Yesterday, all being quiet, we took the canteen car to another part nearer the front. The men were enthusiastic over the supplies. They could buy coffee, cocoa, milk, salmon, pork and beans, sardines, oatmeal, syrup, catsup, peppermints, tobacco, and cigarettes besides such supplies as toothpaste, blacking, etc. I got out of the car and went thru one of the block houses picking up some brass shells for souvenirs. We could see the big potholes where the shells had burst nearby. On the way back, we three ate our lunch. It was the first time that the canteen car had been there for some time, so we did a land office business. I shall take the car down, if there is fighting, so Mr. Hall and Dan Laurie are free to go to the front.

What ever maybe said in unfavorable criticism of the YMCA in France, can not be said here. Here the sec'ys are often in the very front block houses. Nothing has been learned about Mr. Arnold and Bryant Ryall, who were captured near Bolshya Ozerka. We feel that they are living and are safe. We are thankful that the weather has moderated. We have feared that Mr. Arnold may have escaped but have frozen as it was about 35° below the night he was found missing.

In the recreation hall we serve either coca or coffee and crackers every night at seven. The men play basketball, thump the piano until eight fifteen when the movies begin, or some impromptu play. We are going to put on a few canteen specialties while I am here like rice pudding, and oatmeal fritters.

We are fixing up a huge car for reading and writing room for further down the line. The car has been relined and made perfectly warm. Today, I have been making curtains out of unbleached muslin. From Arkangel they will send us heavy linen for table coverings. I have been getting together some pictures and posters for the walls. Tomorrow I am asking the engineers to cut down some empty brass shells for ash trays for the writing and reading tables. When we finish it will be a very attractive little hut. A Russian Sec'y will look after it, while some one from here will go down every other day.

April 6th

It is Sunday noon, the two YM men are visiting block houses. They are distributing candy and holding a short service in each. In twenty minutes I will eat, then leave for down the line with posters, writing material and the *American Sentinel*, returning at five o'clock.

Last night we were thrilled with the excitement when Father Roach, the catholic priest who was captured with Mr. Ryall and 3 company "M" men came into camp. He had been released by the Bolos and reports that

Mr. Arnold and Mr. Ryall and the other American prisoners are safe, well and on their way to Moscow. Dear old Catherine was too happy to contain herself. I think it is quite likely that she will leave on the next boat for home. Which will be not before first of May.

Now more facts are being given out regarding the coming of new, and withdrawal of old, troops, I think that we will be able to make more definite plans for the summer. While I am away from Arkangel I don't know what the various things may enter into the decisions. We certainly under the present circumstance are not talking about going home. But we rather expect that we will.

We need more workers here. If a transportation pass is granted Elizabeth Dickerson, she will come up tomorrow for a couple of weeks, to be relieved by Helen later. I am to stay right thru the month. It is quite the most enjoyable place for us, under the present situation. And I feel wonderfully glad that my turn came just at this time. Tho it is rather selfish, one reason why I wish so much to come home soon is to be able to relate to the family some of my many giant thrillers.

The two Red Cross nurses sailed Wednesday on an ice boat to Murmansk from whence they probably will go by Norwegian boat to Bergin and sail from there home. I will send Miss Foerster's Chicago address. So if any of the family should be in Chicago you could arrange to see her. I do want Sis to write and express the family's appreciation for her wonderful care of me. She helped in the operation and also to look after me when Miss Gosling was away from the hospital. Both nurses have been most thoughtful and considerate of us and have supplied us with some things which we very much needed and couldn't procure. Then we shall miss them as friends and Americans. Only six American women remain here now. Our other sec'ys from London will come in May if we cable for them. Two trunks for us are on the way but have not yet reached us. I will wire when they come. Up here I live in kakai shirt, old blue skirt and dark sweater. This is not a clean place in which to live.

Will the family please do something for me. Last night in course of the conversation with Lt. Bricker, I was horrified to learn that the Red Cross sent their cables from Washington collect. When I was in the Hospital they said they supposed that I would be sending word home often, and there was no reason why I shouldn't send thru the Red Cross, same as the soldiers, and get the benefit of the cheaper rate. Then last night I learned from Washington these cables were sent collect. If that is so please pay Rose Henry and Fanny Armstrong for the cables which I sent them. Here after I will send directly as I did before January. I feel most embarrassed about the expense which my cables since January have cost my family and these friends. Please explain to them.

The woods here are so beautiful. They remind me of the Norway pines of Minnesota and Wisconsin. The snow is very deep four or five feet deep along this track and thru the forest. Now that the clear moonlight nights are coming again, it will be a veritable fairy land here.

Yesterday, I had such a good visit with a Mr. Hootman, Corporal, who is a great friend of Clarence Barbre and Prue Hedden. He attended Eureka, but finished Michigan Agri. He was teaching there when the war broke out. He is a remarkably fine fellow. His two brothers are officers in France. He was drafted just before the 339 left the states.

Tues. Apr. 8

Well we have had a busy day in the canteen this morning, and have waited all afternoon for a colonel to go down the line so we can take another group of men. But it begins to look as tho the car would not go as our canteen in the big recreation hall opens in a couple of hours. We were greatly excited Sunday night when Father Roach, the Catholic priest who was taken prisoner with Mr. Ryall, was permitted to return under a white flag. He brought back the news that Mr. Arnold and Ryall and other American prisoners were safe and well and were on the way to Moscow. Then yesterday morning and today the Bolos and Allies have met to arrange the exchange of prisoners so our men will soon be returned unto their own.

We are having glorious weather and this is just the place to be to enjoy it the most fully.

Will give this to the messenger tonight to be send thru the Pouch.

With a world of love to each of you dear ones at home from your affectionate sister,

Teke

Clara Taylor

The following are undated short letters to Sis written from Arkangel

Dear Sis:

When I receive the home mail and you speak of sending copies of my letters to friends, I have an awful feeling and decide to be very impersonal in what I write, then suddenly news comes that we may send mail, and I forget all, and have in mind only the family. Please cut out most references made to Read, as already gossip has started in the states which has come back thru the Ogden letters. You are in a position to deny any and all reports that may come to you. Furthermore I have written many things that were for family consumption only. I feel sure that you would cut all that out . . . I am sure you have, only I should feel more comfortable if I knew that only the more or less impersonal things were published.

You did not tell me what you took from the things for your birthday gift. What did you? Also put up any and all ikons which you may wish. I am glad to have them enjoyed by all. I am so glad that you all liked the things. There is absolutely nothing to buy here, unless you persuade people to sell from their homes. So I am not collecting anything from here. Laundry and cable grams is about all that we spend money for now.

I had hoped that you and father would go south for the winter, has the Influenza been too bad, to make going away from home unwise. I hope by now the epidemic is over.

Lovingly,

Clara

I surely appreciate the faithfulness with which you Genieve and Fritz have written me, and I can't tell you how contrite and ashamed I am, that I complained about not hearing. I have cabled recp't of letters, that you might know that they were getting through now. If you had numbered them, it would have been easier to report on them. But I am sure practically all are getting thru now. Don't send via Stockholm, or Pacific, just address Arkangel, until boats come here directly from America, all will go via England.

PERSONAL

Dear Sis,

Tell John to inquire at the Bank sometime in June or July if an extra hundred was sent to my credit. Marcia has written NY asking them to grant each of us $100 for equipment which we bought in Stockholm, and to help out on the baggage expense. She requested that mine be sent to Taylorville. After its arrival, perhaps John would have time to send me another financial statement, so I will know just where I stand. I want to get out of debt by September if possible. So as to accumulate a little for those precious six months that I am to have when I return next March. The workers in France got two months on salary. I am expecting three if I stay until next spring.

I shall need a Jersey dress for next winter, shoes and doeskin gloves but will write about them later. I do not want a narrow skirt dress. However, if you and Genieve shop in Chicago and you should see any pretty Jerseys get me one, not narrow. Three of the sec'ys here have had them, and how the rest of us have envied them. They are ideal for this climate and nomadic life. Who knows but that Marcia and I shall be knocking about considerably next year.

I think I shall send the pongie dress home. I think it would fit Genieve. I have worn it only twice and despaired having it altered so it will be satisfactory.

By the first of June we will know more definitely. Then I will write about clothes for Fall. I really would like to see the contents of those trunks in London before deciding on Fall clothes. My velvet is as good as new but that is about all that is left over.

Do you know if my full salary was deposited at home from Dec. to May in full. I am not distressed about finances, I know everything is unusually expensive now.

Did you have to pay duty for the things I sent from Stockholm? If you did, it must be charged to my account. And Sis, you never wrote me, or if you did the letter did not come thru, what you chose for your birthday gift.

I am selling my revolver for 20 American dollars. In most respects it has been a great nuisance and the dollars are worth a heap here.

April 14, 1919

My Dear George:

Your second letter written March 2nd reached me April 9th. Not so bad. It was so good to hear from you directly. I got a bunch of seven letters in that mail, all but one from family letters. And am greedily expecting more by the messenger who comes out three times a week from Arkangel.

You see I am at one of the canteens at the front. Have been here a little over two weeks. Will probably return the first or tenth of May. Our plans for the summer are very uncertain. I have begun to feel that possibly Marcia Dunham and I may go to Odessa during the early summer. However I will wire as soon as we have definite plans.

It was mighty thoughtful of you to send me the candy. It really ought to reach me. The soldiers are receiving packages right along. It will be greatly appreciated, I assure you.

I am sorry that you have received so few of my letters home. I have sent just one letter a week, as the mail doesn't go oftener, to the family, and thought they were always sent the rounds. I have written a very long letter to Leslie which I am asking him to send on to you. It gives the news of my life here, so will not repeat it, in this letter.

I have thought of you boys so often since being so closely associated with the Army. And have tried to picture you men as officers. The army is so full of all kinds, that there is always room for the A no. 1. In our position we get the very frank opinions of the men regarding their officers, and in our social life come to know these men. That is, some of them. And usually our opinions quite coincide with those of the men. The Lt. who says to "go to it" has no standing. It's the "come on!" that wins the loyalty and confidence.

The Russian situation is about as bad a muddle as it could be. If it is true that the cities along the Volga have been retaken from the Bolosheviki, then the food situation is going to be another tremendous factor. The people of Moscow and Petrograd will die like flies, as they did last year when the Cholera was so bad. I am afraid that the English and French slipped one diplomatically over President Wilson. The troops feel terribly bitter towards him. Oh George what a sigh of relief we will give, when we see our boys embark for home in May. It would be too serious to contemplate if anything should happen to prevent their going at the time promised.

Because the men have not known why they are fighting, they have been unhappy at being here. Every mail which the men receive that is full of clippings, stirs them up. All sorts of things both true and untrue have appeared in the US papers I don't wonder that everyone is at sea as to what the real situation here is. Some day, we shall all know and I hope the lives lost here will not have been sacrificed in vain. Some wonderfully fine men have given their lives here.

Mr. Hall, the YMCA man, has gone to the front this morning, leaving Elizabeth Dickerson and me here to run the canteen at two other places. Every Tuesday and Friday our canteen car goes away for the day, to serve two other groups out on this front. We are all stocked and ready for our train to pull out.

I shall be so glad to learn of your's and Trenna's plans for the summer. Shall you be returning to Highland Park again next winter? I know that Trenna has enjoyed teaching. I am so glad that Genieve plans to be home this next year. It will mean so much to Father and Sis to have her there, and she will love being at home. I wish that we girls could have a winter together. Perhaps fate will work to that end.

Well George and Trenna dear, the newsy letter will reach you very soon after this one, altho I am sending Leslie's thru the pouch and this with army mail.

With appreciation for your thoughtfulness, . . . and very much love to you both, your loving sister,

Clara. Clara I. Taylor

April 22, 1919
Arkangel

My dear Fritz:

I am afraid that the family will have a long wait of a month or six weeks between letters at this time, for the melting of the snow has made overland mail impossible, and the ice bergs in the White Sea are very bad at this season. The ice boats are not running very frequently. When the *Canada* does sail, Catherine Childs-Ryall and Consular Davis and wife, with three or four YM men will leave us. Bryant Ryall will sail from Europe, having been freed by the Bolsheviki. The Davises go to the new appointment in Finland. While several of the YMCA men must return to their business, their contracts expiring here with the YMCA. With the departure of Catherine and Mrs. Davis there will be just four American women left in Arkangel. As passports are not yet being granted to people coming into Russia, our secretaries from London are delayed. I doubt if they will come here at all. We look for things to happen within the next month which will determine our plans definitely for the summer. It certainly looks as tho we would not get away from here as soon as we all had hoped. Altho the 339 [Infantry] will probably leave by the last of May or early June.

The new Bridg. Gen. Richardson reviewed the troops here this morning. And in a speech to them, told them they would embark as soon as navigation permitted transports to enter the White Sea. Because of the advance season, the ice will doubtless permit more or less regular navigation early in June, if not the last of May.

Our weather so far this spring has been marvelous. The snow is practically all gone and the sun is delightfully warm. It is still light at 9 p.m. and the sun is up by four thirty. It is most interesting to be here for the long days as well as the shortest. If we are to remain all summer, I think we shall plan to sail over to Murmansk during June, during the days of the midnight sun. The sun here sinks below the horizon two or three hours, but there are weeks when it is light enough to read without artificial light, twenty-four hours of the whole day. Isn't it truly marvelous.

I am going to have some charming souvenirs to bring home from this front. I have four beautifully decorated shells, which three of the men have made for me. They are not all finished yet. I want the boys to allow me to pay them, as the work takes a very long time, but as yet they have not decided. If I have room in my trunk, I shall bring home several brass shells which we can shine up for flower vases. But they are not easy things to carry.

Elizabeth Dickerson who has been here for ten days returned to Arkangel tonight. Helen Ogden will come out on Friday night, so we shall not be alone long. Tonight I am the only woman for many miles around. Sometimes, I can't quite believe that it is true, that I am up here in this corner of the world, and under such unusual circumstances. I long to return home so I can tell it all to the family. I am so afraid that I shall forget the most interesting incidents. My life has been so chucked with them.

Monday I went down to Obererskaya to take some fruit to eight of our men who were ill there. Three were victims of a very sad accident. A squad of men were practicing throwing hand grenades when one, who was throwing, struck one of the men who was standing too near him in the rear. The grenade fell in their midst, killing the hero of the Boshoi Ozerka battle, and wounding these others. Fortunately these others are not seriously wounded. All were taken today from Oberzerskaya to Arkangel. I will look them up next week on my return there.

April 24

Well, Fritzie, I have stocked the canteen for tomorrow. Friday is one of our heavy days as we leave here on the 11:15 train for some versts up the line where we sell fast and furiously for an hour. Then while we travel back to some versts below our base here, we eat our lunch. We return either at three thirty or seven depending on extras and delays. I also have kettles of various kinds of dried fruits soaking, for fruit compote tonight at the recreation hall. In this way, we make a limited amount of fruit serve the greatest number.

I intended to go down to our other cars down the line today, but, they are being used for machine gun schools, teaching the Russians the use of these guns, so I have a little free time, which is constantly interrupted by men who come in to exchange library books and to visit while they do it.

Yesterday, I was standing near headquarters when a Bolsheviki officer came in blindfolded. He had watched the chance to give himself up. They fly a white flag, and under its protection are allowed to come in and surrender. He reported that two other officers were awaiting an opportunity to do likewise.

Well I have just arranged that cocoa and crackers be served within thirty minutes to several hundred Russian soldiers who are passing thru here on their way to the front. It is always such a pleasure to our Russian helpers when it is their own countrymen that are being served. When men are on their way to the front, we do not charge them for their refreshments. Usually we charge one ruble for a mug of coca, with four or five biscuits. We charge a ruble extra if we have fruit compote or something of that sort.

I am going to send home such a touching letter which I received from an anxious mother. This same mail takes the answer to her. She is just one of a host who doubtlessly could duplicate the fears she has for her loved ones. How thankful we are, that all of these troops who have been here all winter are so soon to go home, and furthermore, they are in good condition, for the most part. They are so much better off then most of them admit or realize.

April 29, Arkangel

Sunday Helen and I took some plum puddings, sauce, magazines and stationary to a platoon of Americans down the line. The train stopped for us near a block house. During the two hours while we waited for its return, we visited all the block houses and had good visits with the men. Everybody is in high spirits because spring has come so quickly and so persistently, that we feel that the days are numbered now until our men depart.

Sunday night I decided to return to Arkangel as I feared that I would be unable to cross the river. When I reached Bakeritsa, lo, they said no horses could go across, that the ice was unsafe. So three Engineers who came down on the same train, insisted on carrying my heavy dunnage bag and suitcase, and seeing me safely across. So I arrived home just the day before the ice broke. It is piling up now so communications will be only by ice ferries for the next week or ten days, when the regular ferries begin their usual schedule.

Another boat arrived two days ago, bringing your letter written Jan 1 and 8th, four from Sis, written Jan. and Feb., and one from Genieve, written in early March. The letters written just before and at Xmas time I have not received. The daily couriers are arriving at the rate of ten to twenty on every boat. It is a joy to have them. I hope that by this time that my letters written in early January have come through Nos. 46 & 47. They told of Xmas here.

You will all be disappointed in learning that our long looked for trunks are still in London. One trunk with uniforms came thru a week ago, but no one is interested in uniforms, we sadly need the personal things. Goodness knows when we shall ever receive them. We are really getting very much discouraged about them. The contents sound so wonderful, you all went to such a lot of trouble and pains to get them started, and we so long for them, to say nothing of the need. Catherine Childs-Ryall will leave for home next week, and I think Elizabeth Dickerson will follow in June. Helen will remain until July if needed. Marcia and I are still uncertain as to our plans. It's very difficult to get passports into Russia, so while we are here we feel that perhaps we ought to remain. I shall wire when we make any change. I think there is very little doubt that we shall leave here before July at the earliest.

Our new uniforms are very becoming. A gray blue suit, with a lovely big black cape, and little overseas cap like the soldiers. The caps are most unbecoming. Marcia and I probably will be the only ones to wear them, as our need is that desperate. Canteen work is really very hard on clothes.

Our days are lengthening so fast. When I came home tonight at a quarter to ten, it was still light. The soldiers say at 2:30 a.m. it is quite light. Even now on clear nights, it isn't dark at midnight, as we know it to be.

The home letters are just wonderful, for days after their arrival I read and reread them, and in my dreams at night go back to all you loved ones. It's going to be pretty hard not to get home sick as we see our friends departing for the homeland. Last night one company visited the Hostess House for the last time. They have gone further down the River from where they will embark. They will embark from several different points, so we may not be near to speed them farewell. The men feel quite disturbed because we do not go along, but they forget that still Americans will be here in some numbers during the early summer.

I am so sorry to hear of the wounded and deaths among our home boys. I know what they have been thru and suffered. I wish I could be home at the homecoming. I feel so a part of the army. If I do not return before next March or April, I hope our country will be quite settled after this strife with all the sorrow and pain it has incurred.

I am so happy, Fritz, dear, that you are finding so much joy in your work, that it is satisfying. I never had any doubt about your making good. Do you get any real support from the Field Office. I hope Mrs. Byers and Miss Crittenden are standing by you. After you have been there a couple or three years, I know a bigger association will be offered you. I don't know how you will feel about it, but the medium sized association has always appealed to me as the most desirable. Don't let them send you to Omaha. It has an excellent building and has been a splendid association, but the last few years it has been afflicted with inefficient Generals. It isn't that the position itself is so hard, but I do hate the climate. But you know what it is like. I had forgotten. I am so glad that Genieve is to be at home next year, it makes me more than eager to return this fall, but so much is at stake here, and I never would leave Marcia here alone. But I certainly will be home early next spring, I hope.

Well, dear, this isn't an interesting letter, it has been interrupted so many times, but it brings very much love, and appreciation for all the family letters and a promise to do better next time. I am feeling fine, and no need to worry about me. Our work has eased up considerably the last two months. I expect to put most of my mornings in studying the language. I haven't accomplished a thing along that line this winter.

Do you ever see the *Survey*? Lorian Jefferson wrote she had read an article of mine in it. If you have seen it, please send me copy. I should like to know what sort of things are appearing over my signature, perhaps it is extracts from my Industrial survey of Moscow. *Life and Labor* have written for [asked for] an article, but I don't know as I can write it at present.

With very much love to each and all from your affectionate sister,

Clara

Boat supposed to be sailing April 30th, May 1st.

The enclosed money is a counterfeit 3 ruble Arkangel money. After the Allies came in all money was stamped by the red lines. Some people didn't turn their money in, in time, so have tried to fix it up themselves.

Diary
April 4 – April 30, 1919

April 4, 1919, 455
Fri. Spent day making curtains while Don was at 466 and Fred at front. In the evening had dandy movies. All quiet on this front.

April 5, 1919, glorious clear day
Sat. Helped in Canteen all day. Word came in evening that Father Roach was set free by Bolos & that Arnold and Ryall and 3 "M" Co. men are safe & on way to Moscow. Lt. Brecker came. All men ordered to stand to at 4 a.m. as attack here is expected.

April 6, 1919
Sunday Spent morning finishing curtains. Went to 466 for the afternoon. Movies at 455 in evening. Lt. Brieker here for the evening. Beautiful weather—Men stood to at 3:30.

April 7, 1919
Mon. Visited Block houses at 455. Busy canteen at 455. Officers of both sides held parley for exchange of prisoners, 6 for officers, 4 for YMCA, 1 each for privates—15 Bolo soldier. Sympothies went across the line. Eliz came down from Arkangel & [?]

April 8, 1919
Tues. Took Canteen car to 448–66. Glorious weather. Fired few shots at the Bolo airoplane. Sent letter 58 Eliz and R. L. 6. Parleying about prisoners continues. All quiet along here.

April 9, 1919, Glorious day 453
Wed. Relief day of different companies. Col. Stewart and Maj Nicholas stopped in for a visit. Katya spent day with us. Parley about prisoners continues. All quiet on this front.

April 10, 1919, 453–466

Thurs. Two letters from home. Spent afternoon at 466 visiting with the 'Il' Co. men. It looks as tho southern Russia was going to open up. Curtiss & Clark ordered to Odessa.

April 11, 1919, 455

Fri. Went up to 446 & 48. Rep. of Allied Forces for hostages were on way to Eecclca [?]. Bolo had not heard from Moscow. Saw the Baracade across the track at the very front.

April 12, 1919

Sat. Eliz, Fred & I went to 466 in canteen car. I spent remainder of day there fixing up the canteen car with Ivan. Four letters from home. Parlency between allies and Bolos continues. So all quiet. Bolos sent back two more prisoners. Others in Moscow.

April 13, 1919, gray and damp, 453

Went to 466 for afternoon. Car was filled for afternoon. Service Men Co. "M" do not know that they are to go to the front again. Men desperately bitter against Wilson. But wonderfully loyal to Major Nicholos. Bad attacks on the Bolshya Ozerkia front.

April 14, 1919, 455

Mon. Gorgeous spring day. Snow melting rapidly. Soldiers wearing hip boots. Official order from Gen. Ironsides has closed up parlying. Bolos attacked at 448 and 46–42. Possibility of going to Odessa seems on the horizon.

April 15, 1919

Tues. Soldiers stood to at 3 a.m. but no attack. Eliz & I took canteen to 48 and 66. Sent letter 59 to Leslie. Bolo's sent across another English officer for propaganda mark.

April 16, 1919

Wed. Spent afternoon at 66. Machine gun practice [?] mortars & hand grenades thundered from three different points. Wrote letters in the evening.

April 17, 1919
Thurs. Wonderful warm day, 55. Fred at front, Don 66. In afternoon. Eliz took walk at 4:30 The big 4 inch new naval gun was tried out at 54. All quiet on our front.

April 18, 1919, Oberzerskya
Friday Went to Oberzerskay to take travel candles to Frank. Our troops occupying Balshka Ozerka. Bolo's withdrawing. Wonderful spring weather. Most snow gone. Katya all packed to leave

April 19, 1919, 455
Sat. Busy with canteen in afternoon. All sad because of very bad accident in "M" Co. where Corp'l Russell was killed in hand grenade accident. Two Sargt wounded. Letters from Read and Life & Labor and Soldier's mother. Katya left for Ark.

April 20, 1919, Easter, 455
Sun. Sent letter to Read. Sent letters out by currier. Snowed most of the day. Went to '66 Relief Day. Was there when I came to relieve "M." All quiet on this front.

April 21, 1919
Mon. Went to Oberzerskaya with Fruit for "M" Co. boys who were hurt. Came back with Bridg. [?] Marcia sent word passports were not being issued to Odessa or Ark. All quiet. Light at 9P.M. and 2:30 a.m

April 22, 1919, Verst 455
Tues. Review of troops by Bridg. Gen. Richardson at 8:45. Bols officer prisoner gave self up and brought in during review. Liza & I took care of canteen in afternoon. Frank O. & Liza left for Arkangel in the evening.

April 23, 1919, 455
Wed. Lovely spring day. Made fruit compote; stocked canteen, mended. [?] money & loaned out library books. Mr. Stone came up for a few days—225 Russians stopped for coca at 5:00 on way to front. Much confusion about plans for summer.

April 24,1919, Verst, 455
Thurs. Frank came up from Bolshose Ozerna. He and Eliz. left for Arkangel. Mr. Stone came for two days. Russians taking over the front lines.

April 25, 1919, Verst, 455
Fri. Fred & I took the canteen car to 48 and 66. "I" Co. men had bad accident with hand grenade Helen arrived on the evening train.

April 26, 1919, 455
Sat. Busy day in canteen—Pioneer Stanley brough[t] the beautifully decorated shells. Helen and I had great visit. In Arkangel Dance for new officers.

April 27, 1919, 455
Sun. Helen & I took fruit pudding & sauce, magazine and writing material to Co. G at 458 visiting the five block house. Took the evening train for Arkangel, used trench candle for light—dark hours between 11:30–1:30. warm and mild.

April 28, 1919, Arkangel
Mon. Arrived at Bokereton at 7:00. two A Co. Engineers carried my baggage across the river for me. Ice not safe for horses and no ice boat operating as yet. Hostess House in the evening.

April 29, 1919, Arkangel
Tues. Spent a.m. at bath. Afternoon & evening at the Hostess House. Everything Spring like. ice breakers have broken trail in river ice—5 home letters rec'd

April 30, 1919
Wed. Ice leaving river rapidly boat service begun to Bokeritsa. Visited Hospital 53 and Somolny Lt. Dricher walked home with me at ten. Still bright.

PART FOUR

May 7 – August 23, 1919

Clara had now returned to "her" Soldier's Huts at the Arkhangelsk suburbs of Solombola and Smolny after a few weeks at the front. She noted on May 7 that Smolny will be handed over to the British and the Americans troops will go to "Economy (Economia) Camp," a way station north of the city from which they will embark for home. The men were happy to be off the front lines, but dismayed to find that this was not a rest stop—they were drilled five to eight hours a day in order to be ready to march in parades at home.

New British troops arrived daily in a push to finalize training for the North Russian Army, in preparation for the handing over of all military operations from British to Russian command. Clara assisted at Economy Camp, about thirty versts (approximately 20 miles) upriver from the city of Arkhangelsk, for four or five days at a time, continuing the canteen and library support tasks she had done at Smolny. She went back and forth from there to the Hostess House during this period while soldiers were embarking for home.

In this section of her letters and diary, Clara was much more open about her feelings. We hear the moral indignation and outrage she really felt. She wrote scathing comments about the entire fiasco. She was angry with British command, with their officers' attitudes towards the American enlisted men, and the obvious distain the British showed for the Russians. She was particularly upset that rum and whiskey were available to the men, who gave it to Russian girls. She allowed herself to write about the attitudes of the US men, the political situation, and troop movements and plans. Clara defended some of the socialist policies of the new Russian government, but decried the methods and barbaric cruelty of the Bolshevik regime: "What it has grown to, now, is vastly different from it was in the beginning. All of us devoutly wish now for the overthrow of the powers in Moscow."[47] There were even some uncharacteristically negative comments (albeit mildly expressed) about other American war workers.

Clara and her colleagues were working ever harder, with fifteen hour days and much traveling back and forth among the camps. In addition to their work with the Hostess House, canteens, and a Girl Scout group they had organized earlier in the year, Clara, Helen, Catherine, and Marcia were asked by the British command to find a house and employment for forty Russian female political prisoners. Clara noted that the American women do not, however, assume responsibility of the prisoner's parole—Clara felt that was too much to ask.

In June, the American troops at Vega and Onega withdrew to Arkhangelsk, leaving the fronts to the Slavo-British Allied Legion 1st Battalion. Early in July, those Russian Allied troops mutinied at Troitsa, and later, at Onega. The Russian men murdered their commanding officers and turned over munitions and territory to the Red Army. It was a foretaste of the rapid decline of any gains the Allied troops made in holding Arkhangelsk Province for the White Army. On October 25, 1919, the International Expedition was officially closed by the Allied Command. All foreign troops had left North Russia. After only four months, on February 20, 1920, the Bolsheviks retook Arkhangelsk, and the North Russian Expedition's failure was complete (Cudahy 1924, 210).

The time between May and August 1919 on the world stage was filled with small but intense and bloody conflicts. In May, six hundred people were killed in street fighting as troops of the Weimar Republic crushed the German Soviet resistance in Munich. The Estonian war for independence commenced. The White Russian Army retreated from the eastern front, giving up territory to the Red Army. In June, the Soviet Republics in Russia, Ukraine, Lithuania-Belorussia, Latvia, and the Crimea formed a military union. In other news, on June 15, British pilot John Alcock and navigator Arthur Whitten Brown landed their airplane, a "Vickers Vimy", in Galway, Ireland, after the first nonstop flight across the Atlantic Ocean.

---

47 Letter to Genieve, May 15, 1919.

In June, the Paris Peace Conference submitted an ultimatum to Germany. On June 22, the Allies threatened to cross the Rhine within twenty-four hours unless German Chancellor Gustav Bauer agreed to sign the treaty as drafted. The Germans capitulated, and the Treaty of Versailles was signed on June 28, 1919. All international military hostilities between the Allies and the Central Powers were now officially ended.

Also at Versailles, national boundaries were redrawn and additional peace treaties negotiated. The Ottoman empire was dissolved, which entailed carving up its former territories. Africa, the Middle East, and Central Europe were all distributed among the participants of the Conference: one example is that German East Africa was given to Britain, which agreed to cede part of the territory to Belgium. [48]

In the United States, race riots in south central portions of the country led to the "red summer" of white supremacist's atrocities and racial violence across the country. On June 4, the US Congress voted to send the Nineteenth Amendment to the Constitution (the voting rights act) to the states for ratification.[49]

July found Clara Taylor and Marcia Dunham the last of their group of YWCA women in Arkhangelsk. Clara described a fun-filled July 4 celebration, all the more poignant since troops had been embarking for home each day. The Hostess House now served the sailors from the transports and US warship *Des Moines*. The women also moved their living quarters in preparation for the arrival of a new batch of YWCA secretaries. Clara was still planning on heading back to Moscow, or to Odessa, Samara, or Kiev in the fall to continue the YWCA work.

The new YWCA secretaries arrived on July 14, 1919, and this allowed Clara and Marcia to take a bit of a vacation. They traveled across the White Sea to the Solovetski Monastery for a week of sightseeing and worship at the venerable monastery. When they returned to the city, the women

---

48 The complexities of the issues, the personalities of the negotiators—the massive undertaking of ending a world conflict—is well explained in Margaret MacMillan's 2001 book *Paris 1919*.

49 "The right of citizens of the United States to vote shall not be denied or abridged by the United States or by any State on account of sex" (US Constitution, Amendment XVIII). On August 18, 1920, Tennessee becomes the thirty-sixth state to ratify the amendment, making universal suffrage the law of the land.

heard more about the unsettled state of the British trained Russian troops. Mutinies by the Russian soldiers demoralized the civilians, and Clara noted how upset the local Russian people were that the Allied troops were leaving. The YWCA staff openned a club for Russian women and girls on August 3. Clara wrote in her diary that she had been instructed to be in New York City on October 20 for an "International Women's Labor Meeting" (a.k.a. the International Congress of Working Women, see the introduction to Part Five, below, for more information), where she was to present her Russian findings. She now knew for certain that there would be no further support for women by the YWCA in Russia.

Battles at Puchega, on the Railroad, and at the Seletskoe fronts in late August were the last offensive actions involving Allied troops. These were initiated in order to boost local Russian morale. British General Rawlinson arrived in Arkhangelsk on August 11 and took command of the evacuation of all Allied personnel. Clara's letter home of August 2 told of plans for the YWCA Association Club. The American women planned to offer classes for 200 women who had registered for the six-week-long courses. Clara's upbeat prediction that they would be able to offer two sets of six-week classes before evacuating was crushed when the women were told they all would be evacuated before the end of August.

For Clara, finally leaving Russia's soil turned out to be a more difficult event than warranted. Shelby Strothers, an American diplomat, made trouble for Clara over paperwork allowing her to leave. He had her escorted off the *Kaylon* hospital ship on which she and Marcia had secured berths to England. The women returned to their city rooms, frightened and confused about the denial of their visas. After frantic appeals to Consul Poole and the Norwegian government, the women were granted visas to leave through Vardo, Norway.

The night of August 23, 1919, found Clara and Marica aboard a Russian ship with a few other Americans headed to Murmansk. Clara was questioned again at the port, but her friend Peter Pierce of the American Consul intervened and she was allowed to continue traveling. She and Marcia boarded a ship at Bergen, Norway, for Newcastle, England, on September 6, 1919. Clara Taylor's time in Russia—the "great opportunity of my life"—and the most exciting, exacting, and exhausting but exhilarating experience of her 34 years had ended.

Chapter Seven
"Arkangel will be quite deserted after this week."

Diary
May 1 – May 6, 1919

May 1, 1919, Arkangel

Thurs. market in morning. Hostess house in afternoon. Smolny in evening. Splendid winter tournament of Durham Light Infantry Cheery-O's [a vaudeville-style act who sang and danced for the troops] & Crawford, [?] Frank, & Jim Blawelt came for tea.

May 2, 1919

Fri. Visited Red Cross Hospital in afternoon. and Central in morning. Met new Army officers. Men returning daily from front. Bolos being hard pressed.

May 3, 1919

Sat. Cold but clear. Sun rise 3:30. Spent afternoon at the Hostess House. Evening at Amer. Headquarters dance—with Lt. Bricker. Had a really beautiful time. Glorious sunset at ten and lovely night.

May 4, 1919

Sun. Attended the Russian Churches in a.m. Wrote letters in afternoon went to Central hut in evening. Guests came in for tea at 8:30. Started letter 8 to Read.

May 5, 1919

Mon. Spent afternoon & evening at Smoly preparing dinner for the Cheerie O's and farewell to the men there. Hospital Ships have gone up the river to evacuate hospitals. Capt. Hoyle and Lt. Prechar in for tea. Miss Gosling's birthday.

May 6, 1919

Tues. All went to market in the morning. Sold Grace's dress for 175 rubles. At Hostess House in the afternoon. Marcia & I had tea with Miss Harwich in evening. Russians at Tolgus shot two Eng. officers and went over to the Bolos.

Letters

Arkangel
May 7, 1919

Dear Sis:

Catherine Childs-Ryall will sail directly to London, on an ice breaker on Friday. She will mail some letters for me in England. We are looking forward to the time when mail can go directly thru to the States. Your mail probably comes thru faster then mine to you, for yours is not censored and I suppose ours is. This won't be.

All the ice from here has gone out of the river, but we hear that there will be big ice flows coming down soon. Our river is high but is apparently not causing any disturbances or inconveniences. Boat service is rapidly being established between here and the nearby islands.

I returned on the 28th from the Railroad front after being there a month and two days. The change did me a world of good. Everyone remarks on how well I am looking. I am not often conscious of my side now, and with lighter work here, all pain will soon be gone. I had a very long incision, which accounts in part for so long a time in getting over the effects of it.

Monday night at the Smolny canteen we gave a farewell dinner to the members of the Durham Light Infantry "Cheerie O's" entertainers who have frequently given evenings at the Hut, and for eight men who have given much volunteer service.

The Smolny camp is soon to be evacuated by the Americans and turned over to the British. Our troops who usually have stayed there, when in from the front, are going to Economy [Camp]. From whence they will embark for home. Almost every day brings home other groups from the lines. And happy the fellows are to have returned in safety. Now follow days of hard drilling from five to eight hours a day. Here, of course, they have had none of that. But they need the drilling if they are to make any public marches in England and the States. Some of these men came into this regiment only a few weeks before they sailed, so they are quite green, but they make good fighters. The French and English both speak in high terms of our fighting abilities, but criticize us when it comes to discipline and marching.

We rather expect that all our troops, or most of them, will be gone by

the last of June, if not earlier. They hospital boat went up the River yesterday, to bring back the patients. Every boat leaving now is filled to capacity
with convalescents and others who are scheduled to leave here.

It gives us a bit of home sickness to see them going, but we wouldn't
have it otherwise. I wish all could go. The British troops who came at the
same time as ours, are to be relieved now as well.

The British are coming in, in quite large numbers. And will undoubtedly remain until this affair is successfully settled. There has been so much
bitter feeling against the English and especially among or against the officers. In the first place most of the British sent here were men fit only for
guard duty who had been through two and three years of warfare, so they
were class B & C men. So the Americans, instead of doing guard duty, as
they had been told they would do, have done most of the hard fighting and
it was an aggressive warfare. The forces were too small for the enormous
length of front which was established and maintained until the Shenkursk
retreat. In those early days, the men were insufficiently equipped with
guns, no artillery, inadequate clothing and insufficient food. The men
went directly into fighting lines thru deep cold swamps with no boots,
always advancing, sleeping and eating in these damp, deep watery swamps,
sometimes the men couldn't lie down at night for water. I guess the first
General, General Poole, was largely responsible for the warfare. He was
superseded by General Ironsides of whom all speak in the highest terms.
But the other British officers are a booze fighting bunch, which have made
some sad blunders such as shelling over our own lines, dropping a bomb
that killed one of our men, and giving orders for men to advance into
regular death traps. Not a few Lieutenants have refused to obey orders of
commanding British officers. And most of our soldiers, do not and will not
salute a Britisher.

The disgrace of a country that imports great cargo of rum into a dry
country. When the hatches were needed for onions, fruits and food stuffs
in general, and worse still give it in quantities to the Russian soldiers. The
Legions enlisted and under British leadership among the Russians have
only bitterness against the English. They are so short sighted. The French
well clothed, well fed, and splendidly trained their [Russian] Legion, and
made comrades of them. We all expect to see a good many English officers
disposed of by Russians when the French and Americans depart. The spirit

of brotherhood which has grown up among the Americans and Canadians is just wonderful, and the antipathy of the Canadian for the English is growing. Our men would gladly help Canada cut loose from the Empire.

I am one of a host that needs to go to England in order to see there some of the things which may help me to redeem my good opinion of her. So far as I am concerned, it's down with the English, when it comes to military methods as I have seen them here. I understand why the Russians so thoroughly dislike them, and their treatment of prisoners is anything but admirable.

Our officers' dances at American headquarters had to be discontinued for three weeks in order to get rid of objectionable English who had no better sense than to bring bottles of whiskey in their pockets, to drink themselves and get their Russian girls drunk as well.

Now our dances are by invitation only, which means practically an all American affair. Then the new staff that came in with General Richardson is quite large so we more than comfortably fill the floor, with our own people.

Last Saturday's dance was truly lovely. We danced in the glow of a glorious sunset on the Key until ten o'clock. It did not get dark all night. The darkness is absolutely gone until September. Sunrise is at 3 a.m. I fancy that we shall not have many more dances. In a way we shall miss them very much. We have played cards but very little among the men, of course it has been popular. There has been a heap of gambling all winter.

I have just returned from the dentist where I have had two teeth plugged up, or cavities, rather, and had the teeth thoroughly cleaned. I haven't yet got used to receiving medical professional aid without paying for it. The dentists here have been very busy people and have been handicapped in not having proper equipment.

In the early part of the afternoon Catherine and I went up to the Red Cross hospital to take some sweet crackers to certain of the men, and visit with one who sees no company. We are the only ones permitted to see him. His leg was amputated about ten days ago, poor fellow. His has been a winter of terrible suffering, for he was wounded about the eight of October. It has been a life and death fight all the time, but now he is better.

Oh the men are so happy at the prospect of returning home soon. We expect any day now, to hear that the first group has gone to England. They may be sent to France to embark from there, but it seems quite certain that they will not go directly to the States from here. I am more eager for the hospital boats to go out loaded then the others. Rumor has it that the hospital ship *Kaylon* will leave the fifteenth of this month.

Did I write you that one trunk had come from England, but that it was not the one with our things from home. We have cabled London to do everything in their power to get them through for us. The Uniform is really quite becoming. More so to me, than any of the others. The suits are a gray blue suit and skirt patch pockets and belt. With warm pretty dark blue capes. The overseas cap like the soldiers wear is most unbecoming to us all. Marcia and I are the only ones to wear the uniform for Helen, Catherine and Elizabeth sail for home soon. Eliz and Helen will leave sometime in June, and immediately on arrival of the others, if they are granted permissions.

As a big drive is planned to take place soon, it looks more and more as tho we would go south by the middle of the summer. That being the case, Marcia and I will stay for the present and go to Moscow or Vologda just as soon as possible. So my hopes for returning home this summer are waning. Never mind next March will come early and soon. It is less than a year off, when nothing will prevent me sailing for home. By the way did letter 46 & 47 get thru, also 36 is being mailed in England along with this one. It is old, but the facts are interesting. I hope that it does come through all right.

On the next boat from Murmansk will be a lot of films in the YMCA supplies, just as soon as I can get some I will take pictures and send home. We have been without films a long time. I let one of the officers take my Kodak and films, he was killed in battle so it was a long time before the Kodak came back. The men of the company used up the films. I hope to get copies of pictures which have been taken by the official photographers here. They will be better than mine.

Last Sunday three of us visited two of the Russian churches here. The music was heavenly. When you go to Chicago again and have time to do it, be sure and look up a Russian church, either go at six in the evening on Saturday, or about ten Sunday morning. I have never heard church music anywhere to equal or compare with the average Russian church choir. The service would be most interesting, and impress you as being very medieval.

I shall be most grateful to the WRC for the flag. I think it is lovely of them to give me a second one. I know they would have been glad to have me give the other away, when they know how greatly it was needed by a stranded, very ill American woman, who arrived in Petrograd during the Bolsheviki revolution.[50] I will write Mrs. Merridth on the next mail and hope it will be soon when the [new] flag comes thru [to me].

May 8
A cable came from London at noon saying that some people were coming thru from there, this week and supplies would be sent us. We wired back to send trunks with our personal things, so hope to have them by June first. Catherine Ryall will do everything in her power to start them for here if they have not left by the time she arrives. Our secretaries are still unable to procure permissions, so we can't say when others will come to relieve us.

We are having a little farewell for Catherine tonight. Since dinner we have made a cake and salad dressing for refreshments tonight. We will have salad, cake and tea.

I am sending cable today thru Red Cross. From now on, I imagine that mail will get thru more or less regularly so will not cable often, if I am able to send out letters every week. Another boat is scheduled to leave next week.

I shall be anxious to hear all the family plans for the summer. At present, I believe Genieve intends to be in Dillon, and George hopes to change positions. The rest, I suppose will have fun autoing.

Now, I must write one or two notes and then do some work.

With very much love to each and all from your ever affectionate,

Clara

---

50 Unfortunately, this is the only reference we have to the incident Clara mentions. We do not know who that ill American woman was or how she came to be in Petrograd. It is unclear if Clara means herself here, but she never says that she was ill when she arrived, nor was she "stranded" in the city.

May 11

This letter as you see didn't get off because Katy's boat was delayed sailing, but it actually is leaving tomorrow morning the 12th.

Elizabeth Dickerson sails on the 28th or there abouts and perhaps Helen Odgen. Our troops, the sick and wounded, go about the last of May and in June.

We are having freezing weather again, and we do feel it after these warm days of April.

I have spent six hours this afternoon at the Hostess House. It is now 8:45 and time that I was going over to the other house as we are entertaining nine officers. Three are Wisconsin men.

One of the Wisconsin men today is from somewhere procuring some films for me, so I shall send you some pictures.

2:50

Well during the evening John's, Cora's, and Muirison's letters were delivered. It was wonderful to have them. Another mail is going out next week, "they say." So will answer questions. Send clippings as you like, your mails are not censored. I haven't had a chance to read these but will tomorrow.

Hope this reaches you this month. It ought to. Also letter from Mr. Spindler came in the mail and Field Glass from Margaret O'Connell. What is her address. Will write her when I know.

It is very late. Must go to bed. Tell John, Cora and Muirison that I was so glad to hear from them.

With heaps and heaps of love,

From

Teke

To Genieve also

Arkangel
May 14, 1919

My dear John:

Your letter of April 14th with financial statement enclosed was received on May 11. Pretty good time, "I'll say." The following day came a letter from Geney, written on March 21st. I am hoping more will be delivered, as there are still so many missing. We feel that they just must come eventually. The boats will be arriving every week with mail from now on, I hope.

Thanks so much, John, for the financial statement. For Dec. I find only $35.75 recorded. But I suppose the muff and other things were paid for by New York which would make up the rest of the $100 for December. Ask Mary about it will you? All the rest I understand.

I am instructing NY to pay my May and June salary in full at home as well. So if the extra $100 for equipment is granted I will have sufficient to wipe out most of the remaining debt by Sept. when it is due. I shall just about be even with the world when I return home next March.

I am so glad for you, John dear, that you have prospered. I will be glad when you can buy out Perry and if only Calegrove would cease making abstracts you would have clear sailing with a comfortable income. Some day, I know it will come. All the family seems to have prospered for which I am deeply thankful. I am so happy that Father has cut down most of his debt. I hope there isn't much left to eat up interest. What a joyous day when none of us have debts. Geney is out now and I surely will be by December, if I don't need too many things this fall. I am hoping that I can make things hold out until next spring. If only the trunks would come from London so we could see and know what is in them. They haven't left there yet.

Catherine Ryall sailed on the *Canada* on the 12th. I sent letters with her, which may be confiscated, as the captain and several of the crew were under arrest. They may search everybody.

Our troops will leave by the 15th of June, I imagine. Two large groups are leaving here by the 20th for Economy from whence they will embark. The *Kaylon* Hospital boat sails within ten days. It will take practically all the sick and wounded. Its capacity is 1200 so many of the wounded need special treatment which they can't have here. Oh the whole situation here is so heart sickening. Poor Russia. I hope America is remaining in Siberia, and that we, as a nation, will help Russia in every possible way. Every day her need grows greater.

The bitterness against the English increases daily. The floating of the English rubles, which has had the affect of depreciating more than ever the Russian money, has been another huge stick in the fire of trouble.

And be it justly recorded, that there are fine English here who feel just as keenly as we do over the English situation. This expedition in northern Russia is going to be fruitful for governmental investigations in America, England and France. It's been an awful mess and most awful, unpardonable mis-management of the English. When our boys get home, I hope they will have cooled off, and look at facts as they are, and not distorted and exaggerated as many do now. We have Providence to thank for the care of our men. It has been nothing short of a miracle that they were not annihilated in the fall. What helped to save them was bluff, just as truly as bluff saved the English and French in '14 and '15 against the Germans. Well John, all this which I have written is not for newspaper publication. I am glad to have the Pences and Armstrongs see it, but it is not for general publication.

I am glad to stay on and see what the next chapter is to open with. A big drive will be made here early this summer which will link up with the Siberian forces at Veotka [?] then we will go south and if not into European Russia, then into Siberia.

I think Marcia and I will be here until August any way. Our other sec'ys who were in England, have apparently given up hope and all returned to France for work.

Elizabeth and possibly Helen leave the end of this month. Our work will constantly grow lighter until all troops are gone. With the departure of the Hospital ship, most of the Hospital work will end.

We are suffering much with a very cold snap which is to continue thru the whole month apparently. We are so glad to wear warm clothes, as the houses are not satisfactorily heated now. The Russians seem to think that because it was warm in April, we shouldn't expect fires often in May. The ground was white with snow when Mr. Stove, one of the YMCA men, and I sailed across to Bakeritsa this morning. We are fixing up a clubroom for a group of 150 Americans over there.

May 15

Last night we entertained nine soldiers who entered the checker tournament. They are all such fine fellows. We gave candy to the winner and Lucky Strikes to the second with a feed for them all. Checkers are very popular, there are tournaments being played in several camps.

Elizabeth Dickerson has definitely decided to leave next week on the Hospital ship, but Helen will remain until the army leaves in June.

Arkangel will be quite deserted after this week as two large transports are due next week from England. We imagine that the first group of our soldiers, along with the Royal Scotts and Canadians will immediately leave for England.

I notice by the currier, that the Dappert men are all still in France. What fine lads they are and what remarkably fine records they have made. How very proud Mr. and Mrs. Dappert must be of them, as well as all of Taylorville. I hope Sam Herdman will be at home a year from this summer when I return. It isn't going to be long, Johnie Boy, until I come steaming across and home. I haven't exactly begun counting the days, but I will after xmas. I expect to see much more in the political situation in Russia before next March. We do so hope that August will find us headed south. But you never can tell. This is the land of uncertainty.

Write me often, John, and thanks so much for the clippings. With a heartful of love, from your ever affectionate sister,

Teke

Clara I. Taylor

Did a letter come thru written in Dec. which was cut up by the censor. I had been informed that it had been so cut. Also did letters telling of the Xmas time arrive. I think it was letter 45 or 46. Geney's was the second part and she received hers.

May 15, 1919

My dear Genieve:

Mr. and Mrs. Davis of the Consular staff and one of the YMCA men are leaving on a French steamer for Murmansk from there they hope to go via the Fjords to Bergen, so this letter will probably be mailed in Norway or England. Then next week the Hospital ship the *Kaylon* is scheduled to sail and on it, probably, will be Elizabeth Dickerson. She has made application for a reservation. It will be a charming big boat to go on, and wonderfully nice for her to be where she can visit with the sick on their first lap of the homeward journey. Helen Ogden will not go until after the American troops all leave. So three of us will still remain, thru June. Helen goes in June.

We are still pulling wires, using pressure and doing everything possible to get the other sec'ys up here, but so far, all has been in vain. They simply will not grant them passports, that is, our gov't. One reason for my remaining until next spring is because I probably could not procure a passport to return. I am afraid that Jerome Davis is establishing a reputation for me which would not be all together favorable for our government. I don't think Jerome ought to quote me, that is our personal conversation which he did in some public address which has been printed. Please look up early Dec. or Jan. *Surveys* and tell me what they say.[51] I hear I have articles in them. If I have, the material came from the National Board.

Of course many of the great fundamental socialistic principles for which Russia is struggling along with the rest of the world I am in heartily accord (as most Americans who have been in R) but of course not all. No one with common sense believes in class warfare or sole rule of the proletariat. The methods used for the most part are, have been, criminal. What it has grown to be now, is vastly different from what it was in the beginning. All of us devoutly wish now for the overthrow of the powers in Moscow. It must be done and no one wishes it more than I. I should like nothing better than to appear before the Senate Investigating Committee which I undoubtedly would be called upon to do, if I returned this summer. I think all of us here should give our experiences, our impressions and honest convictions on the subject. The difficulty is that people, who are well qualified top witness, whose judgments carry weight, vary so diversely. This diversity of opinion goes right thru, from newspaper writers, army, government officials and semi officials, under which class, we have been placed. It is a stupendous problem, Geney, and there is no middle ground. Every one feels intensely one way or the other. But I know of no one who isn't more than convinced

---

51 The Survey, a Journal of Social Exploration was edited by Paul U. Kellogg, with Associate Editors Edward T. Devine, Graham Taylor, and Jane Addams. The magazine ran from 1909 to 1952, and published essays, articles, and art relating to social and political issues. "A New Era in Russian Industry" was Clara's Industrial Survey report from Moscow (in The Survey. Vol. XLI, No. 18. Feb 1, 1919. pp. 612-615). Graham Taylor is mentioned in Clara's letters as a friend.

that the leaders of Soviet Russia must be overcome. The situation of Russia and its future not only effects a hundred and eighty million Russians, but it effects the whole world. And of all peoples, the help of Americans is the most acceptable to Russians. The Russians feel that we, in our government, have attained that for which they are so bitterly struggling. They feel also, that we as a nation would help without weakening them thru exploitation. They look upon us, as a sympathetic, democratic, practical people, in whom they can trust. And there are not many, either among officers or men, a few have, who have caught the universal brotherhood of man spirit. Oh Geney, I have fairly envied the officers their opportunities of being leaders. Of developing their men into soldiers, arousing loyal company spirits, of setting standards. Some have done it, but so many were too young to realize their opportunities and their responsibilities.

Our life here after the troops go will be quiet, I fancy. We will put in long hard licks in language study. We hope to go further north to visit a very famous monastery during the last days of June. Of course we can't tell when or how soon we may be pushing into Petrograd and Moscow. We will be ready when the time comes.

This afternoon, I go to the Hospitals and then out to Smolny. Our troops leave there tomorrow. After that I shall go to Solombola where our Engineers and Machine Gunners have their barracks. They haven't received movement orders yet, and not all have returned from the lines of communications. Instead of fighting, they are now putting in five to eight hours of drilling. Naturally, they would rather be at the front, but the drilling will do them a heap of good, and they need the training if they are to do any public drilling. Many of the 339th were assigned to the Regiment just before they sailed, and have had no training along drilling lines.

Our trunks from London have not yet arrived, but we are enjoying the suits and capes of our uniforms. We are trying vainly to get our trunks headed this way. When they come, great will be our joy. Our immediate need of some will be lessened by the fact that after withdrawal of our forces, we probably will have no social life, as we do not, or will not, attend the English dances. Liquor flows too freely.

Your letter written March 21 came a few days ago. Also your March cable came. I have acknowledged all cables and letters, but fear some of my letters may not be getting thru. I do hope my letter written about Jan. 2 or 3d will get thru. Yours 46 or 47 was the second part.

It's cold, and gray so far most of this month. Just after the wind goes to the south, and blows away the ice jam in the White Sea, they say, summer will be here until the middle of July, when it again begins to get cool.

There is no special news Geney as my letter so plainly indicates. Life has ceased to be so strenuous. I am looking forward to time for study and reading. I still have magazines to read and several books. I am not dreading a quiet spell, in fact, I quite look forward to it, but shall feel terribly distressed if all, or most all, Americans leave but no use worrying over that yet.

I hope you will have a delightful summer Geney, and how I wish that I were going to be at home with the family this winter. But spring will come. Oh it would be wonderful Geney if you could come over and return with me. We shall see.

With a heartful of love, from your affectionate,

Clara.

A letter with some other news is being send to John on this same mail. I think it better if you and Sis didn't buy any more clothes until the trunks from London come. I wrote asking for a Jersey for next Fall with mail going faster now, I will wait until June before planning winter clothes. I surely do appreciate deeply all you girls have done, and can hardly wait until our things arrive.

Sunday, May 25, 1919
Economy Camp

My Dear ones at Home:

I am sorry that I haven't time for a long letter, but you will forgive me I know when I tell you that I have gone on a fifteen hours a day schedule for a week. I am now at Economy. Our concentration camp for the returning troops. We are just thirty versts from the White Sea, and about thirty north of Arkangel. It is now one thirty. I am writing in the writing room of the hut. Our men are reading and writing to the accompaniment of the Victrola which never gets tired. And stops only for change of records. In the future I shall always associate my memories of the army with Victrolas. They have been such a Godsend. I am thankful every day for their invention.

Well if this letter is going to be short, because of necessity, I must tell you a little of what I have been doing this week. Last Monday I came by boat to this Camp, where we now have two battalions and others concentrated. The YMCA man who headed up the work was wholly inefficient. I was followed the second day by an experienced YM sec'y. Together we have opened both dry and wet canteens, have moved into new quarters which had to be sprayed, white washed, and lots of carpentering work done. Curtains made and . . .

May 29

Well I was interrupted so will once more try to finish this letter. I am back in Arkangel. Helen came in Tuesday evening to relieve me. I was sorry not to remain over the departure of the first boat load of troops. The *Czar* is now scheduled to leave on Sunday with about fifteen hundred troops who will sail for Brest, France. The second load leaving a week later. All the 339th Infantry are leaving in three sections. The third Battalion going first, followed by the 2d and finally the first. The Engineers (310) men are to remain for some time yet, perhaps a couple of months as are part of the 337th Field Ambulance Corps.

The *Des Moines* Cruiser came in on Monday to the great excitement of us all. "Old Glory" as one of the soldiers said, "looked something swell, as she sailed along." The sailors have quite taken possession of the Hostess House and they are truly a fine lot of fellows. Only one forth are permitted off at a time. The Marines say it is because they fear if all were off they would beat up the "Limies" (English).

Five thousand English arrived at the same time the cruiser steamed in. So Arkangel looks more like a military centre than ever, and is less popular for American soldiers. The feeling between English and American is most bitter. To hear our men talk, you would think that it would be comparatively easy to raise a big army to fight the English. It is only the English they dislike. The Irish, Scotch and Colonials they like.

The cruiser brought in the mail. There was a second dandy letter from Cora and M. F. [Margaret Frances], from Genieve of April 14–16, Sis,

March 22 and April 4th. The first came thru the State Dept. at Washington. It was so good to get them, and their enclosures. None were censored. There have been no out-going boats for two weeks. The ice jam in the neck of the White Sea is still very bad.

I hope after the middle of June my mail will reach you in a month's time at least. Most of them, I fancy, have been mailed in Norway and England since Xmas. We always send out by friends if it is possible. Censorship surely inhibits freedom in writing.

We are having wonderful weather, cool nights and mornings, but warm during the day. The leaves are beginning to appear on the few scrubby trees, the grass is wonderful, and along the rivers are a few wild flowers. Warblers of many different kinds have been appearing lately and ducks have been returning to their old haunts. We all have enjoyed the novelty of the continuous day light. But most of us find it rather difficult to get enough sleep. Last night out doors I could easily read at twelve o'clock. While at Economy, I used to climb the fire tower, about nine thirty, to watch the sunset, and the beautiful after glow which does not die out, until the east is reddened with sunrise about 1:40. From this tower, with glasses, we were able to see the White Sea. I wish that it were possible to go to the mouth of the sea and see the ice bergs, but it doesn't seem possible.

In June after our troops have gone, and the six new sec'ys have arrived, Marcia and I are going to visit an Island in the White Sea, which is famous for a monastery and polar bears. I think it will be possible to plan some little boat trips as this front pushes further south.

Before summer is over, we expect to move south. Petrograd will be open soon, and the rest must soon follow. I hope that we will not go south until things are a bit settled. We won't go until the Embassy moves.

Our new sec'ys expect to sail from England about the 7th of June. They failed to get their passage on the 18th because they were in France. We were filled with righteous indignation. They had been cabled again and again to leave France and go to England so as to be there when permissions were granted. They ought to get here between the 15th and 20th of June. They will take over all the work here, that we have begun, while Marcia and I study on language. I haven't had a lesson for ages, and never study.

This afternoon I went up to the Red Cross Hospital to see our eighteen men who are there. Most of the patients have been moved onto the Hospital Ship, which will sail probably at the same time the first transports go out.

General Richardson and his staff are remaining here indefinitely. They expect to go south when the way opens. The military mission remains here also. There will be quite a colony of Americans besides the marines. You need not worry, we will not go into Russia, unless all is safe.

We are looking for the arrival of two YMCA men who are supposed to have our trunks, or one of them. We may yet get our long looked for things. It has been discouraging.

I am richer for a pair of shoes which I am buying from Marcia. She received two pairs, and one she cannot wear and they fit me finely. And I do need them. The supply company of the Regiment is half soling my winter boots, so they will be ready for another year's wear.

Geney do not try to send me another dress, we shall have very little opportunity for wearing thin clothing this summer, I imagine. The summer here is very short. It begins to get pretty cool by the middle of July. We none of us mind, for it is so much easier to work and study when it is cool, than when hot.

May 31
Memorial day was beautifully and impressively celebrated here. The Red Cross Buick called for us at ten o'clock, we watched the parade first, then followed along with it, in its march to the cemetery. It was a small parade, headed by company "M" and a company of sailors off the *Des Moines*. Then followed platoons of Russian soldiers and sailors, English, French, Italian and Polish. At the cemetery speeches were made by General Richardson, Mr. Poole, Gen. Ironside of British Army, and the Governor General of the Arkangel gov't. All stood at attention at the close of the last speech while the Band played "Star Spangled Banner." The salute was then fired over the hundred evergreen covered graves. The impressive silence that followed was broken by "Taps" that were beautifully given by a fine cornetist.

There are many other graves scattered over the long front, which will never be located, I fancy. There hasn't been the thought and care for this sort of thing here, as in France. It seems that we are the only country which has this beautiful custom. And the only one who takes such good care of their dead.

I devoutly hope that these men have not died in vain. That they have helped in the solution of a grave problem, in a great, helpless and harassed country. Unfortunately some died thru the selfishness and carelessness of others. Oh, it is such a great thing to be entrusted with the lives of others and such an unpardonable crime to fail to live up to the responsibility.

June 2

Elizabeth is sailing 6 a.m. Tues. June 3d on the transport to Brest, France. She will reach America some time in July and will write you.

Yesterday afternoon, Marcia and I visited the Hospital Ship for the last time. 284 of our men are on it. 1600 are sailing Tues. and seven wives whom Eliz. is chaperoning. Most of our best friends go out on this transport. I go to Economy again Thurs. morning to remain a week. The work will be easy this time and the camp smaller. Only six companies will be there after tomorrow.

Our trunks have not yet arrived. Our despair is pathetic for our clothes. Surely the new workers will bring them this month. It is very warm now. I have on short shoes and thin clothes. Summer lasts usually until middle of July.

A friend of Penelope Bond Lee, a Lt. McCarthy of the *Des Moines*, introduced himself to me the other day. I will invite him to the house this week before I go to Economy.

There is so much to do to get Eliz off so will say goodbye until the next boat which goes very soon.

Heaps and heaps of love to each and all from your affectionate,

Teke

Clara I. Taylor

Arkangel, Russia

Diary
May 7–May 31, 1919

May 7, 1919, Letter 60 to Sis
Wed. Spent am. writing letters. In afternoon Catherine and I visited Red Cross Hospital, had teeth filled. Went to 53 & Smolny in evening. Merrill & Tom rowed down from Bernik.

May 8, 1919
Thurs. Spent afternoon writing letters. In evening at Hostess House and later farewell supper for Kotya, Lt. Johnson, Tom, Husky, Frank, G. Somerville and Crawford. cold & raw

May 9, 1919
Friday Central "G" co. returned. Clippings rec'd of I Co. affair

May 10, 1919
Sat. Hostess House & Hospital 53. Everybody getting off mail. Russians making good on R.R. Front.

May 11, 1919
Sun. Finished Kathia's basket. Wrote letters—Spent afternoon at Hostess House. In evening Lt. Mead, Lt. Johnson & Lt. Wood, Tom & Crawford spent the evening. Letter from John. Very cold and raw.

May 12, 1919
Mon. Mr. Stone & I spent morning at Bakuntsa planning club room for the supply Co. men. Kathrine Childs Ryall sailed on the *Canada* at 11 o'clock. Spent afternoon & early evening at Hostess House. Letter from Genieve. Sent letter 8 to R —

May 13, 1919
Tues. Elizabeth making preparations for departure home via Eng. Still difficulties about our secy's coming from Eng. New money has made a mess of things in general.

May 14, 1919
Wed. Mr. Stone & I sent to Bokerita for club room purposes—Fred Hall and Davis sailed for Murmansk. Letter 61—to Genieve & John. Hospital & Smolny in the afternoon and evening. very cold & raw. Getting Peace terms through communiques.

May 15, 1919
Thurs. Spent afternoon at Hostess House and evening at Smolny. a grand farewell to the Americans there at Smolny.—All plans for evacuation of our troops to Economy continue.

May 16, 1919
Fri. Spent morning with Elizabeth on Girl Scout hike. Evening at Hostess House. A cruiser & transport arrived. Most of our wounded & sick removed to *Kaylon*.

May 17, 1919, cold, raw
Sat. Visited *Kaylon* in afternoon. Attended dance with Tom in the evening at Reg. Headquarters.

May 18, 1919, Arkangel
Sun. Hostess House filled all day. In the Evening Mr. Poole and Lt. Spitler of M. G. Co. called with Col. Thurston. We had splendid visit until midnight.

May 19, 1919, Read's birthday
Mon. Had delightful trip down to Economy by boat. Found YM in pitiful condition, lots of friends called in to welcome me, both men & officers.

May 20, 1919, Economy
Tues. Mr. Garlock arrived & together we have slaved to make a proper canteen & Assoc. for the soldiers.

May 21, 1919, Economy
Wed. Had large detail of men moving YMCA into new quarters. Started checker tournament.

May 22, 1919
Thurs. Co. "M" arrived. Five officers came in for supper. Things getting moved & in better shape for serving the troops.

May 23, 1919, Economy
Fri. Getting settled. Men all training hard. Everybody happy over prospect of early departure.

May 24, 1919, Economy
Sat. Thing[s] getting more settled. Had detail of soldiers helping all day getting buildings into shape & condition. Had splendid visit with Lt. Beckett of Wisconsin "G" Co. Lt.

May 25, 1919, Economy
Sun. Glorious warm day. Lt. Drichu & I took a long walk to near by village. ballgames in afternoon. Officers dinner in evening. Band concert for men. Long visit Capt. Moor "M" co. 4 Letters from home.

May 26, 1919, Economy
Mon. Camp went wild with enthusiasm when two transports *Czar* and *Czarina* with British troops passed & the cruiser *Des Moines*. Splendid review of troops by high officials—Had delightful visit Lt. Beckett on tower.

May 27, 1919, Economy
Tues. Returned at 7 P.M. Talked with Herbert Paul about Assoc. work. Entertained two Marine officers at tea in Hostess House. Big British troops parade in Archangel.

May 28, 1919
Wed. spent most of day resting—Evening at Hostess House. Arkangel very much decorated with English flags. Engineer definitely told that they remain.

May 29, 1919
Thurs. Lovely spring like day, trees getting green. Mild. Spent afternoon at Hospital and evening at Hostess House. The Sailors (450) delightful, fine looking fellows. About 1800 men in camp

May 30, 1919, Arkangel
Fri. Parade of Co. "M" & Marines. English, Russians, French, Italian & Polish troops & marines—to cemetery—speeches—graves decorated with greens —"Taps"—very, very beautiful Afternoon Hostess House. Evening Scout meeting. Met Lt. McCarthy friend of Pen [Penelope] Bond Lee.

May 31, 1919
Sat. Growing warmer. Last day of machine gunners at the Hostess House. Splendid visit with a number of the men, a joyous sing during the evening.

MEMORANDA
1919 June entered beautifully. Warm & summery, with men happy at early departure and fall of the Soviet gov't felt more possible every day.

Chapter Eight
"Political prisoners are not the easiest people to deal with in Russia."

Diary
June 1 – June 20, 1919

June 1, 1919, Letter 9 R. L. 1st Summer day, Letter Home 62
Sun. Spent a.m. writing home letters—Afternoon at Hospital Ship. Marcia & I rowed over to pay a last visit to our men. Bitterest of feeling between Eng. and Am. [?] Navy especially. Lt. Beckett & others in for Samovar for evening.

June 2, 1919, Economy
Mon. Marcia & I went to E. with Elizabeth to see her off on the *Czar*. 1600 troops left for Brest Fr [ance]. *Kaylon* sailed with sick. & Stevenson with French. *Des Moines* escorted to White Sea. Big review in a.m. Looks as tho N.A. govt moved back up Kolebalk.

June 3, 1919
Tues. Went shopping for hat pd 350 rubles & traded gloves for 100p. Called at Embassy & banks. In afternoon selected books at YM for YW work. Mr. Pool & Crawford called in the evening.

June 4, 1919
Wed. Spent afternoon at Hostess House. Evening at Girl Scout meeting Cool but lovely. Great difficulty sleeping—Sun sets at 10 o'clock.

June 5, 1919, Economy
Thurs. Went to Economy on the morning boat. Saw the *Sacramento* cruiser & other cargo boats come in. Many new troops, but greatly miss those who have gone.

June 6, 1919, Economy
Fri. Spent day reorganizing kitchen help. H & B. Co. men look at me in perfect amazement. One man looked at me in wonder and exclaimed, "Jesus Christ."

June 7, 1919, Economy
Sat. Evening dandy ball game between Army & Navy, tie game. Game closed at 8:45. Lt. Dricher and Welchover came to dinner. Co. D. & C. came in during night.

June 8, 1919, Economy
Sun. Charming church service in A.M. & band concert in evening. visited with many new men from F. & H. Companies. All getting ready to leave by Wed. All fear trouble with Germany.

June 9, 1919
Mon. Beautiful flowers, lots of mosquitos & warm but good breeze. Returned to Arkangel on evening boat.

June 10, 1919, Arkangel
Tues. All M. men leaving came in the evening for a party. Helen and I went to the Bath in the morning, dropped the wooden pillow out the window.

June 11, 1919
Wed. Helen left for Economy—the H H is filled with Engineers and Medics—all are glad because they are going home. are getting more or less restless.

June 12, 1919
Thurs. Frank & Dan came for dinner. Very cool & mosquitoes bad. Medics had delightful sing in the evening. The sailors are becoming a little more easy to visit with.

June 13, 1919, Arkangel
Fri. Snowed most of day. Frank, Don, Mr Stone came to dinner and again until midnight in evening. Lt Graham & Forester called in evening off Eagle No. 2. Letter came from Fritz telling of Aunt Etta's death. Mr. Pool sent word that he was leaving.

June 14, 1919, Letter 10 R. 63. Genieve
Sat. Rainy day. Met Girl Scouts in A.M. Frank & Don with finance people left for Economy on route home. Afternoon new nurses called— Farewell dance at Reg. H.Q. in evening. All three went with Lt. Johnson an extremely happy party. Every one was in high spirits.

June 15, 1919, Archangel
Sun. The rest of 339th sailed on the *Menomie* & *Parto* for France. Crawford, Arison & Tom came to dinner. Lt. Johnson & Mr. Albertson in the evening. Lt. Johnson gave us each pictures of the Front. Cold rainy and home sick weather.

June 16, 1919
Mon. Marion, Helen & I had a charming luncheon on board the Eagle No. 2. Capt. Wheeler, Lt. Johnson, [?], Forester. Began report in the afternoon & evening.

June 17, 1919
Tues. English going to the Front—preparation to move H.Q. to Beronifi's. Have been asked to do same prison work for 40 women by the English

June 18, 1919
Wed. Spent most of day consulting about girls in prison. 3 torpedo destroyers arrived. All the officers came in to call at the Hostess House.

June 19, 1919, Archangel

Thurs. Marcia & I visited the prison 40 young women some of them in their teens classified as political prisoners with long hard sentences. Attended Scout meeting at 5—finished report. Warm & lovely. The 6 Red Cross nurses came to a Russia luncheon.

June 20, 1919

Friday Went to Hospital to talk to Major Henry about Matrons for prison women. Eng. troops & staff leaving Archangel for the fronts.

Letters

June 21, 1919

Dear Ones All:

I wonder what you are all doing on the longest day of the year. It has been truly glorious here. Warm but not hot. With a cool breeze blowing most of the day. This morning I taught eighteen little Russian Girl Scouts baseball, refreshing myself immediately afterwards at the Russian bath. This afternoon while at the Hostess House, one of the sailors who does guard duty at the Embassy brought me Sis's letter mailed May 17. Fine time "I'll say." I have read the letter three times already and will as many more tomorrow. It is now eight thirty with the sun three hours high in the heavens. Helen and I are awaiting our escorts to the last officer's dance. Last week we danced farewell to the Infantry, and tonight to the Engineers and part of the General's staff. Rumor has it that even the General will leave within the next two weeks. Since half of his staff sail this next week, and as the YMCA has purchased all their supplies, I guess there is truth in the rumor. I frankly have gotten to the point where I want all who are going to depart at once. This seeing one's friends leave one by one, or more truthfully speaking, by ship loads, is conducive to restlessness in those of us who must remain.

We have enough to do to keep us all going all summer. When the ships are in port there are a thousand sailors. Three Destroyers came in the early part of this week. At present most of the boats, Cruisers, Eagle boats and Destroyers are in the White Sea for a few day's target practice. There are lots of Illinois boys among the sailors. On the whole they seem younger than the soldiers. Poor chaps, they only have four hours on land every fourth day. There is so very little, almost nothing, for them to do to amuse themselves, so they are already restless and are joining the chorus wailing for home. I think undoubtedly they will be leaving these waters in September if not before.

Sunday 22
Well once more it is eight thirty in the evening. We had a delightful time at the dance. At midnight we were dancing without lights, with the sky rose colored from eleven until one thirty, when again the sun was above the horizon. Just as we came out of Headquarters building, we faced a movie machine. If I had had a Kodak I could have taken a "time" very easily. We returned home at one thirty. We shall all be grateful for darkness again. It is too light to sleep with rest and comfort.

This morning I went across the river to the American supply Co. to buy some provisions. Tomorrow every thing will be turned over to the English. These supplies came in a week ago, too late for use for the Infantry. Thousands of spoiled lemons and oranges have been dumped into the river. The poor Russians have tried to rescue them in spite of the guards. About a dozen were sent to us and oh were they good. We find lemon powder is quite satisfactory as the lemons which come here. The fresh lemons seem to have lost much of their acidness.

I returned home just in time for dinner. Two YMCA men were here along with Col. Thurston, Chief Advocate and Lt. Johnson of the Engineers. At four I went over to the Hostess House where I have been doing hostess duty. It is the last Sunday here for the Engineers. They sail for Brest, France the end of this week. These men have done a great piece of work. They are, taken on the whole, a better class of men than the Infantry. I am afraid that our Americans here have not proven to be very good sports. It is due, of course, to the friction between the English and Americans, and especially to the commanding officer of our forces. If we had a better Colonel, our own officers would have been more loyal. The officers are almost wholly responsible for mutinous times which occurred this spring. This expedition up here has been such that will not reflect any great glory on us. And now is no time for us to be pulling out. I don't blame the war-tired English soldiers for contemptuously calling us quitters. We are. We ought to see this thing thru, if Germany is to be thwarted in her intrenchment in Russia. Somebody has to help the Russians. Why leave so much of it to England. I don't of course know what you people know of our help in Siberia. Up here we hear of much friction with the Japanese and much disagreement among the members of the Stevens railroad commission with really very little help given the Russians.

The English are in quite large numbers, about fifteen thousand. They hope their work will be over by September. Their Headquarters has been moved from here up to Beresniki on the Divna river. The big drive will probably come very early in July. We all devoutly hope that Kalchalk will be in Moscow in August and that we may pack up our things and move south.

Last Thursday Marcia and I visited the prison here in the interest of the women prisoners. There are about thirty confined, many on very minor charges, with severe judgment, eight or ten are suspected "of Bolsheviki sympathies" all have not been tried altho they have been confined some months already. One twenty years old young woman is sentenced to several years of hard labour for having been connected with a Bolosheviki organization. Two sisters, sixteen and twenty, are imprisoned for two years for the murder of the oldest sister's new born babe. Another twenty year old woman sentenced for two years because of killing her three year old baby when she fled Bolosheviki territory. Three are in for several weeks because their passports were not right, and others for petty theft. There were four mothers with babies less than a year old. Scurvy already has effected four, and other will follow if relief isn't granted soon. A British Col. Major have asked us to get a house and be responsible for them, expecting that one of us would live there. We are going to find or hope to find a responsible Russian housekeeper, and do all that we can for the women in finding them work. While they are on parole. We sincerely hope to be helpful, but there are some very serious difficulties which make us refuse to assume the responsibility of the parole. Political prisoners are not the easiest people to deal with in Russia, especially when probably two thirds of the population here, are secretly Bolosheviki in their sympathies.

We are in the midst of plans to move into other quarters. We want to have three rooms papered, but alas there is no paper. The place where we have lived all winter is becoming unbearable as regards relationships. We have lost too many things all winter both as to personal things and food.

Then when the six new secretaries come about the middle of July, we will need more room. They are at last actually sailing from England via Bergen the 26th of June. So they ought to be here by July 15th. No our clothes have not arrived. We hear that they are now on the way due July 1st, but I can't believe it. Only one trunk of uniforms came thru and they have been life savers. They are gray blue suits of medium weight. Really very attractive and have met a very real need. There was shirt waist material so we each could have two new shirt waists. We will get thru the summer with what we have, but we have the absolute minimum. Next summer I shall have to have everything new. Summers here are probably short. At least we are hoping there will be very little of weather as hot as today.

There have been six Red Cross Army nurses here for two weeks. They were ordered here while General Richardson was still in England. The British heretofore had not permitted women to come to this region. When they arrived there were just two convalescent patients in our empty hospital. The nurses are all 1915 graduates of the Springfield Hospital. One of them is Miss Gergenson, niece of Mrs. Waddells. She will come to call just as soon as she returns home, which she hopes is immediately. As all our forces will be gone with the departure of these last troops there is no reason for their being here. They sail from here Wed.

We learned this morning that the American Red Cross is hoping to receive orders to return. They have wanted to go for a long time, but the embassy and others have tried to show them some of the many reasons for their remaining here. There is plenty of work for them. Their attitude is, let the British do it. The Red Cross here had come in for some very severe criticisms. A few days ago someone stole the lens from my Kodak and none more are to be procured I fear. I am cabling our sec'ys to bring one if possible. Since the war, it has been difficult to get them.

Tuesday, there is to be a big parade of Engineers and of all troops here in behalf of our departing engineers. The Russians are decorating their colors, and quite a number are to be decorated. The 310th Eng. are not keen to be further associated with 339th Inf.

Well, right here our Red Cross Ambulance came, I have just returned from taking a young girl to the Hospital for an operation. I have an awful fear that she will die. It was to a Russian Hospital, I wish that it could have been our doctors to have performed the operation.

One reason I haven't sent pictures is because there is no paper here to print. I think perhaps the men on the boats can do some for us.

John will you send my dues of two dollars to the Wisconsin Alumni Association. I get the magazines regularly, but it is the only one that I do get.

Last Monday, we three had a wonderful dinner on one of the Eagle boats. The first olives in months and other good things were served that were rare delicacies for us.

We like the officers very much from the boats. They are all fine clean looking men. And much more democratic with their men than is usually seen in the Army. The men aren't enthusiastic over the Eagle boats. I don't know whether it is mostly prejudice or that the boats are not what they are designed to be.

Well, family dear, I hope there will be other boats going out so I can send mail home every week.

As far as I know, I will be in Arkangel all summer, and our hopes are for returning to Moscow in September. If the way doesn't open up, I shall return home.

Rev. D. C. Beatty, of the Episcopal Church, Decatur, has been a YMCA sec'y here all winter. He sails home via France. He will be home in August. He would give you an excellent account of conditions and situations. Also if you should drive up there, take time to call on W. F. McDougall 466 So. Haworth Ave, Decatur. He is one of the Infantry soldiers and would love to report to the family on my welfare. He ought to be home early in August. You might drop both these people a card telling them when you are coming. I am wondering if you are in California or Montana, Geney, and when you will be home Fritzie for your vacation. How much I wish that I could be with you all. Everything over here is so uncertain that it is quite impossible to tell what our plans will be very far ahead. Sometimes I feel so strongly that I will be home this Fall and then again, Moscow looks very possible and probable. Please put up plenty of fruit in case I do come. Oh I almost envy you your fresh fruit. Well, Russia has its compensations and if our sailors are to be here, we may save some broken heads by remaining and giving them a safe as well as charming place in which to loaf. The sailors fight on much less provocation than the soldiers.

We have urged Helen to remain until July 15th when she can go with the last group of American YMCA secretaries who leave here this summer. They will sail from Bergen the last of July. So Marcia and I will not be left absolutely alone.

Have you received all my mail and is it censored. Some was mailed in Norway, I imagine, and others in England. This leaves here June 25 to be mailed by Miss Fergenson in England. Part of your mail is censored and part not.

Now I must run over to the Hostess House before it rains and take this to Miss Fergenson who is to meet me there.

With a heartful of love to each and all, and best wishes for happy vacations and a cool lovely summer for you all, from your affectionate,

Clara

Fritz how come the finance campaign. I'll wager your Board and committees learned a heap about the Assoc. themselves when they had to present it in their campaign. I am so sorry to hear that Mrs. Byers has been ill. We have no Boards, no staff meeting or anything of that sort. We are just a family doing it. Of course we will have a Board when we resume Assoc. work.

What are your plans Geo. and Trenna. I think you each and all should write me a letter of your plans and doings again. It would almost be worth another operation.

June 30, 1919

My dear Family:

Altho it is nearly eleven thirty, I am going to write a short letter home. Today the Embassy phoned us that [the] mail [will] close at 5 o'clock tomorrow.

I am wondering if you could possibly be enjoying as fine a summer as we are having. It gets hot early as the sun is up early, but by five o'clock usually a light wrap is comfortable. In the shade it is perfect. We have no complaints to make with the weather man. I only wish that it were not so light. Today we got some Japanese curtains, or shades I should say, so we will have more darkness in our sleeping room. We will have only about four more weeks of hot weather. Then Fall again. Really time slips by here unmercifully fast. These are the days which seem to be full, yet I don't accomplish much. I don't seem to get at the things that I want to do most. At present we are busy getting new living quarters ready for the new secretaries who will be joining by the middle of July. It means a lot of work. We have to have rooms papered, electric lighted, water piped upstairs, and enumerable other things done. Russian workmen are so painfully slow that you despair many times before the thing is actually accomplished. Today some new furniture was delivered which was ordered just four months ago. Things will look attractive and pretty for these new comers.

Well Family things are discouraging here so far as the immediate future is concerned. The Russian fighting with the Allies is not very aggressive. The long planned, and long expected, drive for July doesn't look promising and because there is lack of loyalty on part of many Russians and still, after all the past year's experience the enemy's strength has been and is constantly underestimated. They even still outrange us in artillery. With Katchalk's [Kolchak's] recent retreat,[52] we begin to think that the end is not to come this summer as had been expected. Here, every one is anything but optimistic and the Russians feel resentful that the Americans have withdrawn. It's rather difficult to explain our situation and policy. We explain it one way, while deeply regretting withdrawal of our troops.

Well the situation is this. Now on the first day of July I think that early in September Marcia and I will be leaving Archangel. We may go together to Finland to size up the situation there, or Marcia may go there while

---

52 The Anti-Bolshevik Russians and the Allies' plan was for all factions of Russians working against Bolshevik expansion to combine, and together restore the Constituent Assembly, first by crushing the Red Army. Admiral Alexander Vasilyevich Kolchak (1874–1920) had been named the White Russian Military Dictator in November of 1918 and led troops from the Omsk region. It was hoped that Kolchak's forces would connect with the Czecho-Slovak troops who were holding the Trans-Siberian Railway near Samara, connect with Generals Korniloff's and Denekin's forces from the south and Ukraine regions, and all come together to meet the Allied expedition in the center of the country. The plan failed. An excellent summary of the situation is given in Cudahy's 1924 book, Archangel: The American War with Russia.

I continue on to London. I will plan to remain in London for a week at least, then go up to Scotland for a week and sail from Liverpool early in October. I think there is but little question but that we shall be leaving here in September, unless the drive gets thru. I have a very strong hunch that I will be home by Nov. if not before.

Do you know if Tom Taylor is still sailing the *Orduna*. Maybe I can arrange to sail home with him. This thing is certain, Marcia and I will not remain in Archangel thru another winter. There is a very important reason why we do not come at once, but I think it wiser not to write about it. We would give much to raise the veil and peep into the future of the next eight months. But I do think you are safe in counting me in on plans for most of the winter months. Unless the unexpected happens, we will be here until sometime in September. And I do want to visit Father's old home on the way back.

Archangel seems quite deserted now. The British headquarters is up the River. All but about thirty American soldiers have gone. The sailors come ashore, one fourth of them, from four thirty to ten. All the official offices have dwindled in numbers, so life is quiet.

On Friday, July 4th I believe the Navy is to have a Field day meet. From 5–7 we attend the reception at the Embassy. At nine in the evening, there is to be a dance at headquarters. I suppose that we shall attend all of these festivities. We were glad to see the return of the boats. The first one, the Eagle boat, returned on Saturday. All the officers, five of them, came to the house for the evening to enjoy a Samovar and drink lemonade. They were glad to come back altho it was for only two days time. It has since gone to Murmansk. We haven't gotten acquainted with many of the officers from the other boats. I believe the *Des Moines* is supposed to be here for a month.

The latest rumors have it that all the boats leave here with the withdrawal of the last troops. There are still seven hundred of our Engineers on the Murmansk line. They are to leave between July and Aug. 15th.

Thursday, our house for the prison women will be ready. Eight will be turned over immediately, with others following, until we get the whole thirty or forty of them. The British have sent to England for a couple of women to take charge of the work. We are anxious to turn over all responsibility of it to their workers.

Once more I am housekeeper, and oh how I long for fresh things to cook. Prices are still outrageously high. Today I traded two glasses of sugar for ten eggs. If I had had to give money, they would have been fifty five ruble or $2.50. So of course we don't use them in any quantity. By the middle of this month we will have some lettuce and other small fresh vegetables. Little green onions are thirty five cents apiece. So we continue to eat canned goods for the most part. We are getting good milk, so we have milk every night for supper.

The last of July, Marcia and I go to the Soliveski Monastery which is on an Island in the White sea, near Onega. You can find it. We will be there a week or ten days. Depending on conditions here. It is necessary to take bedding, food and everything that we shall need.

Our new clothes have not come but probably shall with the sec'ys. We thought two YMCA men who arrived yesterday were bringing them, but we were, for the thousandth time, disappointed. We are learning with how few things we can get along with. My summer wardrobe consists of Geney's old blue voile and a white voile, old linen skirt, and blue and green striped shirt. By having them washed frequently, I am getting along. In fact there is no choice. I have to. I shall certainly have to be completely re-outfitted next summer. And dare not leave here until hot weather is over. Archangel, fortunately, doesn't make many demands. You see all styles worn here from the early medieval to the latest. Perhaps somewhat advanced. There is no place in the world where such independence is exhibited as regards clothing. Even to swimming where it is dispensed with entirely. It is most embarrassing to walk anywhere along the river, either in or out of town, men, women and children, bathe when, where and with whom, as it strikes their fancy. Even the poor sailors confess to being amazingly shocked, admitting that it takes much to shock them.

July 2, 11:05 p.m.

Well this didn't go off, but tomorrow it will be mailed so as to go on Friday's boat. Yesterday, Sis' letter written May 21st arrived, and today two more, April 28 and May 6, thru Embassy. The Embassy mail is very slow, be sure to mail one open mail every time you send to pouch. Oh they were good. As you may have guessed, once more letters are coming in slowly and far between. Those sent thru the open mail come in a month's time.

I am terribly sorry that I have disappointed you regarding my early return home. It did look as tho we would or might be leaving here early in the summer. Now I am counting definitely on September. But don't you all [count on Sept.] until I write that plans are definite, and send a cable. Don't sent mail care of YWCA, always c/o Am. Consul or Embassy. In London the Consul seems to be the most convenient location. I am writing them to forward mail here, if there is any there for me.

Oh your letters were so very good. I literally eat up the words. And you are all so busy with the doings of interesting things. This month I know Fritzie is home, and there will be drives, picnics and lots of lovely things doing. Then late August more home coming with Geney's arrival. Oh, to be home for the autumn time. Who knows. The unexpected always happens in this land, we may leave earlier than we plan. Let's hope anyway.

I had a letter from Cousin Sam Taylor[53] today inviting me to visit them. I shall write at once. Its nice to have the invitation and feel that I am in touch with them. Thanks so much Sis for writing them.

Well, today, Family, the women prisoners came riding on a truck to the house that we have helped to prepare for them. They were so pathetic with their little bundles of things. Two have young babies. Two we put to bed at once, they have scurvy, one strong active middle aged woman will be a great help to the other four.

You would have laughed to see me making up beds last night, with the help of a British Colonel, who took off his coat and Sam Browne,[54] and helped make beds, and unpack dishes, clothing and equipment sent up by the British Red Cross. I spent most of this morning shopping in the market, trying to get flat irons, wash tubs, baking dishes, baskets etc. for their use. The women will live at this house, but go out for day work as they are able to do so.

July 4th

Well the Grand and Glorious Forth is over. It has been a lovely day here, only a little cool. At eleven thirty we crossed on a subchaser to go to Kego Island where the YMCA sec'ys beat the S.S. *Des Moines* officers 8–7 [at baseball]. Then, after a picnic lunch, we watched boxing and wrestling, and

---

53 Of Aberdeen, Scotland; the Taylor's "Scottish Cousins."

54 A wide leather belt with a cross strap over the right shoulder.

all kind of races put on by the sailors. The afternoon ended with a game between the sailors of the *Des Moines* and *Yankton*. We returned just before the last game in order to go to the Embassy reception. I didn't get there for the Hostess House was crowded so I stayed to act as Hostess and had a much better time than if I had gone to the reception.

The ships looked lovely in their flags in honor of the day. The sailors are so proud of them. There is a wonderfully fine spirit between the Navy officers and their men. Those that we have met, among the officers, we admire very much. And for the most part, the sailors are a splendid lot of fellows. I have had a delightful evening, talking with a group of them tonight about Russia. We shall miss them very much indeed when they come to leave, which is within the next few days.

Helen is definitely sailing for home now. She leaves on the *Czar* which goes between the 12th and 15th. We dread very much to see her go. Of all the group that has been here, I am the most fond of Helen. She is an old dear.

Now must say goodbye and good night. It is twelve and time that I was in bed. In spite of the fact that it is daylight outside.

Am feeling fine, and not working hard. There isn't a great deal to do.

With a world of love to each and all from your ever affectionate,

Clara

Arkangel
July 9, 1919

My dear Fritz:

While waiting to see if our three sailors come from the Cruiser *Des Moines* for supper, I will start a letter for Helen to mail to you when she reaches New York. For she is at last sailing on Friday of this week via Vardo thru the Fjords to Christiana from whence she sails for home. Well the men did come. They invited us for a spread at our house, bringing with them wonderful beef salad, asparagus, and salad dressing from their ship. It was the first meal at a table with napkins and service that they had enjoyed for many months. We all had a happy time. They were our first guests in our new rooms.

Our rooms look very attractive with net curtains and crepe hangings which came from London. We were able to rent some furniture so we really look quite American. It is a pity that we didn't have as attractive a place all winter long when we had needed it so much.

There is very little news here, all but forty of our soldiers have gone and they are leaving this month. Most of the boats have gone, all but the *Des Moines* which is to leave at the time of the last soldiers.

Archangel is like a village once more as very few soldiers are here since the Headquarters have been moved up the river front. So that after our new sec'ys arrive and are settled, we ought to have a little quiet and rest. It is certainly going to be lonely without Helen. We shall miss her sadly. She has been quite the most congenial one of the group to me. She is really very anxious to go. Every mail and every departing group makes staying a little harder. It will be the first of September before the last of our old YMCA friends depart. And I sincerely hope that we follow in September. We all feel so annoyed because the girls missed the boat in May. We expect them in five days time, and with them comes our trunks.

The military outlook here is very discouraging. There seems to be very little hope of the drive being made this summer. If the south opens up, I think we probably shall send the sec'ys who are not on the high seas, to Odessa. They probably will get established in Russia before we who are in the north. I think likely we shall leave four sec'ys here for the winter. While two will leave with us in September if we go then. Oh, it is so dreadfully hard to know what is the best thing to do. There are so very many things involved. It is quite possible that it will be wise for me to be in London in November for a big meeting of the World's Committee. It meets only once in every four years. A long time ago New York advised us that both Marcia and I should attend. So you see how very indefinite my home coming plans are. I still think that I shall leave here sometime in September.

The River is very low so that the British gun boats are ineffective. Several are returning to England within a few days. And several are stranded on sandbars unable to return to the base. The English are dreadfully discouraged, and there is much talk of their leaving early in the Fall.

This afternoon we three were invited over to the English hospital ship for afternoon tea. It is a beautiful ship, much finer than the *Kalyon*. It is the finest Navy hospital ship in the British Navy. There are four very attractive nurses there, two of whom came to see us very often. We plan to have them all here for a samovar one afternoon next week.

July 11

Well this letter is doomed to many interruptions. I left early for a girl scout meeting, returning home just in time to fix welch rarebit for the two men who are leaving on the same boat with Helen. They brought some nuts and figs which had just been brought in by some new secretaries. Some candy came for us, but most of it was moldy and unfit to eat. George's candy purchased on my birthday never came thru. Probably some mail clerk decided that mail wasn't reaching Archangel and disposed of it himself.

We have no end of trouble about mail because many officials who ought to know better, think this is still a closed port. We are having some very hot weather the past few days. It's like Duluth, when it is hot, every body complains for cooler weather. We hope there will not be much like it, for we start work for young women next week, and it is so much easier to work when it is cool.

We had to postpone our trip to the Monastery because those stupid secretaries of ours have not cabled when they expect to arrive. Thru a cable from Bergin we know they have left there. So Marcia and I decided to split the party when it comes and take them there, as they really ought to make the trip.

Oh Fritzie, I wish that I were home to "vacate" with you for we will have so much to talk about. But I promise this if you are too busy to come home when I arrive, I'll come soon after arrival to see you. I never could wait till Xmas, if I come this fall.

I am sending my pongee suit home by Helen for Genieve. I think it will be more becoming to her. Anyway she or Sis can do with it as they please, it simply won't do for me. It's most unbecoming.

You all can write Helen any questions which are in your mind about Archangel or me. Her address, Helen Ogden 31 Highland Ave, Orange, New Jersey.

I haven't heard from Geney in ages, am still wondering if she went to California or stayed in Montana.

Now must run and finish Helen's food basket for the boat. She goes to

Bergin on boats that do not have very good meals, especially the first four days on the Russian boat to Vardo.

With a world of love to each and all from your ever affectionate sister,

Clara

The 339th is in the States so we hear. Wonder if you have seen Mr. Hallcock or any of the Decatur boys. Watch for Miss Fergenson, Mrs. Waddell's niece. I will send pictures when we can get paper to print. Did Kodak pictures come with the things I sent in the Fall. If not, they were lost.

Solivesky Monastery
July 21, 1919

My dear Family:

Here I am in this wonderful ancient Monastery out in the White Sea. At present four of us are sitting on a steamer rug on the shore looking out over the harbor. It is a very rocky harbor with crosses standing like sentinels on the various rocky islands. Screaming, crying, gulls on the rocks. Being protected, the gulls are here in great numbers.

We left Archangel on Friday evening, food basket, bed rolls and all. We watched a glorious sunset at ten o'clock and then sought a comfortable place on the floor of the deck to sleep as we all had a "tendency" to sea sickness so didn't want to go below where we had a hot stuffy cabin. Instead of arriving on schedule at eleven o'clock the next morning, we found ourselves stranded in the fog. After anchoring for three hours waiting for the fog to rise, the priests held service praying for the sun, so we might make a safe landing. Finally, a small boat put out to find land, but did not return for three hours. Our boat was small and most everyone was sea sick. It was not until the next morning that we were able to land.

This Monastery was founded in the fifteenth century and is famously rich in Jeweled ikons. There are many ikons of gold and silver studded with diamonds, pearls and all kinds of precious jewels. The paintings, too, are in some cases very, very rich and lovely. While the very ancient are weird and hideous in their conception, many of the ancient wall decorations classify with Dore's "Dante's Inferno." They are curious, and interesting rather than beautiful.

Today was a very great holiday here. The anniversary of the deliverance of this monastery from the attacks of the English, at the time of the Crimean war. At the service this morning, the monks were clothed in their golden robes. At the end of the service, they marched with several of the sacred ikons, around the walls of the monastery, followed by many monks dressed in black, chanting some of their sad, but very beautiful songs.

Yesterday we took a glorious drive to a monastery ten miles from here. We passed thru woods, very like northern Wisconsin, and Minnesota. Miles of beautiful pines, birches, and hundreds of lakes. Interesting rocks and glacial moraines add greatly to the beauty of the scenery.

Today we were greatly disappointed not to be able to drive to Golgotha twenty miles away, we were not entitled to go today, as there are only six carriages, and several hundred people to use them.

From the monastery are lovely roads leading to innumerable little churches that are picturesquely located in the high banks of some of the lakes. Last night we walked three miles to one of the peaceful little sanctuaries returning at sunset and to behold a gorgeous sunset over the sea. All the beautiful shades of lavender and pink were reflected in the water from the sky and the White monastery with its green roofs gleaming in its forest setting. Family mine, I thought of you all very hard, and wished that we might all be together here and that you might know that I was enjoying a really memorable experience.

July 23

On the day of our arrival at the monastery we were delightfully surprised to meet a group of fifteen American engineer officers, who had come over for the day from the Murmansk front near Keam. We were the first American women that they had seen in months, and were as pleased and excited about it as boys. They trailed us everywhere. Like the officers on the Archangel front, they do not approve of our forces being withdrawn and no one sent to take their places.

I have had the opportunity of talking with quite a few Russian people on this trip who simply cannot understand our leaving them in a critical hour. Since we forced our entrance here, in the first place, we have no right to withdraw all troops and leave them to the fate which a successful Bolsheviki drive may deal to them. These poor people are filled with a very great fear.

Once more I am on the boat nearing Arkangel. The rain has made it mightily unpleasant for the crowds that sleep and eat on deck. On the bow and stern of our boat are painted ikons and a big cross tips the mast. The priests came on board to pray for our safe journey, as we left the shore of the monastery.

About six hours after we left Solevisky, we were hailed by a stranded British boat. We dropped anchor and waited until the small boat was finally able to reach us. This boat has been on the sand six days. Fortunately it is not far from a light house so if worse came to worst, they can easily row to safety in the life boats. We are taking a letter and information to the naval authorities. It is a small boat, freighter. It didn't seem quite right not to aid her, but our captain feared that we too might be stranded.

Both going and returning, we have seen the alert, dog like faces of seals as they have come quite near our boat. The children on board were much excited at seeing them.

At this monastery, are about two hundred little boys about Muirison's age who are sent here for two years to work and pray. Many have been ill and so were sent here in gratitude for their recovery. These little fellows wear heavy grey coats, belted with a black leather belt, heavy boots, and a peaked black velvet hat. Then there are men who have come here to live who are not monks, who wear long hair and long black coats belted and the peaked cap. The monks have beards and long hair, wear long, very long full black robes, with tall round caps with black veil hanging down the back. Many of these monks have been here for twenty, thirty, and forty years. One old monk came in 1840. He is said to be a soothsayer.

Yesterday we took a long walk thru wonderful woods, carpeted with flowers of all kinds, bluebells, a kind of goldenrod and many swamp flowers. Also a wealth of pink berries which looks like a flower in its coloring and its formation, and everywhere mushrooms.

Almost every passenger has a box or basket of either berries or mushrooms and bouquets of lovely flowers.

July 25
I have time to add a note before taking the mail to the P.O. It seems good to be back where it is cool and we have other than canned goods to live on. I have just finished packing food baskets for the second group who leave this afternoon.

Also many things seemed to have happened, first the *Des Moines* left, we have made beginnings of girl's work, when lo, the *Des Moines* returns again today to remain indefinitely. The Hostess House is closed and three hundred sailors will be greatly disappointed tonight when they come and find this shut. We put it up to the military mission that we had staff enough for the work if they would procure us a place to do soldier's work. It remains to be seen just what will be done.

Second of great importance. Marcia will probably leave within two weeks for Odessa. I am to remain here until the end of the six week's experiment as advisor to this new staff. Then if all is well, will leave for home about September 20th, at the present writing the prospects for a peaceful Fall, are not reassuring. I understand that the *Des Moines* has returned to stay as long as we have gov't representatives here. So if anything should happen, we will go out on the *Des Moines*. Two Eagle boats came back also, and other boats may return from England, of our fleet. It is wonderful to have so many people here to do things. They are a wonderful group of girls and all eager to pitch into things. I expect an easy time for the next month. Don't stop writing here. Very much love from your sister,

Clara

Arkangel
Aug. 2, 1919

My dear Family:

This is to say that I am really and truly coming home. Unless a bad situation develops between now and the first of September, I shall leave on the first boat sailing for England in September. I will plan to spend a week in London, visit the relatives a week in Aberdeen and then sail for home. Oh, Family, I have been terribly home sick all summer. Especially the last two months I have thought of it, dreamed it, and childishly longed for it. And I frankly admit that I am very, very tired. I will get rested this month and on the journey home. By the 15th of Aug. I will cable for the first possible sailing in October either in France or England. Marcia leaves on the first Russian boat going to Vardo, which probably will be this next week. We are getting her papers and everything ready for her to leave on the 6th. She will try to go to Odessa via France. Perhaps Rome, and may land in Turkey before getting to Odessa. Or if the political situation becomes bad, she will go to the States.

The new girls are all fine. They are taking ahold of things in a splendid way. I have been relieved of the housekeeper's work. So after Marcia leaves I will do only advising. The girls have taken over most of the responsibilities. We have two interpreters for them, but of course I have to help them out a great deal.

Tonight we are having a farewell party for Marcia and the four YMCA men who are sailing tomorrow via Vardo and Christiania. Christiania would be simpler and easier for me, but I want to come via England. I ought to reach New York by the 15th of October, will be home until the big Industrial Conference in Washington, part of Nov. and early Dec. then home again. Think of it. Home. Oh Family you can't possibly want me home as badly as I want to come. You just can't.

The political situation has been very depressing here once more. As you probably know the Onega front went over to the Bolsheviki en masse. We have two Am. YM men there, but we know that they are perfectly safe. They probably are working for the Bolos. Arandon [?] is indiscreet enough to do it.

Just a year ago today Archangel was taken by the Allies. It was celebrated here after a fashion. Most people greatly feared trouble, as did the military authorities. There is unrest throughout this gov't. People are sick and tired of war and foreigners. The river, Dvina, is so low that the gun boats are unable to do a great deal. The British are simply holding their positions. On the Rail Road front the Russians plotted to give over their positions to the Bolosheviki at the same time as on the Onega front, but the plot was discovered a few hours before the fatal time. The Company occupying the frontline positions were withdrawn to Verst 455, (where I was in April) and every tenth man shot. The Australians were sent up to recover the frontline positions which were eventually lost. It is all very discouraging to the Allies. Almost everyone here feels convinced that alone the Russians cannot or will not combat the Bolosheviki, and a big foreign Army must be sent here if any thing effectual is to be done. There are only twelve thousand British troops here now, and they are very discontented.

The English expect to withdraw in November which means all foreigners getting out before the city is taken. Unless compromise is made, the revenge which the Bolos will wreak here, will be too awful to contemplate. For so many Bolo sympathizers have been ruthlessly killed. The Allies are morally obligated to protect the lives, at least of those who have been loyal to them. They must deport many from here to southern Russia. And America is just as obligated as England. Just think, a year ago July, our Allies and we were instigating a revolution here!!! And we were in it just as deep as England and have left England with the bag.

Our club has been redecorated, and is most charming. The girls have been registering the last three days for the various courses. Over two hundred are registered for the six weeks course. We probably shall have time for a second six weeks before having to evacuate. The [YW] girls here will go south to Odessa, if the way is open, when they leave Archangel.

I have no longings to see more of Russia until I see home. I fancy I shall have to do a little conference work during the year while home but it won't be much. I surely expect the N-B[55] to give me three months vacation at their expense. The rest I will take at my own. Nothing seems to matter now excepting to get home.

I am wondering if you have seen Miss Fergenson, or if she hasn't reached Taylorville yet. Three months seems like a long time to wait, but by the time this reaches you, I probably shall be on the high seas started for home.

Tomorrow, Sunday, the Priest comes in accordance to Russian customs, to bless the club rooms and sprinkle them with Holy water. Mr. Cole representing the Embassy, will give a short talk, followed by Marcia. Then we will serve tea.

Hastily ended 12:30 night. Heaps of love to each and all from

Teke

---

55 YWCA National Board.

Arkangel
Aug. 14, 1919

Dear Girls:

These have been wonderful days, not that I have gotten so much mail, but what has come thru has made me just crazy to start for home. I have cabled England for passage from there for the last of September, not later than October first. Further more I am hoping to sail from here not later than the first.

Yesterday I had Geney's letter of July 1st and today Mary's and Fritz's of July 5th and yesterday an envelope full of letters from seven different people written June-July and Aug of 1918. Where do you suppose it has been. From things you elude to there are many letters which have gone astray. Thank you dear people for the stockings, films and money. I don't know when I shall "meet up" with them, for the secretaries who probably brought them will soon be leaving Christiana for Finland. As you know people are no longer coming to Arkangel, but rather leaving. Poor Marcia has been so delayed. Now she hopes to leave on the 20th if she can get passage. We may get to leave together. She hopes to go to Christiana, while I will take some fifteen or twenty pieces of baggage to London. It will be equipment which we will not carry around until we know when and where it will be needed. Marcia, I wrote you, is not coming home this winter. She goes to Paris first. I imagine that she will remain there several weeks. Then she hopes to proceed around to Denikin's country in the south of Russia,[56] stopping in Greece and Constantinople. Today some very splendid news came for me. My salary was raised last Nov. but the news of it just came today. In fact it was the May meeting of the Overseas Com. that voted the raise and that it should apply beginning with Nov. 1918. It was a raise of $400 a year so my salary is $1600 plus living expenses. Which has meant about $75 a month. This means completely clearing up my indebtedness and giving me enough to buy the necessary new clothes. I need two new dresses, a suit and winter coat, shoes, hat, gloves, etc. And I have wondered how I was going to meet the expense when Lo, here comes the raise. Isn't it grand. I owe that to Marcia. She wrote for it months ago but said nothing

---

56 General Anton I. Denikin succeeded Kornilov in April 1918 as commander of the southern White forces. At this point the region of the Don River (Ukraine) was a stronghold for the anti-Bolshevik effort.

about it to me. Also the $100 for equipment which we spent in Sweden is going to be allowed.

I am so tickled that Father has sold the Missouri farm and had gotten rid of that burdensome debt. My how I wish Mother and Sam could know. We just ought to have some very wonderful celebration in honor of so important an event. Why not celebrate it, by escorting me back to Europe when I return next summer.

Yesterday I learned from the *New Republic* that the big meeting in Washington takes place the last week in October. That is disconcerting for it will give me only about ten days at home, and no time to get a few necessary clothes. If I should be delayed getting home, I may have to go to Washington for a couple of weeks first and then get home about Nov. 15 for three uninterrupted months. I expect to do some traveling to present the work in Russia, and only yesterday, we learned that our big Nat. Convention was to be in April, so I will be in the country for that. I hope not to return before June or July of next summer.

If you get this letter as early as the last few please send sizes of gloves for the feminine members of the household, so I can buy in London for you. Also let me know if there are other things which I can buy for you in London. There is absolutely nothing here and the prices are simply prohibitive of the few things that can be bought. I have picked up two or three little copper things in the market. You will all love the two charming brass shells which the soldiers did for me. And the towels which my landlady gave me for a little needed help I was able to give her. I have looked in vain for things for the three children, but it is almost a hopeless task. I will find for them something in England.

Diary
June 21 – August 31, 1919

June 21, 1919, Archangel
Sat. Spent early morning playing with Girl Scouts. Then Bath—In evening Helen and I went to the dance with Lt. Johnson. Sunset 11:15, rise 1:30. Went to bed at 2 a.m. Too light to sleep.

June 22, 1919
Sun. Went to Archangel Prestan [?] with Tom, Col. Thurston, Lt. Johnson. Jim S. & Tom came to dinner. After busy day at H.H. spent evening at Home. All boats but one Chaser have gone from Archangel. Letter from Sis.

June 23, 1919
Mon. Spent a.m. writing. Helped to take Katya to Russian Hospital. Afternoon & evening at Hostess House. Germans signed peace treaty.

June 24, 1919, Letter 64 from Father
Tues. At eleven saw presentation of Honor metals to Engineer. Very hot. At nine o'clock Major Henry, Hurlbert, Hale, Metkiff, Butrick came to have Samovar and visit.

June 25, 1919, cooler
Wed. Lesson with Will Hourwich. Interviewing people regarding Prison work. New Sec'ys on the Way to Archangle

June 26, 1919
Thurs. Many Engineers in to say good bye—Lt. Johnson, Crawford, Tom & Jim came in for the evening.

June 27, 1919
Fri. Prison work—Met Girl Scouts for baseball. 1st shot for typhoid. One o'clock Engineers marched to boat. At eight we went down to wave them goodbye. Marcia & I called on Col. Ruglis.

June 28, 1919
Sat. Warm and summery, lots of flowers in bloom. H. H. [Hostess House] very much deserted. Feel sure that I will go home in the Fall.

June 29, 1919
Sun. Spent day reading *Red Planet*, Locke. arranged some household affairs. Spent afternoon at Hostess House. In evening all officers of Eagle Boat No. 2 came in for evening, along with Crawford, Tom & Russian girl.

June 30, 1919, Arkangel
Mon. Glorious Day. MOD & I called at Embassy. Got hint that doubtful if we get into Petrograd from here this Fall. Boats have returned—if true all go out in Aug. We too shall soon go.

July 1, 1919
Tues. Russians can't understand Allie's withdrawal. Murmansk Engineer came up to help others troops get out & are sore because they have never even seen the other troops & are still here.

July 2, 1919
Wed. Marcia and I went to Ikemiesky Prentr at the time when prison women were freed. Spent evening at the Hostess House. Sailors more and more making use of the House. 2 letters from home.

July 3, 1919
Thurs. Husky Merrill came to dinner. He & I went to Kego Island with Mr. Preston to arrange about 4th picnic. Crawford & Jim came in the evening. Cold & rainey.

July 4, 1919, Archangel
Fri. Went to Kego Isl. where *Des Moines* Officers played YMCA Sec'ys 7–8 in favor YM. Picnic meal. Sailors boxed & had sports. Gave Navy ice cream. In evening reception at Embassy 5–7 a perfect day. Did not attend the dance. Had good talk about Russia with sailors.

July 5, 1919, Letter 65 Mary
Sat. Cold & rainey—several Navy boats departed for Murmansk and England. No change in situation here or in Siberia. Denikin pushing North with success.

July 6, 1919, Archangel
Sun. cold and clear. Spent morning writing letters to people in Am. who lost friends in war here. Most of the old crowd in for the evening. In evening packed many things for moving.

July 7, 1919
Mon. Moved into new quarters above the Hostess House. Several men in to visit with us.

July 8, 1919
Tues. No word from Sec'ys. Busy getting settled. Helen packing ready to leave daily for home, getting very hot again.

July 9, 1919
Wed. Two boys from the *Des Moines* brought steaks for a wonderful dinner. They were delighted with a home meal.

July 10, 1919
Thurs. Spent afternoon at English Hospital Boat with English nurses and farewell spread for Tom, Husky, and Helen. Very warm.

July 11, 1919, Letter 66 Fritz. R. 11–
Fri. Helen, Tom & Husky Merrill left for home. Curtiss, Clark, Hach & Warner arrived very unexpectedly at noon & brought the long looked for trunk. Girls are dandy. Prospects for going home look good. very warm. Political situation very depressing. Kolchalk retreated. Drive here not possible. Maj. Scules & Lt. Tucker called

July 12, 1919, Letter from Sis
very hot Busy getting everything settled in new quarters. More troops

arrive from England. Girls settling things. Plans talked of for opening girls work. Soldiers arrive to move graves of dead

July 13, 1919
Sun. Marcia & I tried on our new dresses. Spent most of day at Hostess House. Gen. Richardson & Col. Bury called in evening and took us on a ride on the launch up the River. Muriel Beckett married. The new girls are all peaches.

July 14, 1919, Letter 67—Sis & Genny, Archangel 94°
Mon. Dreadfully busy with final house arrangements. renewed passport. Engineers off from front line. Mobilizing at Murmansk.

July 15, 1919
Tues. Lt. Preston called in afternoon. Lt. Klieforth & Mrs. Klieforth spent the evening. We are so enthusiastic over new girls. Labour situation in England may force withdrawal of Eng. troops.

July 16, 1919, Letter 68—Genieve
Wed. Bought provisions of S. S. *Des Moines*—very hot. Planned girls work program to be given August first. Received letters from Genieve & Lonnie A.

July 17, 1919, left for Solovetsky
Thurs. Took food baskets & left for Solovetski. The *Des Moines* left for Murmansk with Eagle boats—very hot.

July 18, 1919, On White Sea
Fri. At noon anchored because of fog. Every body sea sick—lay on floor of deck. At three Monks held service praying that the sun would shine. Then set off boat. All night we lay anchored. Everyone very thoroughly miserable.

July 19, 1919, Solovetski Monastery
Sat. After eating, we went through the monastery—took long walk at four. Went to eat with pilgrims, of cabbage, quas (beer made of black bread), fish soup. Met Am. Engineers from Kem

July 20, 1919, Solovetsky Monastery

Sun. Attended service at Monastery. In afternoon took long drive to visit two other churches—Wonderful scenery. In evening walked to little chapels built on site where founders of Monastery lived. warm & wonderful.

July 21, 1919, Solovetsky

Mon. Glorious day. Drove 13 verts to two beautiful little churches thru lovely pine & birch woods, passed many lakes & glacial moraines. In the evening we walked out to another little sanctuary, returning to witness very wonderful sunset. A very unusual service.

July 22, 1919, Solovetsky

Tues. Took long walk thru beautiful woods covered with flowers & mushrooms. Sailed for home at 4. Saw stranded boat—also seals. Sunset at 10:10. Cold.

July 23, 1919

Wed. Arrived home from Solovetsky at noon. Learned Onega had been taken by Bolos. R. R. situation critical. 250 Russians soldiers withdrawn from front. Many people in Archangel throwing their loyalty to the Bolos. Jim S. called also Lt. Burnam & Lt. Packard. Cable from Read. Letter from Cora.

July 24, 1919

Thurs. Marcia plans to go.—Staff meeting Miss Curtis to take charge—In evening meetings of girls who were very enthusiastic over club prospects.

July 25, 1919, Archangel

Fri. Marcia & Miss Clark & Neva left for Soleveski. Miss Bredau & Miss Farnecrok arrived. The *Des Moines* & two Eagle boats unexpectedly returned—Olga Nicholai came in during the evening. Letter 69 Cora.

July 26, 1919, cold

Sat. Called at Military Mission. Col. Rugles very depressed. arrests made and city in state of unrest & fear. Had dinner at YMCA. called at [?]

Preute. Rec'd cable from Helen. letter from Sis. Sailors lost without a place to go.

July 27, 1919

Sun. Worked at Hostess House, entertained boys in P.M. Many callers in the evening.

July 28, 1919

Mon. Began Russian lessons with Olga Dubanabna.

July 29, 1919, Archangel

Tues. Made call arranging for teachers. Mr. Dunn and [?] from *Des Moines* called in evening. Mr. Hurburt & Mr. Butrick came for dinner.

July 30, 1919, Archangel

Wed. Called on Priest of Cathedral Arranged for Ikon and for speech given by Mr. Cole. Girls came to register. Attended central com. meeting and went to Rperome [? in Russian: Ппероме]. Crawford called.

July 31, 1919

Thurs. Marica returned from Soleviski. club rooms lovely—Crawford came to spend the evening and read his diary of Beresniki trip—Everything stranded because of low water. Forest fires bad. People of country about growing more pro Bolo.

MEMORANDA 1919 Archangel

Thurs. am. Feeling keenly the situation of Allies pulling out and deserting the faithful—Especially since a year ago Lt. Kleisforth was here helping to stir up the Revolution. Big Russian battle ship stripped of munitions. *Des Moines* here indefinitely.

August 1, 1919

Fri. Registration for classes. Final preparations for opening of club. Mr. Dutting, Russian Capt. and Jim came in for evening. Wrote Eliz. and Helen. Wonderful weather. Airplane circled during night.

August 2, 1919
Sat. Anniversary of Allies taking Archangel. Russians parade but much uneasiness. Every thing carefully guarded in city. Farewell party to Crawford & Jim—15 Sec'ys came for evening. Had movies. Marcia decided to leave on first boat and for me to go Sept. Areoplanes circled all day.

August 3, 1919, Letter Father 70. Letter 12 R. L.
Splendid opening of Club with Priests Ikon presented by Soleviski Monastery. Rec'd cable stating that I should be in N.Y. by Oct. 20th—awful case of homesickness. Officers from *Des Moines* called. Sun set 9:40.

August 4, 1919
Mon. Mr. Cole advised us that we all probably should evacuate before end of Aug. Marcia & I offering [?] all preparations for departure. Talked with Coil who had just been freed from Bolos. at Onega. He was enthusiastic about Bolos.

August 5, 1919
Tues. Had tea on *Des Moines*. Loads of wonderful mail from home. It seems cruel & heartless to go on gaily where so many people are so soon to be uprooted [?] from their homes in a foreign land. While others will be left to a hard fate here. Very hot.

August 6, 1919, Letter 72 M. & Gen.
Wed. Went through trunk & tore up all letters.[57] Decided how to pack clothing. People being allowed to leave Archangel both via Siberia & abroad. Eng. to leave on Sat. Everybody greatly excited and fearful. Many wonderful home letters.

August 7, 1919, Archangel
Thurs. Rainey day. Went through supplies & finished going over baggage preparatory for packing. Got gray coat & found Xmas box from Genieve.

---

57 Tearing up her home letters must have been difficult for Clara. We surmise that she was fearful her baggage would be searched and trouble ensue if her letters were read.

August 8, 1919, Archangel

Fri. Spent morning studying. afternoon selling supplies preparatory to evacuation. Many people leaving on every ship. Local people terribly distressed at prospect of Allies leaving & Bolos coming.

August 9, 1919, Archangel

Sat. Sold. & sailors dance at Hdqts. Marcia & I talked with Olga Slepanova about training school. New gov't going into effect here. People on street threatening. Shooting again at night.

August 10, 1919

Wonderful day. Packed supplies. Everybody very uneasy about political situation locally. Marcia & I called on Military Mission for news. Col. Rugles backing us up. 3 officers from Army & 3 from Navy came in for evening.

August 11, 1919, Letter 73 Father

Very cold and rainey. Marcia probably delayed another week getting off. Evacuation officer arrived. 7,000 Russians to be allowed to leave. Nov. 10 probably last date for Eng. occupation.

August 12, 1919

Tues. Marcia & I spent evening at tea with Olga Stepanov. after calling on Miss Hoururch. Had wonderful day shopping in the market. June–July & Aug. 1918 letters received

August 13, 1919

Wed. Studied hard—read and took notes on Russia—took picture & shopped with girls in market. Carnegie has died. Letter from Geni.

August 14, 1919

Thurs. Rained all day. Spent afternoon reading *New Republic*—feel depressed over peace terms. Spent early evening studying. Maj Lively & Capt. Robinson came for samovar. News reached of raise in salary. Had wonderful letter from Sis and Fritz.

August 15, 1919
Fri. Spent afternoon studying and evening packing my trunk and selecting things for packing bags. YMCA situation continues to be unpleasant.

August 16, 1919, Letter 73 M. & G.
Raw and rainey. The sailors came in for entire afternoon & evening. The officers, Miss Woodworth & Miss Knox, Lt. Packard, Preston Quinn, Dunn, Hazard for cards, playing until two-thirty. Militia men stopped in as we went home.

August 17, 1919, Archangel
Sun. Cold and rainey. *Czarina* transport left with 1200 Russian refugees. Spent evening studying Russian History. House full of girls from 5–8. Wrote Bess and Crawford. officers in from the *Des Moines.*

August 18, 1919
Mon. Were told by Consul that probably the evacuation would be completed so far as Am. concerned by Sept. 15.

August 19, 1919
Tues. The new Russian gov't more liberal. People selling all their possessions. All feel so tragic over their future. 390 girls members of the club— Continued cold and rainey. Scout demonstration.

August 20, 1919
Wed. Marcia & I called on the Kliefoths. Everybody very panic as to what is to be done. Whether the gov't will move out or stay. British decided to withdraw all goods & ammunitions. The Eng. nurses from Garth Casthe came for tea.

August 21, 1919, sent Letter 76
Thurs. Packed. Lt. Packard called in evening regarding helping girls in evacuation. Mr. Poncefard and Komlozy & two British flyers called for Samavor. Marcia & I packed until 2 A.M. Very much rain.

August 22, 1919

Fri. Spent hectic getting everything ready for departure. Learned at 2 that I could go. Went on board on the *Kalyon* Hospital Ship at 5. The *Des Moines* sent little boat to *K* for me. Delightful dinner party on *Des Moines*. All the YMCA men in at 9 for Samavor.

August 23, 1919, Archangel & White Sea

Sat. was called at 6 o'clock [a.m.] on *Kalyon* & told consul ordered me off because lacking Amer. visa. U.S. car met me. 2 British officers escorted me off.[58] At 3:15 Marcia & I left on Russian boat for Vardo & Christiana. great crowds, furniture, cow, and a multitudes of baskets. a British Maj. Russian & child. Marcia & I occupied one state room.

August 24, 1919, Ксебелл C.C. [name of ship] White Sea

Sun. Sea Sick. Spent most of day sleeping or lying down filled with indignation more I think of s.[Strother] making passport trouble. General Morachifsky, Bishop of Arch. Cath. & a no. of other interesting people on Board. Lt. Col. British off. who had charge of mail service, delightful traveling companions

August 25, 1919, White Sea

Mon. Spent a wretched day. rain & sunshine by spells.—having stops at isolated fishing hamlets. Boats row out to ours, a cow & a goat were lowered into row boat this noon. A woman doctor dressed in men's clothes the chief person of interest. She has doctored innumerable sick as a good Samaritan.

August 26, 1919

Tues. A glorious day. Feeling fit first time in three days. Saw interesting jelly fish. Wonderful aquamarine colored waters, interesting [?] on board. Boat

---

58 This is a very much shortened account of what happened. Clara later told David K. Martin that she went straight to Council Poole, who was shocked at Strother's behavior. Poole spent the greater part of the day tracking down a clerk from the Norwegian Consulate to write the required visas for Clara and Marcia. Strother's mischief was not complete, and he had Clara threatened with arrest in Murmansk. Luckily, the US Consul in Murmansk was Peter Pierce, an old friend of Clara's who knew Strothers and the situation.

crowded with fishermens' families, baskets & fish. Arrived Murmansk at 8 after call at YMCA. Went to call on Pete Pierce who had received telegram from Strouther to delay us if possible. He fixed up our passports. Returned to boat at 1 o'clock.

August 27, 1919, Murmansk

Wed. Spent the morning lying off Murmansk. city. [. . . ? . . .] frame houses scattered over the coast line, foot of beautiful green foot hills. A very beautiful harbour. Mild weather—Sailed for Vardo at 4 P.M. All day bright & clear. There was much roll to the sea.

August 28, 1919, Arctic Ocean

Thurs. Arrived Vardo at noon. After Passport reg. & customs Marcia and I explored the town & sent telegrams. Vardo windows full good eatables. Glorious bright day. Slept on board the Cbep 6 until two A.M. *Erling Jarl*—Steam Ship.

August 29, 1919, Arctic Ocean, Norway

Fri. Left Vardo at 4 A.M. Glorious golden twilight all night. At 3:00 rounded the Northern most point seeing North Cape off in the distance. 30 Fishing boats were off the Point—altho rainey & misty. It was very impressive sea color. at 6:30 we came for 3 hours at Konocurga vang. Glorious harbour & a [?] flat road traversing mts.

August 30, 1919, Trosomor (Tromso), Norway

Sat. Left Hammerfest at 6 A.M. All day in glorious Mts. with many glaciers in sight. Passed the highest Mts. & biggest glaciers in northern Norway. At Tromso we spent 4 hrs. Went to the movies. The stores were filled with lovely things. In our gray coats we attracted a great deal of attention. Stopped at Sjers at noon.

August 31, 1919, Norwegian Fjords

Sun. Heavy clouds most of day. Marcia & I took long walk at 6 o'clock getting drenched. The Mts. and the clouds very beautiful. Had delightful walk with one of the French men early in the morning.

MEMORANDA Mon. 1919 on board ship

Hard rain part of the day. about six, passed the rock famous for the whole [. . . ? . . .]—very rough a part of the night. We enjoy very much the Captain at whose table we sit.

PART FIVE

September 1–December 31, 1919

Clara and Marcia arrived safely in England on September 7, 1919. Clara spent a month visiting her cousins the Laws in Aberdeen, Scotland, and attending meetings in London. Then, to her great relief, Clara finally set sail for America on October 8. One month and two years after she had left, she was back home. Understated as usual, her diary entry for October 19, 1919 notes ". . . arrived home at eight o'clock, . . . all family at house for dinner & supper. Perfect, wonderful to be home."

However, Clara didn't get much rest yet. After only four days at home in Illinois with her family, she was on a train back east to Washington, DC. There she connected with Bessie Boies, gave her report on the YWCA Russian work, and attended the International Congress of Working Women (ICWW). The ICWW was a ten-day conference of 200 prominent women labor leaders, who traveled to Washington, DC from nineteen countries across the world.[59] The meeting was organized by the National Women's Trade Union League of America (Margaret Dreir Robins, President), with the support of British and French organizers. The purpose was to prepare resolutions to present to the League of Nations and the first meeting of

---

59 Eleanor Roosevelt was at the ICWW, acting as a translator for the French contingent. In 1922, she joined the Women's Trade Union League and set about using her Washington connections to bolster the organization's public relations and finances, and to improve working conditions and wages for women. Jane Addams gave the opening remarks at the ICWW (see reference Stevenson's Digital Library: "The Working Women").

the International Labor organization (ILO). The ICWW was scheduled to meet congruently with the ILO, making the point that, although the ILO, charged by the Treaty of Versailles to formulate labor policies, used language such as "to protect children and women," it did not make provision for women to be represented at its deliberations. Women labor organizers felt that they must not be silent as men held meetings at which policies that would directly impact women's lives were developed. Hence, the women of the ICWW met ". . . hop[ing] to transcend differences of nation, culture, and ideology and formulate a set of international worker rights and entitlements that would benefit working women everywhere" (Cobble 2014).

In her diary entry for October 28, 1919, the opening day of the women's conference, Clara mentioned that Mrs. Robins gave a tea at her hotel. The following day, Clara noted the opening of the International Labor Organization's Conference, at which she was expecting to speak. The week in Washington was busy for Clara: she attended the Women's Conference in the mornings, the "Int't Labor" meetings in the afternoons, then went sightseeing or attended the theater in the evenings.

After the conferences, Clara took the train north to New York City. She spent time at the YWCA headquarters helping to plan further work. Also, she met with US officials in the State Department about "the situation"—a reference to the rumors about her alleged Bolshevik sympathies promoted by both Jerome Davis in his speeches using her comments in support of soviet factory organizations[60] and the vitriolic animosity expressed by Shelby Strother after she barred him from social activities in Archangelsk.

Clara got home to Taylorville, Illinois, for good on November 20, 1919. She noted visits from family members, small gatherings of good friends, and the serious coal shortage that gripped the Midwest that winter. Her diary entries are short and simple: "Read. Wrote. Went to Eastern Star with Sis. Coal strike continues." There are even blank pages—for December 1 and 2, Clara did not write an entry. This gives us the sense that she had "let down", and no longer needed to anxiously record events. She had returned to the safety of her family home in a small secure town in the middle of America, and there was not much to note. Spending the holidays at home with her dearest ones brought a sense of joy and a deep appreciation for her healthy, happy, lucky, and loving family. Christmas Day found the whole

---

60 See Clara's diary entry for November 7, 1919.

family at home, sharing presents, decorating the tree, playing children's games, and having a family sing around the fire. She could not have been more content.

Our last letter from Clara written in Russia is dated August 14, 1919. Sadly, any letters she might have written from England or while aboard ship have been lost. The rest of this volume contains her line-a-day diary entries from September 1 through December 31, 1919.

Chapter Nine
"Spent entire morning seeing officials."

Diary
September 1 – October 19, 1919

September 1, 1919, Trondheim

Mon. After glorious morning arrived at Trondheim at noon. Spent day visiting cathedral. The shops—took train for Christiania [Oslo] Norway at 7:45—beautifully situated in the Mts. very quaint streets, but very modern houses.

September 2, 1919, Travel thru Mts. & Christiania

Tues. Arrived Christiania at 1:30. Miss Roelofs & Miss Prichard meeting us. Had dinner. Took walk, attend movie while waiting to get hotel room. C. charmingly situated on hills & Mts

September 3, 1919, Christiania

Had conferences with new Secys—Did shopping & a little sight seeing. Sent cables—Decided to go Am. with girls and give up trip to England.

September 4, 1919, Christiania

Thurs. Decided to go to Fin(d)land, called Mr. (Col.) Matax at Embassy for information. Shopped. at eight o'clock, opened supply trunk, found films, silk stockings, flag, candy

September 5, 1919, Christiania
Fri. Spent most of a.m. calling at Consulate. Strother had wired him. after, out on the Mts. where we held a staff meeting. Rec'd cable the Curtiss party had left Archangel. All plans for Finland had to be given up.

September 6, 1919, Bergen, Norway
Sat. Travel all night & morning thru magnificent Mts. with innumerable waterfalls, Fjords & lakes—Many of the birch trees & ferns yellow with first colors of frost. after two hours sailed for New Castle.

September 7, 1919, English Channel
Sun. Boat rolled until two P.M. We were unable to dress until 3 when sea became smoother. We sat all evening on deck and enjoyed the first moonlight in six months. Decided to try and get sailings from Eng. or France. Docked at 2 A.M.

September 8, 1919, New Castle & Edinborough
Mon. Came off Boat *Irina* at 8:30. Went to R.R. Hotel, checked baggage & took 11:20 train for Edinboro. Delayed by wreck long time outside city. Beautiful rolling country. Neat fields, wonderful gardens. Interesting rock fences & neat hedges. Took carriage for two hour drive over city, passed castle, palace & homes of many famous men in Scottish literature.

September 9, 1919, Edinborough
Tues. Spent entire morning seeing officials and arranging to get Russian girls off early to Christiania. 2,000 troops landed & all Embassies—All YM & YW. Took night train for London.

September 10, 1919 (Fritz's birthday) London
Wed. First day in London. Visited three offices regard sailings, called at consulate and Embassy—had tea at World Office with Miss Spencer. Found a lot of mail there from Read, Helen & Liza.

September 11, 1919 (John's Birthday) London

Thurs. Called Embassy—consulate, shopped, rode about over the city. In evening Prentice - Jones - & MOD & I went to hear *Abraham Lincoln* at Hammersmith Theatre.

September 12, 1919, London

Friday Went to British Museum. Bk of Engl. Drove thru old part of city, visited St. Pauls Cathedral. went up the Strand to Trafalgar Sq., passed Halls of Justice. Went to Liberties & shopped in afternoon. Did acc'ts in evening.

September 13, 1919, London

Sat. Spent morning in Nat'l Art Gallery, Parliament Bldgs. Walked up to Buckingham Palace. in afternoon, went out to Kew to the Royal Gardens. Saw *Daddies* at Hay Market Theatre in evening.

September 14, 1919, London

Sun. Marcia and I got up at 6 AM to see off three Russian girls to Am. Miss Prentice & Jones went to St. Marks in the Field with us to church. Walked thru Hyde Part, down Pall Mall to Hotel. Left for Aberdeen.

September 15, 1919, Aberdeen

Mon. Arrived 8:50. Sam & David met me. In afternoon Beatrix, Bettie & Bob & I visited old churches, Uni[versity] Bldgs and met Sam & David & all went out for afternoon tea. Spent evening visiting.[61]

September 16, 1919

Tues. Glorious day. Sam, Beatrix, Bettie, Ruth & I left at 8:30 for [the village of] Maud. Took auto New Byth. Then to Pernlau [?]. Wonderful view of the sea, & quaint fishing village. Stopped at Aberdour for dinner. Then on to Cartes to call on Marmond House the Jim Taylors. Thence back to Maud & train home. Wonderful hills, lovely heathers, and perfect day.

---

61 These are the "Scottish Cousins": Sam Law was the son of Clara's paternal aunt Jane Taylor Law. Sam was married to Betty and their children were Beatrix, Ruth, and David.

September 17, 1919, Aberdeen
Wed. Slept late, had breakfast in bed. Beatrix and I visited interesting parts of town, went out to the beach—guests came in for six o'clock tea. Alex (Uncle).

September 18, 1919, Aberdeen
Sewed and visited in A.M. David & I motored thru country fifty miles for tea at hotel on the Dee River, returning by another road. We returned at seven to find the McGregors here for tea at seven. Spent evening talking about Russia.

September 19, 1919, Aberdeen
Fri. Spent morning reading and sewing. Very cold, raw East wind blowing. Had homey time sitting in front of a grate fire. Had big dinner & early tea.[62] The whole family came to the train to see me off.

September 20, 1919, London
Sat. Did a little shopping in the morning. Took Neva to see the Tower of London in the afternoon. Spent the evening puttering about my room. Have an at home feeling about London.

September 21, 1919, London
Sun. Left at noon for Esher to visit Lask. It was a glorious day spent in a lovely old house amid charming surrounding, great old oak and beach trees—high ferns & beautiful rolling country. The family was exceedingly delightful.

September 22, 1919, London
Mon. Procured passage sailing 25th. Marcia and I called on Miss Phillys

---

62 In Europe, "dinner" could be either a formal mid-day meal, or the very formal late evening meal, where women dressed in evening gowns and men in tuxedos. "Luncheon" was a lighter, informal mid-day meal often eaten at a restaurant or café, and "tea" was a light snack in the late afternoon/early evening. "Supper" was a very late night meal, often eaten at a restaurant after a theater performance. As an American, Clara interchanges the terms "supper" (informal) and "dinner" (formal) for an evening meal. The Taylor family also used the term "a spread" to indicate a special meal with treats, such as for a holiday celebration.

of Nat'l YWCA who put us in touch with interesting people. Then we had tea at Fullers. Walked down to the Cheshire cheese for dinner and to see *Caesar's Wife* at the Royal Theater in evening

September 23, 1919, London

Tues. Had passport visaed. shopped for pictures, visited Trades school, Newbury in afternoon. Bought English Labour Bullitins. Read some Bul. in evening. London is lovely. Boat postponed from 25th to 30th. Spent evening with the Klieforth's.

September 24, 1919, London

Wed. Marcia and I visited East End London Settlement, Canning Town Women's Settlement. Having luncheon with Mrs. Parker-Crane. Thence to Silvertown thru Keeler's Jam Factory. Home across the Dock's thru East End, home. Evening visited Industrial Club at Highbury gave talk on Russia. Boat postponed sailing until 7th.

September 25, 1919, London

Thurs. Called Women's Trade Union League Headquarters and Russell Square hoping to find Paul Dulces.

September 26, 1919, London

Friday Called on Mr. Shotwell and got information regarding Int'l Conference in Wash. Staff meeting. Everybody terribly depressed because Marcia is called home by State Dep't

September 27, 1919, London

Sat. Big R. R. Strike began at midnight. While city greatly inconvenienced, very orderly & philosophical. Sympathy seems to be favoring R. R. Saw big parade of Ex servicemen who were protesting against gov't. Had tea with Mr. Golamaske and Smith from S.S. *Des Moines*. Marcia & I went to theatre in evening.

September 28, 1919

Sun. Marcia & I went to church but found Dr. Gouret ch[urch]. closed. Took walk to the River. Afternoon went to Kenningston Gardens, saw

Peter Pan monument. Met Miss Spencer at College Club for tea. Went to hear Dr. Orchard who spoke on the strike. The city is wonderfully self contained over strike.

September 29, 1919, London
Mon. Called at Express Co., bought hat. Had lunch with Miss Spencer. Staff meeting, then lecture on the Russian people by Baron Mirendorff & after late dinner Marcia & I had a grape fruit to celebrate our 2nd Anniversary of sailing from Am.–Russia.

September 30, 1919, London
Tues. Staff meeting at 3, followed by Lecture given by Baron Mirendorff. Spent evening visiting the Jewish Club. Club established 21 yrs. ago. Exclusively Jewish—considered best girls club on London. Called at Trade Union Bldy.

MEMORANDA
1919 London The R.R. strike is amazingly orderly, apparently without bitterness or destruction. [?] philosophically. The R. R. men are so very evident in the right. Ch. with them.

October 1, 1919, London
Wed. Presented Ind[ustrial] Ed. program at Staff meeting. Baron Mirendorff gave his final lecture on the Russian church. Everyone following R. R. strike closely. Marvelous the splendid Labor Leadership.

October 2, 1919, London
Thurs. MOD & I presented Russian work to the World's Committee. Many guests invited in for tea. We went to Cheshire Cheese for dinner and to see *Three Wise Fools* in the evening.

October 3, 1919, London
Fri. Spent day visiting Richmond and Hampton Ct. & Bushy Park. Perfect Day. Chestnut trees lovely. Miss Picton Turbeville & Miss Causird came to dinner & spent the evening. Learned boat again postponed.

October 4, 1919, London

Sat. After meeting Miss Poets at Amer. Embass, ironed [?] at 22 Inverness. Mr. Heiser called in afternoon. Mrs. Porter & I went to Ye Old Cheshire Cheese for supper. Spent evening working on reports of staff conferences.

October 5, 1919, London

Sun. Packed baggage for S.S. *Vauban*. MOD and I went to luncheon with Miss Cauiards, Miss Robtan [?] Turbville, guest also. Attended Temple Ch. where Masonary started. Had tea, then went to city Temple Ch. for evening service to hear Maud Royden. She announced the end of strike. R. R. won out.

October 6, 1919, London

Mon. went to Express office *Vaubun* indefinitely delayed. made application on *Adriatic*. Walked down Mall, passed St. James Palace in evening.

October 7, 1919, London

Tues. Spent morning & day until 3 getting passport & ticket for *Adriatic*. Staff meeting at 4, packed & did last few things. While happy to go, sorry to leave Marcia. The thought of going home!!

October 8, 1919, Sailed

Wed. MOD & I went to train 7:30. Big train of Boat people. Sailed from Southhampton on *Adriatic*. White Star. Mrs. Eddy roommate. Boat Big and beautiful. Wonderful weather. passed Ile of Wight. stopped at France. Col. Rugles, Cole, Lee, Rise on Board.

October 9, 1919, Atlantic

Thurs. Made excellent time. Making 411 knots—Spent entire day reading *The Secret City*. Feel numb [?] from throbbing of engines. Many commercial travelers, few officers, few Red Cross people returning home.

October 10, 1919, Atlantic

Fri. Gloriously warm, calm & beautiful; finished Walpole's *The Secret City*. Read manuscript of Dr. Eddy's book on Russia—Reading Ransome's *6 weeks in Russia in 1919*.

October 11, 1919, Adriatic S.S. Atlantic Ocean
Sat. 2700 people 300 + 1ˢᵗ, 300 2nd , 1400 3rd. 600 crew. Everybody getting acquainted. Smooth journey. made 411[knots].

October 12, 1919, Atlantic Ocean
Sun. Early—Sea smooth—heavy head winds in afternoon. Church—morning & evening. Jolly group at table, Mrs. Barker, Miss Porter, Dr. & Mrs. Eddy—Mr. Huribert, Mr. Pratt 388.

October 13, 1919, Atlantic O.
Mon. Fairly clear, calm sea—played deck tennis. Rec'd signal that ship burning. Another ship got to the rescue. Dance in the evening. Heavy rain & wind in early evening.

October 14, 1919, Atlantic Oc.
Tues. Choppy seas, everybody quiet. Finished reading Ransome's *6 Weeks in Russia*. Finished deck tennis tournaments. In evening Dr. Eddy, Mr. Stead, Morgenthu spoke & Welsh chorus sang! Lt. Platt & I were partners in tournament.

October 15, 1919, Atlantic Ocean
Wed. Wrote & read all day. Danced on deck in evening. Continued fine weather.

October 16, 1919, Atlantic Oc.
Thurs. Spent morning packing. Everybody wonderfully happy. wrote letters. Fog all morning. Beautifully clear & smooth in P.M. Anchored at quarantine 11 o'clock.

October 17, 1919, New York
Fri. Glorious landing. Harbour wonderful. Bess & Helen—4 Secret Service men who apologized for interviews. Saw Jim Somerville. Attended Overseas com. meeting—Dinner with Bess & Henrietta R. Left for home at 12:25.

October 18, 1919, Thru Ohio Travel Home

Sat. Spent morning writing Marcia. Read stack of mail—wrote to Read. Country beautiful in radiant foliage. Can scarcely believe that I am homeward bound.

October 19, 1919, Home

Sun. Found Fritz on train. We arrived home eight o'clock. Family all there—all family at house for dinner & supper. Perfect wonderful to be at home. All look so well.

Chapter Ten
"Father's 80th Birthday"

Diary
October 20 – December 31, 1919

October 20, 1919, Home

Mon. Did errands. In afternoon Fritz, Genieve & I drove to Assumption for Father. In evening Father left for Jerseyville. Cora & Eliz. came in for the evening.

October 21, 1919, Home

Tues. Took drive in morning. Mrs. Powell, Ellen, Lena called in afternoon. Guy & Tannie in evening. Had many phone calls.

October 22, 1919, Home

Wed. Mrs. Anderson, Celia & Isobel Bulpet called in a.m. Packed trunk & did errands in afternoon. Eliz., Sam, John, Genieve & Sis & I drove out North Lane for chicken fry. Told family situation.[63] Dr. Pence & Grace came in to spend evening.

---

63 We think that by "the situation" Clara is referring to the ramifications of Strother's alle-
gations that she was a Bolshevik sympathizer. Later she learns that her sometime friend
Jerome Davis has given speeches and quoted her Industrial Survey Report. She is upset
that her remarks in support of some of the structural aspects of Soviet economic life
are taken out of context (see below, November 7 entry). Reading her comments from

October 23, 1919, Travel B & O to Washington

Thurs. Left 7:30 via Flora. Spent time on train thinking out the Russian situation. Gray day, country beautiful with its radiant foliage. Took long walk in Flora.

October 24, 1919, Washington, D.C.

Fri. Spent morning working on Expense acct's. Gloriously beautiful country, arr. 2:30. Mrs. Robbins spoke. Saw many old friends. Had good talk with Bess

October 25, 1919, Washington, D.C.

Sat. At noon hr. Bess & I visited Senate. In afternoon went to Mt. Vernon to see monument. YMCA Recreation Hall in evening. Stayed all night with Anna Owers.

October 26, 1919, Washington, D.C.

Sun. Spent at Vacation House in beautiful suburb. Miss Cratty & Miss Siurus led Vespers—Bess came back to N.Y.

October 27, 1919, Washington, D.C.

Mon. Closing meetings. Girls spoke splendidly & drew up great resolutions to present to N.B. [National Board of the YWCA] Lt. Rise, Packard & Rogers all stopping at hotel. Beautiful pageant.

October 28, 1919, Washington, D.C.

Tues. Opening of Int'l Congress of Working Women. Many great women in Labor World from European countries. Mrs. Robbins presided tea at her hotel.

October 29, 1919, Washington, D.C.

Wed. Opening of Inter'l Labor Conference in Pan American Bldg. King of Belgium visiting capital. Bess left for N.Y. Mrs. Summers came to luncheon with Bess & me. Lt. Rise visited us in evening.

Archangelsk, it is clear that she abhors the violence of the Soviet regime and does not agree with the Bolsheviks.

October 30, 1919, Washington, D.C.
Thurs. Read arrived in afternoon. We had long walk and dinner together getting caught up on all the past months. Bess received satesf state[satisfactory statement?] from Meblou [?] office.

October 31, 1919
Fri. Attend Women's Congress in morning & Int'l Labor in afternoon. Read & I visit Corcean Gallery. Spent evening walking up Capital & Cong'l Lib. city delightful with folk in Hallowe'en costumes.

November 1, 1919, Wash. D.C.
Sat. Spent entire morning in Sec'y conf. decided to employ Sec'y & work for good meeting in Cleveland. Read & I went to St. Mark's for dinner and then to theatre.

November 2, 1919, Wash. D.C.
Sun. Spent day with Cassius L. & Edie. Had tea with Jennie P. packed trunk to leave. Took glorious drive thru Rocky Creek & Arlington cemetery

November 3, 1919, Travel N.Y.
Mon. Left on 11 o'c train for New York. Called on Russian girls. Spent evening on acct's & writing diary.

November 4, 1919, N.Y.
Tues. Spent morning shopping. Bess and Tom [Cotton] were at home to Russian tea to Russian girls & several men. Miss Gosling and I had dinner & talked until late.

November 5, 1919, N.Y.
Wed. Spent day going over Russian material & getting letter off to Marcia. Had dinner at training School with M. McKinley, Parks, Robe & Russian girls.

November 6, 1919
Thurs. Spent day with Bess going over Russian work & plans.

November 7, 1919, N.Y.
Fri. Jerome, Dan & I had dinner with Bess & Tom. J. admits having quoted me in talks over country. Learned that my [Industrial conditions] survey was used for Bol. propaganda.

November 8, 1919, N.Y.
Sat. Went shopping until 4. Met R. & Mrs. Rob at Lib, had tea. Read & I went to see *Hiring Line* in the evening.

November 9, 1919, N.Y.
Sun. Met R. at Grand Central at 9:40. Took train to Ossing. Lunched on Hillside. Walked up to Dam. Had wonderful supper & evening at the Robinson.

November 10, 1919, N.Y.
Mon. Worked on article. Had dinner with Read & went to see De Classe Ethel Barrymore, in evening.

November 11, 1919, N.Y.
Tues. Visited Metropolitan Gallery in P.M., worked on paper. Read & I attended Philadelphia Symphony in evening. Spoke at big Auditorium meeting 4–5:30.

November 12, 1919, N.Y.
Wed. Walked across Brooklyn Bridge at night, called for G. Roche, had dinner at Tree Top Inn. Attended *Clarence* in evening. Bought *Survey* with article.[64] Visited Rands School.

November 13, 1919, N.Y.
Thurs. Visited East Side, attended Olgin's lecture at New School. Had dinner at Penn Hotel, attending opening concert of N.Y. Philharmonic.

November 14, 1919, N.Y.
Fri. Spent afternoon with Read in glorious walk up the Hudson, having

---

64 Clara's Industrial Survey Report written to her bosses at The YWCA was adapted into this article for The Survey magazine. (See bibligraphy)

dinner up at Bieacake and calling on Mrs. Robinson in evening, walked home along drive. More new(s) from State Dept.

November 15, 1919, N.Y.
Sat. Had lunch with Miss Gosling & spent afternoon with her in her room. Met Read & Mrs. Robinson for dinner at Cosmopolitan Club, attending neighborhood Play House on East Side seeing Russian folk dances.

November 16, 1919, N.Y.
Sun. Read & I left on early train up the Hudson, had luncheon on Bull Mt., walking cross to Baege ? Mt. at sun down. Heard Humphries lecture Jewish hall in evening.

November 17, 1919, N.Y.
Mon. Tom & Bess & Read had luncheon with me at College Club. M. O'Connell & I had five o'clock tea and visited until 6:30. Went to Roof Tree Inn with Read for dinner & to see *The Last Lady* at Greenwich Village Theatre.

November 18, 1919, N.Y. travel
Tues. Spent morning at 600. Had meeting with Miss Cratty on State Dept. Situation. Met Read for luncheon. Went up Woolworth tower, took 4:30 train for home!

November 19, 1919, travel
Wed. Spent day reading Bessie Beatty's book *The Red Heart of Russia*. Met Mrs. Shumway & Etta Newcomb in Pana. Arrived home 7:30. What joy!

November 20, 1919, Home
Thurs. Unpacked. spent day being lazy & enjoying the fact of being home. Glorious weather.

November 21, 1919, Home
Fri. Glorious fall weather. unpacking baggage. Treaties defeated in Congress & miners situation still unsettled. Took drive in afternoon.

November 22, 1919, Home
Sat. Mrs. Colegrave, Eliz & us three drove Ednbough, returning to have oyster stew at Eliz. In evening Lt. Primm & Hallock came to call & spend the evening.

November 23, 1919, Home
Sun. Steve Link buried with honors. All soldiers marched with Father. Saw lots of old friends.

November 24, 1919, Home
Mon. At home. Several called in afternoon. Lou and Zell spent evening. Mrs. V and Eugenia called. Noi & Bird.

November 25, 1919, Home
Tues. Mrs. Calegrove, Lis, Eliz & I took long lovely drive. Called in the Downeys & told them about Link & Russia.

November 26, 1919, Home
Wed. Went up to Eliz. in afternoon and Spates. Attended prayer meeting with Father. Bought records in morning.

November 27, 1919, Thanksgiving and Home
Thurs. All family all together at Leslie's house for lovely day. Sang, had wonderful time. Did our Xmas drawing.[65]

November 28, 1919
Fri. Everybody resting up after big Thanksgiving day at Leslie's. Mail from R. R.R. and coal situation. Serious Bol. gaining. Yudurivitch completely routed.

November 29, 1919
Sat. Stayed in bed all morning. Genieve & I called on Noi in afternoon. Cold, hard wind & change in weather

---

65 Because the Taylor family was so large, they traditionally drew names from a hat so that each had only one special person to buy for.

November 30, 1919
Sun. Glorious winter day. All drove out to Spetes for dinner. John & kiddies called in for evening. Cold & clear.

December 1, 1919
Blank

December 2, 1919
Blank

December 3, 1919
Tues. Wed. Father's 80th birthday. Had dinner party—Major Mr. Richardson, Charles Young, & Mrs. Powers

December 4, 1919
Wed. Thurs. Cold & raw. Spent entire day finishing article for Assoc. Monthly. Spent evening with Eliz.

December 5, 1919
Thurs. Fri. We three girls spent afternoon at Fannie's. Spoke in evening for Christian Church. Missionary Society. Schools closed. Little fuel.

December 6, 1919
Fri. Sat. Read. wrote. Went to Eastern Star with Sis. Coal strike continues.

December 7, 1919
Sun. Reception of Women's Club at Mrs. Shumway. Mrs. Turman presenting beautiful roses. Leslie & Eliz. came in for evening.

December 8, 1919
Mon. Mrs. Parker & Mrs. Ray, Mrs. Tiney, Mrs. Deming—Ella Milligan came in afternoon, and Grace & Doctor to play cards in the evening.

December 9, 1919
Tues. Very cold & blizzardy. Mrs. Hoover & Arney spent the evening.

December 10, 1919
Wed. Very cold 4° below. Spent day reading & writing. All went to Presby. ch. for dinner. Big coal strike settled.

December 11, 1919
Thurs. Attended dance with John & Cora at the Fortnightly Club.

December 12, 1919
Fri. Warm & balmy. Lena came in for the day. Leslie & John came down to discuss land proposition with us.

December 13, 1919
Sat. Father & Boyd Dappert left for La. farm. Spent evening reading.

December 14, 1919, Home
Sun. Very cold & little coal. John's family came down for day because cold. We girls went up to Eliz. for evening.

December 15, 1919
Mon. Wrote Xmas letters all evening—gloriously mild and beautiful.

December 16, 1919
Tues. Daisy Mulberry died. Went to Gang party dinner at Celia Bulpit's; The Herdmans & Armstrongs in for evening to visit & play cards.

December 17, 1919
Wed. Drove out to Spates. Letter from Read. Afternoon tea party at Julia Anderson's. Spent evening writing.

December 18, 1919
Blank

December 19, 1919
Thurs. Met train for Daisy Mulburry's remains. Sis & I called in evening. had visit with Pearl & Frank.

December 20, 1919
Fri. Spoke at Baptist Ch. Missionary Society. Daisy Mulberry buried. Had visit with Jay Bond.

December 21, 1919
Sat./Sun. Spoke at Presbyterian Church in the evening, visited at John's in evening.

December 22, 1919
Mon. No callers. Finished shopping. Geo. came on evening train & Father returned from South. All came in for evening. Boyd Doppert & boys talked over farm.

December 23, 1919
Tues. Fritz came on evening train. Spent most of day writing letters & cards, receiving letters from many old friends.

December 24, 1919
Wed. Trenna came. Spent day visiting & doing last things for Xmas. Spent evening playing cards. Trenna & I went to Eliz. for Sam's Xmas.

December 25, 1919, Home
Thurs. Family came about eleven. after dinner had the tree & played games with children. Took walk, called on Armstrongs & Henry's. Had sing around grate fire until 12:30. Beautiful times together. (Last xmas all together.)[66]

December 26, 1919
Fri. All Taylor girls & Mrs. Henry spent afternoon with Fanny Armstrong. Lovely mild weather, pictures from Read, gift from Helen.

December 27, 1919
Sat. The big family party for cards & singing. Had one of the best times that we have had.

---

66 This last parenthetical note may have been added later, perhaps after her father James's death the following year.

December 28, 1919
Sun. Mrs. Henry & Sarah Marjorie came for dinner. All of us went up to Eliz for family supper. Geo & Trenna left for Decatur.

December 29, 1919
Mon. Callers in afternoon to see Muriel. Reds continue to be arrested. Peace Treaty not settled.

Dec. 30, 1919
Tues. All the Spates, Anselms & McCashel came to dinner. Dalbys in evening. Everybody dead tired. Weather like early Spring. Less [Leslie] and John went to La.

Dec. 31, 1919
Wed. Fritz left for Terra Haute. Weather remarkably mild & lovely.

APPENDIX I

Foreign Intervention into the Russian Civil War 1918–1919

We found three chronicles about this period written by US servicemen that were valuable in putting Clara's experiences into context.[67] All three of these books provide a scathing portrayal of the military events in Northern Russia between November 1918 and July 1919 when the last US troops withdrew from Arkhangelsk. The International Expedition in North Russia was officially closed on October 12, 1919, when the last British civilians left Murmansk.

Ralph Albertson's 1920 book, *Fighting without a War*, is a particularly harsh account of the events. Albertson was a Congregational minister from New York City who was sent by the YMCA to work in Russia in the fall of 1918.[68] He was put in charge of all YMCA work for the Vaga column until June 1919, after which he headed up the evacuation of Allied YMCA personnel, supplies, and equipment from the Dvina and Vaga fronts. He was among the last of the US civilians to leave northern Russia on September 2, 1919. In his book, he lays the blame for the mission's failure firmly on the British:

> The expedition called for military skill and it called for leadership, sympathy, social skill. There was a sad failure to realize that

---

67 Links to these open access e-books are found in the bibliography.

68 Albertson is listed under noncombatants on the Honor Roll of Volume 3, Number 4, September 1918, The Quill: A Magazine of Greenwich Village. He visited the YWCA women (see Clara's diary, June 15, 1919), and was among the regular visitors to the Hostess Houses.

an expedition of this sort is bound to run into social and political problems that are quite as important, perhaps more so, than
mere military practice. The management of this campaign has
ignored all social and political considerations that might have
contributed to its success or failure and has blundered stupidly
whenever these matters have forced themselves to the front. . . .
The failure of the North Russian Expedition was the failure of
the British to make friends of the Russian people.
(Albertson 1920, XIII "The White Man's Burden,")

Albertson's reasons for the inability of the international intervention to
succeed in the goals of the mission are echoed by Moore, et al., throughout
the 1920 book *The History of the American Expedition fighting the Bolsheviki:
Campaigning in North Russia 1918–1919*, and in Lieutenant John Cudahy's
1924 book *Archangel: The American War with Russia*. All three sources agree
that the mutual distrust and downright hatred between the Russians and
the British was a significant contributor to the mission's failure. The British
officers despised what they saw as a barbarian culture of the Russians. The
Russians resented the interference in their politics. The British hated the
rough food; the Russians resented the superior attitudes and colonialism
of the British. There were few successful partnerships between the British
military command and the Russian troops.

A terrible example of this tension occurred on December 10, 1918.
Moore called the event "both pitiful and aggravating" (Moore, et al., 1920,
161). Men of the Slavo-British Allied Legion expressed grievances against
their British officers and refused to leave their barracks in Arkhangelsk
when called to the front. Orders came from General Headquarters to the
American HQ Company to fire on the Russians in their barracks. The
Americans were horrified but followed orders. Several Russians soldiers
were killed. (See above, introduction to Part Two for more details about
this event.) Other mutinies by the Russians serving under British commanders occurred at Troitsa and Onega in July 1919.

Albertson states that the inability of the British to understand the
Russian mind, the lack of respect for the Russian character, a generalized
tactlessness in dealing with the Russians, "the stupid propaganda conducted
by the British," and perhaps equally as significant, British war-weariness

combined to create hostile feelings between the groups that were meant to be allies against the Bolshevik Revolution (Albertson 1920, Chapter XIII). It was not just the Russian troops who bore hateful actions from British officers. Moore's book contains accounts of American servicemen who were on the receiving end of nasty and at times dangerous orders by the British command. Clara's diary and letters also mentioned the tension between the American and British command. She was uncharacteristically forthright in her letters in June and July of 1919, as things were winding down for the Allies. As always, she strove to be fair and, while chastising the British command for their dangerous ineptitude, she also recounted the kindness and consideration of some of the Englishmen (see letter dated May 14, 1919, above).

The men of the North Russian Expeditionary Force were from America, England, Canada, France, Italy, and Serbia. The British War Office was in command. The story of why nearly 2,700 American soldiers were killed or wounded in an undeclared war, after the November 1918 armistice ended the "Great War," is complex. Due largely to the effective censorship by both the US and British governments, the lack of domestic political support, and the vagaries of the communication systems,[69] the general public knew little to nothing of the events.

What we do know is that the action was never sanctioned by the US Congress—war was never declared against the Bolsheviks or Soviet government—and that President Wilson only reluctantly committed US troops to the effort. This reluctance and underestimation of the forces required was noted as a contributing factor to the mission's failure to contain Bolshevik activity.

The 5,500 US troops committed to the mission consisted of the 339th US Army Infantry, one battalion of the 310th Engineers, the 337th Field Hospital, and the 337th Ambulance Company under the command of Col. George E. Stewart. Many of the men were from Minnesota and Wisconsin. The assumption was that these men would be better accustomed to the harsh winter weather found in northern Russia than other servicemen. The troops were detached from the 85th Division (on its way to France) and sent

---

69 Although diplomatic, general, and military postal services functioned quite well by this time, along with the operation of a telegraph system, the difficulties of communicating with icebound Arkhangelsk upriver from the White Sea cannot be overestimated.

to southern England in the summer of 1918. After a short period of training, they left Newcastle upon Tyne, England, for Arkhangelsk, Russia, on August 25, 1918. The US troops arrived at Arkhangelsk, a teeming port city on the Dvina River in North Russia, on September 4, 1918.

Landscape and history of the region

Arkhangelsk is the capital of the Arkhangelsk Oblast (an administrative region or province) of Northern Russia. The city lies fifteen miles up the Diva River (nearly due south of the White Sea coast) and 600 miles north of Moscow, and is approximately 140 miles below the Arctic Circle. Unlike its closest sister city, Murmansk (319 nautical miles north east, and 2° north of the Arctic Circle), the Arkhangelsk port is icebound much of the year.

The land at the mouth of the North Dvina river boasted an established trading port as early as the tenth century. In the 1100s, Novgorodians from the south founded the Mikhailo-Arkhangelsk (Saint Michael the Archangel) Monastery. The city that then grew from the trading port was given the name Arkangelsk.

Tsar Ivan IV ("The Terrible")[70] had a fortress built in 1584, and thereafter Russian trade with British and Dutch interests was solidified. Arkhangelsk was the only seaport for the Muscovite Kingdom until Tsar Peter I ("The Great")[71] established St. Petersburg in 1703 (in part due to the fact that the port at Arkhangelsk was icebound five months of the year). The establishment of St. Petersburg and subsequent restrictions Peter placed on trade in the White Sea diverted most Russian sea trade to the Baltic. Thereafter, as a kind of compensation, Arkhangelsk became the capital of the Oblast, giving the city both diplomatic and administrative status. In the 1800s, the city became a large cosmopolitan center, grounded in the fisheries, sea mammal harvest, fur, and timber trades, with a well-established and busy cargo vessel port. Thousands of pilgrims still journey to the Solovetsky Monastery in June when the seas around the monastery's island are free of ice. This center of Orthodox Russian contemplation was founded in 1436 and was to become one of the richest and most influential of the country's

---

70 Ivan IV Vasilyevich (1530–1584), first Tsar of Russia.

71 Peter I Pyotr Alekseevich (1672–1725) ruled the Tsardom of Russia and then the Russian Empire.

monasteries. The visit Clara and her friends made to the site in the summer of 1919 was one of her favorite memories and was a welcome interlude of respite during that intense year.

From the late 1800s into the mid twentieth century, the city had the largest timber industry (harvesting, milling, and exporting) in Russia. According to contemporary accounts, there were twenty-six sawmills employing 11,000 workers in 1914. In addition to being a thriving port for trade goods, Arkhangelsk became an important home base for the exploration of the Arctic. The Northern Sea Route for shipping also was developed at this time, facilitating the delivery of military supplies from Western Europe and the United States into the Russian Empire during the early stages of World War I. In 1915, an icebreaking bureau was opened, with thirteen ships that provided escorts into the White Sea from Arkhangelsk during winter navigation.

The landscape of the interior areas of the Arkhangelsk Oblast is made up of taiga (spruce, larch, and pine lowlands) with extensive meadows and swamps between the rivers. The Northern Dvina is the largest river flowing north to the White Sea. It drains most of northwestern Russia. Its tributaries include the Pinecha (Pinega), and Vaga rivers, along which fighting fronts were established in 1918. Further to the east, the Onega River (along which another front was built) also flows northwards. It connects Lake Lacha with the Onega Bay on the White Sea southeast of Arkhangelsk.

By the time of the Russian Civil War and Clara Taylor's involvement with the Expedition, the city of Arkhangelsk was a flourishing metropolis of markets, hospitals, sawmills, and industries, with an established population of merchants buying and selling goods. There were soldiers, farmers, industrialists, journalists, diplomats, transportation infrastructures, religious and educational institutions, prisons, and churches—all of the elements of a busy society. In 1918, possession of the city was contested by the new Soviet government, the Red Army, the White Russians, and the international interests of the Allied Northern Expeditionary Force. It was into a military mission Clara and her colleagues of the YWCA were invited during what Russian historians refer to as the Foreign Intervention.

Here is what the US soldiers saw from the harbor as they arrived on the British troop ships Sept. 4, 1918:

. . . the city of Archangel affords an interesting view. Hulks of boats and masts and cordage and docks and warehouses in the front, with muddy streets. Behind, many buildings, grey-weathered ones and white painted ones topped with many chimneys, and towering here and there a smoke stack or graceful spire or dome with minarets.
(Moore, et al., 1920, 39)

Moore describes the city as built on a low promontory jutting into the Dvina River and notes that the city appears to be mostly waterfront: "In fact it is only a few blocks wide, but it is crescent shaped with one horn in Smoly (a southern suburb having dock and warehouse areas), and the other in Solombola in the north, a city half as large as Archangel and possessing of saw-mills, shipyards, hospitals, seminary and a hard reputation" (Moore, et al., 1920, 40).

"Why are we here?"

To step back a minute, it is important to understand the political climate in Arkhangelsk during and after the 1917 Bolshevik revolution. Once Moscow and Petrograd fell to the Reds in November, 1917, there was a short time before any Bolshevik decrees were received in northern Russia. This gap was enough time for anti-Bolshevik members of the former Provisional Government to set up a Revolutionary Committee in Arkhangelsk that sought to maintain the status quo. For three months they succeeded in ignoring Bolshevik directives (Rhodes 1984, 393). However, by February 1918, there was increasing unrest. There were 6,000 Russian soldiers in the White Sea fleet who were pro-Bolshevik, and they were on edge. Felix Cole, the American Vice Consul in Arkhangelsk, reported that those sailors began to "conduct themselves more and more arrogantly" in January 1918 (Rhodes 1984, 393). Once Commissar Mikhail S. Kedrov arrived from Moscow, the Bolsheviks gained complete control over the region on February 8, 1918.[72] He appointed Mikel Tchikowski as president of the Arkhangelsk Soviet. It was a bloodless coup. Directives from Moscow

---

72 Kedrov was a psychopathically brutal man and is credited with establishing the death camps where White Army personnel were murdered en masse. Those camps started

merely eliminated the office of Naval Commander, and the Worker's and Soldier's Deputies of the Arkhangelsk Soviet voted the Revolutionary Committee out of existence. It was at this point that the Bolsheviks began to ship the military stores left in Arkhangelsk by the Allies (for the purpose of defending the Provisional Government against the Germans) south to the interior of the country. The stores were moved concurrently with the signing of the Brest-Litovsk treaty between the Soviets and Germany (March 3, 1918), which removed Russia from the still ongoing Great War.

To the dismay of Allied command, the military stores that they sent over 14,000 international troops to guard had simply been shipped south and neatly fell into the Red Army's coffers. In April, US Consul DeWitt Poole arrived in Murmansk to lay the groundwork for US intervention, and on May 24, 1918, British Major General Fredrick C. Poole landed in Murmansk with troops to bolster the British naval forces already holding Penchenga and the Kola Peninsula, west of Arkhangelsk. Officially, the Allied mission was to guard the region against the potential establishment of a German submarine base, to draw off German troops from the European theater of war, to thwart the potential exploitation of natural resources by the Germans, then to seize the war munitions at Archangel and Vladivostok (Cudahy 1924, 24). Neither the diplomat nor the commander realized that the military supplies they had been sent to secure had vanished months before.

In July, US president Woodrow Wilson agreed to a send a limited number of US troops to support the Allies against the Red Army. The ensuing US State Department document defined the role of US participation: three infantry battalions and three companies of army engineers would be sent to Arkhangelsk to join the British. A small force would also be sent to Vladivostok, which Czecho-Slovak troops had claimed as an Allied protectorate early in July. The US State Department outlined the Allied responsibilities in Russia this way: "Each of the associated powers has the single object of affording such aid as shall be acceptable, and only such aid as shall be acceptable, to the Russian people in their endeavor to regain control of their own affairs, their own territory, and their own destiny" (History.com Ed. 2009). A memo from President Wilson dated

---

the labor camp system of the Gulag which the Soviets utilized to kill or contain their enemies throughout their time in power (Golysheva 2020).

July 17 limited participation to only two tasks: in the west, US troops were to guard military stores, and in the east, they were to aide the Czech legions. The ambiguity of this memo later allowed British command to infer that the Americans were to protect the stores wherever the supplies were located—justifing the assignment of American troops to chase down the railroad lines in pursuit of the Red Army, which had removed the stores southward (Rhodes 1984).

The first US troops arrived in Arkhangelsk on September 4, 1918. They were told that they would take on guard duty for military munitions and provide protection for American diplomats in the city. In addition, the US troops were to protect British and French forces currently under fire from Red Army troops south of the city. Commander in Chief General Frederick Poole did not receive information that restricted the placement of the Americans, and Ambassador David Francis did not so inform him until it was too late to recall the US troops from the front lines where they had been sent upon arrival (Rhodes 1984). This was just the beginning act of further miscommunications and misunderstandings between British and American military men that would create havoc and much bad feeling.

After the Armistice of November 11, 1918, the morale of the international troops in general, but of the American soldiers in particular, plummeted. The men endured severe snow storms, below zero temperatures, swampy mud, densely forested landscapes, and an enemy who was well organized and equipped. The futility of the venture became more and more apparent to the men and to their commanders. The primary accounts from soldiers and officers read for this book are distressing. No one could tell the men why they were fighting, the British command was widely seen as incompetent, skirmishes with the Bolshevik soldiers native to the region were disastrous for the Allies, and the entire show was ill-managed. American servicemen greatly resented being under British command, and British officers had nothing but contempt for the US troops. This contempt did not, however, preclude sending US troops into battle in unconscionably unsafe, stupid scenarios with fatal consequences.

Results of the Expedition

According to a dispatch sent October 25, 1919, from Major General Maynard, Commander of the Allied forces in Murmansk, to the British War Office, "The most satisfactory of all results obtained, however, was the creation of a Northern Russian Army, which, if properly handled, promises to be capable of dealing successfully with any Bolshevik attempt to regain power within the Murmansk Region" (Maynard to Rawlinson 1919). This prediction would prove to be vastly overstated. Murmansk was abandoned by the British on October 12, 1919, after successive failures to recruit soldiers for the Northern Russian Army, repeated defeats in battles on the Kola peninsula from stronger than expected Red Army forces, and a collapse of Allied relationships between Serbs, Finns, Russians, and British.

American soldier Lt. John Cudahy (of the machine gunners of the 1st Battalion of the 339th Infantry) believed that the defeat of the North Russian Expedition was due directly to the incompetence of command. Cudahy noted that there was an inadequate number of men who were thinly spread on six fighting fronts with limited communication between them, severe underestimation of the strength of and local support for the Red Army, ignorance of the overall situation and Allied commitment, want of a definite moral purpose, and British conceit and arrogance that destroyed initially trusting relationships with local Russians as well as Allies. His book portrays a failed mission that had no support from the American public, that was unwanted by the local populations, and that ended ignominiously for the survivors.

We had waged war upon Russia. . . . had engaged in an unprovoked intensive, inglorious, little armed conflict which had ended in disaster and disgrace. . . . and great was the cost of the campaign [with] 2,485 casualties of killed and wounded and sickened men, its financial loss, over ten times the price paid Russia for the vast dominions of Alaska. There was not a man in the ranks who did not sense the disgrace in our ignoble desertion.
(Cudahy 1924, 211)

On the 27th of March, 1918, the Allied military attachés of Italy, France, England, and the United States had met in Moscow and unanimously agreed that intervention into Russian affairs was required. The Supreme War Council at Versailles agreed. Troops were ordered to both the eastern and western edges of the Russian Federation's borders. In April, US Consul DeWitt Clinton Poole arrived in Murmansk to organize American military involvement. On May 24, British Major General Poole arrived in Murmansk to assume command of the Allied Forces in North Russia. US troops arrived in Arkhangelsk on September 4, 1918. One tumultuous, deadly and disastrous year later, by October 12, 1919, all international troops had shipped out of North Russia. On February 21, 1920, the Red Army swept into Arkhangelsk to the cheers of the populace, completing the defeat of the Allied Intervention, and assuring the military success of the Bolshevik Revolution and the subsequent establishment of the Union of Soviet Socialist Republics.

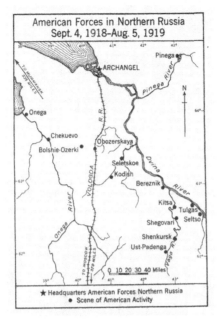

Sketch map showing the fighting fronts and railroad lines south of the city of
Arkhangelsk where the men of the US "Polar Bear" expedition forces of North
Russia engaged the Red Army.
(The Battery Press, Nashville, TN https://wdet.org/
posts/2018/12/28/87636-tale-of-the-michigan-polar-bears/)

Verst 455 on the railway south of Arkhangelsk (Vologda Railway) where the YWCA
staff assisted the YMCA canteen car service. This outpost was nicknamed "Fort
Nichols" in honor of the commanding officer Major Brooks Nichols.
He was a frequent guest at the YW parties.
(US Official Photograph 161108, found in Moore, 1920)

Soldiers receiving snacks and supplies out of the Canteen Car at Verst 455, "Fort Nichols". Clara Taylor served at this site in April, 1919.
(US Official Photograph, found in Moore, 1920)

Soldiers writing letters and relaxing at the YMCA Hut at Obozerskya.
(US Official Photograph, found in Moore, 1920)

These are the women of the YWCA staff in Arkhangelsk, stationed with the North Russia Expeditionary Forces from October 1918 to August 1919. (Clara Taylor, center back row.)
(Unknown, YWCA papers, Sophia Smith Collection, Smith College Archives)

APPENDIX II

Principal Persons of the North Russian Expeditionary Force

Fighting Participants:

British Royal Navy

British Royal Marines

French Artillery Brigade

French Foreign Legion

Canadian Troops

Czech-Slovak Troops

North Russian Army

Russian Railroad Guard

Slavo-British Allied Legion (local volunteers and former POWs from Red Army in Kola Peninsula region organized by Poole, May 1918)

United States Infantry and Engineers

Italian Expeditionary Force

Serbian Troops[73]

Total international troops: 14,000

White Russian troops: 1,500

---

73 The Italian and Serbian forces joined the Allies on the Kola Railroad in the summer of 1918; they were not players in the Arkhangelsk conflicts.

Slavo-British Allied Legion: 3,000

US Forces:

339th Infantry

310th Engineers 1st Battalion

337th Ambulance Company

337th Field Hospital Company, Consisting of 5,500 men under Col. George E. Stewart (replaced by General Richardson in April 1919)

Fighting against:

White Finns (supplied by Germany *and* anti-Bolshevik)

Red Army

Red Guards

Russian sailors

Lett troops

Allied Military Leadership
British

Major General Frederick C. Poole: Commander Allied Forces, Arkhangelsk May 24, 1918, to September 30, 1918.

Field Marshal William Edmund Ironside: Commander of Allied Forces, Arkhangelsk March 18, 1919; takes command at Obozerskaya (Vologda Forces); replaces Maj. Gen. Poole September 30, 1918, to October 26, 1919.

Major General Maynard: Commander of Allied Forces, Murmansk, June 23, 1918, to February 28, 1919.

Brigadier General Robert G. Finlayson: Deputy Commander, North Russian Force, June 23, 1918, to 1918.

General Lord Rawlinson: Commander in Chief of Allied Forces, August

11, 1919, to October 12, 1919. Objective: to complete the orderly evacuation of Allied Troops from North Russia; decides to begin with Arkhangelsk, then withdraw from Murmansk.

British Rear Admiral Thomas Kemp.

Americans

Captain Zachariah H. Maddison, of US Cruiser *Des Moines.*

Col. George E. Stewart, Commander of American Forces in North Russia.

Russians

General Miller, the Russian White Army Commander at Archangel.

People's Commissar Mikhil Kedrov (1878–1941), head of Arkhangelsk Soviet and ardent Bolshevik.

Special Commissar Natzaremus, sent by the Moscow Soviet to Murmansk in May 1918 to negotiate the protection of the Kola peninsula by the Allies.

Russian General Georgi Tchaplin, assisted Poole with August 1918 revolt in Arkhangelsk allowing the Allies to land and secure the city; monarchist.

Other important people at Arkhangesk mentioned in Clara Taylor's letters

Diplomats

US Ambassador David R. Francis.

US Vice Consul Felix Cole, Charge d'Affaires, Arkhangelsk, 1917 to 1919.

Consul Peter Pierce, University of Wisconsin graduate, and friend of Clara Taylor's.

Lieutenant Colonel Fredrick Burry, US Chief of Staff.

Consul Shelby Strother, Harvard University alum (sometimes spelled "Strouthers" in Clara's diary); see note at beginning of Chapter Five, above.

Consul DeWitt Clinton Poole, Jr. (1885–1953) American diplomat and spymaster. Expert in anti-communist propaganda and psychological tactics in political warfare. Special Assistant to the Ambassador at Arkhangelsk with rank of Counselor to Embassy. University of Wisconsin graduate. (Oral account of his experiences in Russia 1917 to 1919 at UW Press Blog: *An American Diplomat in Bolshevik Russia*).

Red Cross

Lieutenant Colonel Raymond Robins, Head of the US Red Cross Commission to Russia from December 1971 to May 1918.

Major Allen Wardwell, Head of American Red Cross from May to October 1918.

Miss Gosling and Miss Foerster: Nurses at the US Red Cross Hospital.

Others

Jerome Davis (1891–1976) arrived in Russia in May 1916 as a YMCA worker in prisoner of war camps. In June, 1916, appointed national Army Work Secretary for Russia. He supported the Bolsheviks and was opposed to US intervention. He later became a Professor of Divinity at Yale University, where he was fired in 1936 for his labor organizing activities.

APPENDIX III

The Military Mission in North Russia
The Fighting Fronts

In addition to the forces fighting on the Kola Peninsula commanded from Murmansk and the actions southwest of Murmansk in the Karelia lands, the following fronts were established that radiated to the east and south from the city of Arkhangelsk. The timeline below incorporates all of the major actions at each front. Included for reference are notes about the movements of the YWCA women and their colleagues.

River Forces:

Dvina River Front: The railhead at Kotlas, 300 miles southeast of Arkhangelsk, was the objective; these forces advanced to Toulgas, 200 miles up river.

Vaga River Front: This was the most advanced front line, 40 miles south of Toulgas at the town of Shenkurst.

Forest and Railroad Forces: Rail lines from Arkhangelsk to junction at Vologda. The objective was Plesetskaya, 130 miles south of Arkhangelsk; but that town was never taken by the Allies.

Vologda Forces:

Onega Valley: 90 miles west of Arkhangelsk at mouth of Onega River. The Bolshie Ozerki battle was the last major fighting for Allies.

Pinega Valley: Near the White Sea coast 80 miles east of Arkhangelsk.

Kodish Front: Between the railway and the Dvina River; town of Seletskoe, center of Yemtsa River area ~100 miles south of Archangel.

Guard Duty within the city of Archangel was maintained throughout the Expedition.

Overview of Major Battles and Political Events in North Russia 1916–1919

1916

August/September US Vice Consul Felix Cole arrives Arkhangelsk, replaces Carl Loewe. Cole argues that military intervention is not a good idea, but that the US should send food to North Russia. Ambassador Francis disagrees.

October 4 The Murman Oblast becomes a semi-autonomous region of Russia. The Arkhangelsk Oblast is anti-Bolshevik at this time.

1917

Winter The British North Russian Naval Squadron under Rear Admiral Kemp arrives in Murmansk at the invitation of the local Soviet to secure the Kola Peninsula against German and White Finn forces.

April 6 US declares war on Germany.

November 5 The Anti-Bolshevik Revolutionary Committee in Arkhangelsk seeks to maintain the status quo. The British North Russian Naval Squadron proceeds to hold Kola Peninsula and Pechenga in cooperation with the White Russian Army against White Finns and Germans.

Goals of Allied Command:

1. Prevent Germany from establishing a submarine base at Murmansk

2. Prevent German troops in Finland from joining the Western Front

3. Support the Russian Army [pre-Armistice]

Clara Taylor and Marcia Dunham join Bessie Boies, Catherine Childs, Muriel Heap, Elizabeth Dickerson, and Helen Ogden of the YWCA in Petrograd.

December 1 The 6th Bolshevik Army (Red Army) stationed at Vologda is the primary Allied enemy after the Armistice.

YWCA women leave Petrograd for Moscow.

December 15 The Bolshevik-Central Powers Armistice is signed.

December 30 The YWCA headquarters in Madam Morozoff's house in Moscow is opened.

1918

January US President Wilson gives "Fourteen Points" speech to Congress outlining his vision of post-war Europe.

Soviets change their calendar: February 1–13 is eliminated so that as of February 14, 1918, Russian dates match up with the Western Gregorian calendar.

February 8 The Arkhangelsk Soviet's Revolutionary Committee is overturned by Bolsheviks; Commissar Kedrov takes command, sends the munitions and food stores in Arkhangelsk to the south via railroads. (Those supplies had been sent by the Allies to support the Provisional Government against the Germans. To protect them against Germans capture was the point of sending US troops to North Russia.)

March 3 Soviets sign Brest–Litovsk Treaty, creating a separate peace with Germany. Pressure on the Allies to send troops increases. Vice Consul Cole is opposed, but Ambassador Francis becomes pro-intervention.

March 7 YWCA women and other Americans evacuated from Moscow by train to Samara.

March 12 Bolsheviks move the capital city to Moscow and establish a central government, and declare Russia a Soviet State.

April US Consul DeWitt Poole arrives in Murmansk to organize American involvement in the North Russian Expeditionary Force.

April 9 Clara Taylor and colleagues return to Moscow from Samara.

May 2 Ambassador Francis wires the US State Department to initiate military intervention in North Russia.

May 10 American Consul Summer dies in Moscow.

May 1 Clara Taylor receives permission from Commissar Melanchanski to visit factories in Moscow.

May 24 British Major General Poole arrives in Murmansk and assumes command of "Allied Force in North Russia." The Kola peninsula is held by the Allied ground force. The City of Pechenga is held by British Naval forces.

May 29 400 Royal British Marines arrive in Murmansk. Special Commissar Natzaremus is sent from the Moscow Soviet to negotiate an agreement with Allies for protection of Kola Peninsula. (Natzaremus is a "slippery, treacherous fellow," writes Ambassador Francis.)

June Clara Taylor visits 220 factories in and around Moscow in June and July.

June 7 Allied troops drive White Finns out of Kem and occupy the area. (White Finns were the forces representing the refugee government under Pehr Evind Svinhufvud and the 1st Finnish Independent Senate. Whites opposed "Red Finns," who were the Finnish Socialist Worker's Republic during 1918 Finnish Civil War. Svinhufvud was pro-German and anti-Soviet.) Moscow is put under martial law. Bolsheviks arrest 1,000 counter-revolutionaries.

June 8 The Moscow Soviet announces that the Allied presence in North is a breach of the Brest–Litovsk Treaty, and demands the withdrawal of international troops.

June 9 100 US enlisted men and 8 officers land at Murmansk, Lieut. Henry F. Floyd in command.

June 18 Russian General A. Zankevitch is rescued from murder by his own troops, joins General Poole's "Slavo-British Allied Legion."

June 23 Major General Maynard and troops arrive Murmansk. (These troops stay in Murmansk for the duration of the campaign.) Brigadier General Finlayson arrives in Murmansk; troops are sent to Arkhangelsk fronts. Commissar Kedrov demands the immediate withdrawal of Allied war ships at Arkhangelsk. Maynard stays at Murmansk with 7,000 Allied troops + 9,000 local Russians. Finlayson and Poole, (later, Ironside) are stationed at Archangel with 37,000 Allied troops:

June 25 Red Guards in Kola Peninsula are disarmed, and Karelina district is secured by Allies.

June 26 The pro-Bolshevik Arkhangelsk Soviet declares martial law in the city.

June 30 The Murman Soviet severs relationships with the Moscow Central Government, defies Moscow's orders to force Allies out; requests assistance from Allies to hold the district against Germans. Allied command agrees to stay and assist. Allies believe that Arkhangelsk is being fortified by the Red Army (Bolsheviks), but in fact is being evacuated, supplies and armaments taken south and the river railroad bridges destroyed. The Dvina River is mined by the Red Army as they retreat.

The YWCA staff moves into a new apartment in Moscow, Clara Taylor visits silk and candy factories.

July 6 US President Wilson agrees to send troops to Siberia in Northern Russia. German Ambassador Mirback is assassinated in Moscow.

July 7 Murman Soviet signs agreement with the British, French, and US, formalizing the Allied Expedition on the Murman coast.

Clara Taylor reports gunfire in the streets of Moscow. The telephone and telegraph offices are captured by counter revolutionaries in morning, but re-taken by Bolsheviks in the afternoon.

2nd week July Maynard takes full command of southern portions of Kola Peninsula.

July 16 The Russian Czar and family are murdered at Yekaterinburg. Clara Taylor notes in her diary that the Bolsheviks admit to killing the Royals. President Wilson signs a memo limiting US troops to guard duty and aiding Czech troops only. Tensions rise in Arkhangelsk as Kedrov discovers the British presence in Murmansk. Wilson's memo is never communicated to British Brig. Gen Poole, and therefore American troops are immediately sent to the river and railroad fronts south of Arkhangelsk when they arrive.

July 26 A French battalion arrives in Murmansk.

July 30 Poole receives intelligence that "friends" (including Russian Gen. Georgi Tchaplin) will stage a revolt in Arkhangelsk on the night of July 31. The coup's leaders request that the Allies occupy city immediately. Poole and 400 troops sail from Murmansk to Arkhangelsk.

July 31 Poole's troops capture island of Modyugski [Morzhovets] in White Sea (just outside of the mouth of River Dvina).

August 2–3 1,450 British troops and 50 US servicemen arrive in Arkhangelsk and secure the city's waterfront. Poole takes command of city. Bolsheviks complete their retreat by boat and rail. Allies are welcomed by government and President M. Tchaikovsky.

Clara Taylor reports "conditions very serious" in Moscow, disturbing times in Petrograd.

August 8 Clara Taylor, Marcia Dunham, Bessie Boies, Catherine Childs, Muriel Heap, and Helen Ogden of the YWCA, plus other foreigners in Moscow, are evacuated by rail to Niji Novogrod for safety from German and Bolshevik soldiers who are occupying Moscow.

August 25 US troops embark from Newcastle on Tyne, England, bound for "guard duty" and to protect diplomats in Arkhangelsk.

YWCA women and other foreign nationals travel back to Moscow from Niji Novgorod.

September 2 The YWCA women and all foreign nationals from Moscow cross the border bridge into Finland from Petrograd, out of Soviet territory.

September 4 British troopships *Somali, Tydeus, Nagoya* land at Arkhangelsk with US forces. The Allied "Vologda Force" occupies Oboserskaia. US forces and Slavo-British-Allied Legion under Lt-Col. Guard occupy Onega. The 2d Battalion of the US 339th Infantry disembark at Smolny to "protect Diplomatic Corp and guard supplies." However, the troops receive orders by British command to protect British and French troops who are under fire from Bolshevik forces south of the city, and are immediately sent to succor those troops. The Red Army establishes five fronts south of Arkhangelsk on railroads and rivers.

September 5 US 339th Infantry Companies I, L, and K fortify "Kodish Front" after traveling from Arkhangelsk via railroad to Obozerskaya (British Major Young in command). Russian Col. Tschaplin stages a coup d'état against president. Tchaikowsky's Arkhangelsk government. Labor strikes in the city turn violent.

September 7 The US 310th Engineers arrive in Arkhangelsk.

September 8 120 US troops under Donoghue move out to rescue Scottish, French, and American sailors surrounded by Bolsheviks in area east of Oberzerskaya.

September 11 Allied "Railroad and Forest Front/Vologda Forces" encounter Bolshevik Red Army at Verst 466; Allies take the bridge at Verst 464. US Company K engages Reds at Seletskoe-Kodish Front. President Tchaikowsky is returned to power after US Ambassador Francis convinces Tschaplin to stand down. The Strategic Plan was to connect the Kodish-Onega and Railroad Fronts and push onto Plesetskya, however, this push failed.

The YWCA women rest in Stockholm.

September 15 US "River Forces" of 339th travel up Dvina River from Beresnik, engaging Red Army troops. Company A ("Vaga River Forces") travel via steamship up Dvina to Skenkurst. Company H ("Onega Front Forces") take possession of Onega city.

September 16 Kodish Forces (US Companies K and D) fight at Seletskoe.

September 17 US Company A takes possession of Skenhurst from fleeing Red Army troops.

September 18 US Company H is ordered to Chekuevo.

September 19 The Allied River Forces engage and dislodge Reds at Seltso; then return to Yakavlevskays (north of Seltso).

September 20 The Vaga River Forces advance to Rovdinskaya under fire.

September 23–26 The Allies occupy Seletskoe. US Lt. Ballard arrives with American gunners. They engage in fierce battles, and establish entrenchments. Companies K, L, M, and G report six killed, 24 wounded.

September 24 The Battle at Chekuevo occurs, and the Allies hold the city.

October Gen. Ironside takes over Command from Poole. A Provisional Government is established in Arkhangelsk. Gen. Maynard is at Murmansk with 7,000 Allies and 9,000 locals. Gen. Ironside is at Arkhangelsk with 37,000 Allied troops.

October 2 Clara Taylor, Elizabeth Dickerson, Helen Ogden, Catherine Childs, Marcia Dunham, Bessie Boies, and other foreign nationals begin journey to Arkhangelsk railroad through northern Norway.

October 8 Vaga River Forces take village of Puiya, then retreat to Rovdinskaya. The Strategic Plan is to have railroad troops push down to Plesetskaya. Vologda troops go to Velsk, but R. R. troops are stopped by the Bolsheviks near Yemtsa settlement. Other troops are on the Dvina River at Toulgas. This distribution of troops caused the smallest force (at Vaga) to be stuck at the most forward position, and therefore the plan failed.

The American women and colleagues board a ship at Narvik and travel around fjords to Kirkenes on their way to Arkhangelsk.

October 9 US Company H (Onega River Forces) under Cpt. Gevers' command establishes Headquarters at Onega.

Oct. 4–Nov. 15 The Dvina River Offensive occurs.

October 12 US Companies K and L (Kodish Forces), and 3d Battalion of 339th Infantry under Cpt. Donoghue cross River Yemtsa and engage Bolsheviks. Reds flee Kodish with extensive losses.

October 13–16 The Forest and Railroad Forces consisting of US and French troops advance to Versts 455, 457 and 458, skirmishing with Red Army troops along the way.

Clara Taylor and her colleagues arrive in Arkhangelsk.

October 14 The Dvina Forces (1st Battalion of 339th Infantry) retreat to Toulgas after the Bolsheviks return down-river and regain Seltso. **October 17** US forces dig in at Kodish.

October 18 The Plan is abandoned, and Allied troops all withdraw from Rovdinskaya to Ust Padenga.

October 19 The Onega River Forces advance on both sides of River from Chekuevo. Bolsheviks retreat to Turchesova. Verst 445 is won by the Allies. Allies at Onega dig in to wait out winter; throughout December they engage in skirmishes with Bolsheviks.

The American women settle into work for the war effort, get the Hostess House set up, and establish routines of canteen and hospital work.

October 20 US Company G (Penega Valley Forces) is dispatched from Arkhangelsk to Penega, where they set up a garrison and recruit 300 local volunteers. Bolsheviks gather forces up Pinega Valley. The townspeople beg Allies for protection and to secure stores of flour.

October 23 US Company B and Scottish troops defeat Bolsheviks at Touglas.

October 29 The Red Army troops retreat to Avda.

October 30 The Vaga Forces Company A is relieved by Company C plus

Canadian artillery. US Company F under Captain Ramsay, which had been on guard in Arkhangelsk since September, now move out to Yemetskoe up the Dvina River to protect communications and trails; these troops are scattered from Khalmogori (90 versts North of Yemet) to Morjegorskaya (55 versts South).

Bessie Boies and Muriel Heap leave Arkhangelsk. Boies to London and NY seeking more help; Heap goes to her family in France due to her mother's death.

November The Railroad Front/Vologda Forces dig in at Verst 445.The port of Arkhangelsk is now frozen in. 25,000 Russian forces have been trained by British officers. There are over 100 American civilians now in Arkhangelsk.

The Red Cross, military command, YMCA, and the Russian government all ask for help from Clara Taylor and her colleagues for hosting parties, hospital work, morale support, propaganda, and library work.

November 1–3 Kodish Front forces engage in fierce battles with Bolsheviks at Verst 17. Lt. Ballard and his gunners engage with enemy.

November 4 The Bolsheviks take Verst 17. Forest and Railroad Forces repel Reds at Verst 455. An accidental bombing of Allied troops by an Allied plane occurs. American and French troops build blockhouse quarters along rail lines.

November 5 The Battle for Kodish occurs. The Bolsheviks drive Ballard's men back "verst by verst." Allies fight to hold the bridge over the Yemtsa River.

November 7 US Ambassador Francis leaves for America.

First musical evening at hospital organized by Clara Taylor.

November 9 The Allied Kodish Forces and Bolsheviks both dig in on banks of Yemtsa River. US Engineers arrive to build blockhouses for winter shelter. US Company K relieved by Company E to hold area for the winter. Company K men and Lt. Ballard return to Arkhangelsk, marking the end of the Fall campaign on the Kodish front.

Clara Taylor and her colleagues work at YMCA huts and canteens, hospitals, Red Cross HQ, and Embassies throughout November and December.

November 11, 1918 Armistice Day
The "Great War" ends at 11:00 on the 11th day of the 11th month of 1918 with the surrender of Germany. Allied Dvina Forces are attacked at Toulgas, and the Bolsheviks are repelled with high casualties on both sides.

November 12–14 Bolsheviks in gun boats fire on Allies on the Dvina River. Siege conditions prevail at Toulgas with counterattacks and sorties by Allies that capture some of the Red's forest gun nests. Bolsheviks are routed and Allies hold Toulgas. Bolshevik Commander Foukes killed in action. Allies report 100 troops killed.

November 15 US Company G ("Pinega Forces") sent to clear valley and occupy Katpogora.

University of Wisconsin Alumni party organized by Clara Taylor in Arkhangelsk.

mid-November Vaga River Forces actively engage with Bolsheviks in skirmishes with no clear results. Spanish Influenza sickens villagers and troops. Allied men are extremely demoralized.

November 24 Allied Pinega Forces take Katpogora.

November 27 American Thanksgiving Day Holiday. The troops are given a half-holiday at the YMCA block house (built by the US 310th Engineers). Maj. Nichols has Helen Ogden read President Wilson's proclamation. Consul DeWitt Poole addresses troops.

Clara Taylor helps serve pie at hospitals, hostesses a party at HQ, writes: ". . . we danced until one."

December The Bolsheviks troops hold Turchesoura and Plesetskya.

December 1 US Company C/Vaga River Forces relieved by Company A.

December 4 Bolsheviks return to Karpogora in Pinega Valley, and the Allies retreat down the Valley.

December 5–10 Continual skirmishing occurs between the Bolsheviks and Vaga Forces at and around the village of Ust Padenga. Company C with White Russian troops drive towards Senkurst and Kodima, where they are forced to retreat due to frozen guns (temperature is 50° F below zero). US soldiers are upset because of the death of troops by British friendly fire. Some Russian soldiers refuse to leave their barracks in Arkhangelsk, and US troops are ordered to fire upon them by the British Command.

Bessie Boies sails for London.

December 11 Allies attempt to help Senkurst but are again defeated by the weather. A Cossack foray at Kodima fails with many killed.

December 18–27 US 1st and 4th Platoons force march from Arkhangelsk to Pinega.

The Smolny Soldier's Hut opened by Clara Taylor and Lt. Bracket on 18th.

Christmas preparations for the hospital parties take up the time of the American women.

December 30 Clara Taylor is hospitalized for appendicitis.

1919

January The Vaga River Forces (US Company A of 339th Infantry, Platoon A of 310th Engineers; Canadian Artillery; British Signal Corps; White Russian and Cossack troops) establish a main post at Netsvetiafskya.

Jan. 19–March 10 The Shenkurst Offensive is planned and executed, but proves to be a disaster. All troops are evacuated north to Arkhangelsk in March.

1st week January US 2d and 3d platoons force march from Arkhangelsk to reinforce Company M and Pinega Forces. The Bolsheviks fortify Trufanagora. This area "very complex with divided loyalties and personalities" writes the British Command. Throughout January skirmishes occur, with back-and-forth victories for small villages of Priluk, Zapocha, Pochexero, Soyla.

Helen Ogden, Catherine Childs, Marcia Dunham, and Elizabeth Dickerson open the YWCA Hostess House for American Soldiers.

January 1–7 The Bolsheviks hold Kodish with 2,700 troops. It is finally recaptured in "Hellish battles" by Americans with Canadian, "The King's Liverpools," Russian "Dyer's Best," and French officers. Seven US troops are killed and 35 wounded in these actions.

January 1 A fierce battle at Kleshevo occurs, and Company H/Onega forces are forced to withdraw.

January 6 The Bolsheviks are in retreat from Kodish and Plesetskaya, which are now held by the Allies. The fighting is now over on the Kodish front.

January 19–22 V aga River Forces are bombarded at Nijni Gora, with house-to-house fighting and much carnage. Americans withdraw to Ust Padenga and join Russians and Cossacks there but must withdraw further to Spasskoe.

Clara Taylor is released from the hospital on January 14.

January 23–24 The Shenkurst siege and retreat occurs with the evacuation of Allies. American troops were over 15 versts away from Shenkurst in a "disastrous situation": The Allied Headquarters was at Beresnik, a river base +100 miles from Shenkurst; the Kitsa outpost was +20 miles away; and the Shegouarie base was +44 miles from Shenkurst—all too far away to support the fighting men at Skenkurst.

January 24 Bolsheviks nearly take Pinega and the Allies are forced to withdraw to fortifications at Peligora.

January 26 US Vega River Forces arrive in Vistavka (6 versts from Kitsa) on Vaga River's east bank, dig in, and defend it until the end of March.

February 1919 The Government of Pinega and local people enthusiastically support Allies. All men 18–45 years old are drafted in accordance with decree from Arkhangelsk.

The Military Mission in Pinega is deemed complete, due to the completion of training for 2,000 White Russian troops.

February 7 Lt. Ballard is killed at Kodish.

2d week February Bolsheviks inexplicably retreat from Trufanagora.

February 10 The Allied Onega Forces drive Bolsheviks from Khala.

Jan. 29–March 1 Bolshevik attacks on Toulgas are repulsed by Dvina River Forces.

March Throughout the month, all attempts made to connect Allied troops with Russian General Kolchak near Kotlas fail. The Dvina River is abnormally low, which prevents Allied ships from moving. The British government decides to withdraw all troops. Commander in Chief Rawlinson establishes plans for offensives to cover the evacuation. British Command expect White Russian "North Russian Army" to carry on after Allies leave.

March 1 Patrols of Dvina Forces at Toulgas are ambushed with eight killed. Allies still hold Toulgas.

March 3 US Vaga River Forces lose Yeveeskya. Vistavka is now surrounded by the Red Army.

March 6 The Cossaks sally from Kitsa and try to punch through Bolshevik lines to succor Americans at Vistavka but fail.

March 9 Bolsheviks cut and run from Vistavka but then return. Americans withdraw to a position 3 versts away in the forest and dig in until April.

March 16–17 The Bolshe Ozerke Front is the newest fighting front for Vologda Forces.

March 16–April 18 In the Vologda River Offensive French troops at Bolshe Ozerke are overwhelmed by the Red Army. A Bolshevik "fighting wedge" is created between Onega and Railroad Forces. Many French troops are killed.

March 18 British General Ironside takes command at Oberskaya.

March 18–20 Battles occur around Bolshe Ozerke. The Allies withdraw to Chinova.

March 23 Heavy fighting around Versts 18 and 19 occur.Bolshe Ozerke is fortified with men and artillery by the Bolsheviks. US and White Russians hold Verst 18. The Smolney Barracks burn down.

March 28 Clara Taylor serves on the Railroad canteen car at Verst 455 front.

March 31 The Bolsheviks attack Allied rear at Verst 18.

Catherine Childs Ryall's husband captured by the Bolsheviks and sent to Moscow as a prisoner.

April 1 A major offensive by Bolsheviks is attempted, but the Allies hold Verst 18.

April 2 Bolsheviks try to cut Allied line to get to Obozerkaya in a "vicious drive." The British launch an attack at the Bolshevik's western edge but are repelled and retreat to Chekuevo and Onega.

April 4 US Company M is relieved at Verst 18 by Yorkshire Men and White Russian forces, and are able to hold the Bolsheviks at Bolshe Ozerke. The Red Army abandons the attempt to capture Obozerskya. Of the 7,000 Bolshevik troops at the Battle of Bolosheozerki, 2,000 are killed or wounded.

April 19 The Americans and Cossacks of the Vaga Forces near Vistavka retreat and blow up the villages of Kitska and Maximouskya. The Vaga River ice breaks up, which allows Company F to withdraw across the river to Ignatavskya, then to Mala-Beresnik and Nizhnikitsa (8 versts from Kitska).

Clara Taylor travels to and from Oberzerskaya with the Railroad canteen car.

April 25, 26 North Russian Army troops mutiny at Toulgas. Bolsheviks take control, but Allies and loyal Russians open fire on the city and retake it.

May 1 Clara Taylor returns to Arkhangelsk from the Railroad Front.

May 10 Ice out of Vaga River opens the way for gun boats and the withdrawal of Allied troops back to the city of Arkhangelsk.

Catherine Childs Ryall's husband is released and she leaves for London on the 12th.

May 17 British Royal Navy troops steam up Vaga River to Toulgas to relieve Americans.

May 19 Allies of Vaga Forces re-take Ignatavskya from the Bolsheviks, in the last action on the Vega Front.

May 25 Camp Economia is established upriver from Arkhangelsk and starts to receive men scheduled to depart for home.

May–June Clara Taylor, Marcia Dunham, and Elizabeth Dickerson help out at canteens opened by the YMCA at Camp Economia.

The YWCA Hostess House and YMCA Hospitality Huts close down.

Clara Taylor and Marcia Dunham are asked to provide for Russian women prisoners.

June 5 US Company H leaves Onega for Camp Economia.

June 15 US Company H disembarks for home.

June 28 The Treaty of Versailles is signed in Paris, thus ending the "Great War."

July 7 A mutiny at Troitsa by Slavo-British Allied Legion 1st Battalion troops is quelled, but not before the officers are murdered.

July 20 A mutiny of Russian National Army holding Onega sector succeeds in handing over the town, port, and other territory to the Red Army.

July 26 The last of US servicemen ship out for home.

New YWCA secretaries arrive in Arkhangelsk, and all visit the Solovetsky monastery.

August 10 The attack on Puchega, and Borok (on Dvina River) is successful as a last offensive to boost Russian morale and set the stage to withdraw remainder of Allied troops from all fronts.

August 11 General Rawlinson arrives in Arkhangelsk to take command of the evacuation.

August 14 Clara Taylor posts her last letter from Russia.

August 23 Clara Taylor and Marcia Dunham leave Arkhangelsk for Murmansk aboard a Russian freighter.

August 29–30 Offensives against Railroad and Seletskoe Fronts occur.

September 1 Attacks by the Red Army on Bolshoi Oserke are repelled by North Russian Army without Allied help.

September 9–10 Bolsheviks appear to leave Onega Valley. The evacuation of British troops and civilians from Arkhangelsk commences.

Clara Taylor, Marcia Dunham and others arrive in Newcastle, England, then travel to London.

September 16 British General Sadler-Jackson turns over command to the North Russian Army.

Clara Taylor visits her Scottish cousins in Aberdeen.

September 22 All British troops are off the front lines and at Arkhangelsk.

September 25 The last British civilians leave Arkhangelsk.

September 27 Allied evacuation of Arkhangelsk is complete. All transports are out at sea headed for Murmansk at 6:00 p.m.

October 3 The Murmansk evacuation begins.

October 8 General Rawlinson leaves Murmansk.

Clara Taylor sails aboard the USS *Adriatic* to New York from London.

October 12 All foreign troops are out of Murmansk, and the western mission of the North Russian Expedition is ended.

Great Aunt Teke (Clara Taylor) in New York City, 1955 during a visit from Patricia.
(Photographer: Patricia M. Maloney)

Patricia Martin (later Maloney) visiting her Great Aunt Teke in New York City, 1955.
(Photographer: Clara Taylor)

Maloney siblings with Great Grand Aunt Teke, on the occasion of her visit and a picnic in Connecticut, 1964. Left to right: Tim, Aunt Teke, Julie, Katrina (Kathleen) (Photographer: Patricia M. Maloney)

Bibliography

Albertson, Ralph. *Fighting without a War:* An Account of Military Intervention in North Russia. New York: Harcourt, Brace and Howe, 1920. http://www.gutenberg.org/files/46191/46191-h/46191-h.html

Allison, William. *American Diplomats in Russia: Case Studies in Orphan Diplomacy 1916–1919.* Greenwood Publishing Group, 1997.

Buchanan, Meriel. *Petrograd, the City of Trouble 1914–1918.* London: W. Collins & Sons, 1918.

Bunin, Ivan. *Cursed Days: A Diary of Revolution.* Translated by Thomas Gaiton Marullo. Chicago: Ivan R. Dee, 1998.

Cantacuzene, Julia. *Revolutionary Days. Including Passages from My Life Here and There 1876–1917.* Edited by Terence Emmons. Chicago: R. R. Donnelley & Sons Company, Lakeside Press, 1999.

Cobble, Dorothy Sue. "A Higher Standard of Life for the World: US Labor Women's Reform Internationalism and the Legacies of 1919." *The Journal of American History* 100, No. 4 (2014): 1052–085. Accessed June 28, 2021. http://www.jstor.org/stable/44307858.

Cudahy, John. *Archangel the American War with Russia.* Chicago: A. C. McClurg & Co., 1924.

Golysheva, Natalia. "Red Terror in the North." BBC. 2020. Accessed March 17, 2021. https://www.bbc.com/russian/resources/idt-sh/red_terror_russian

Moore, Joel R., Harry H. Mead, and Lewis E. Jahns. *History of the American Expedition Fighting the Bolsheviks-Campaigning in North Russia 1918–1919*. Detroit, MI: Polar Bear Publishing Co. 1920. Polar Bear Digital Collections https://quod.lib.umich.edu/p/polaread/history.html

MacMillan, Margaret. *Paris 1919*. New York: Random House, 2001.

McEwen, Yvonne. "When British Forces Invaded Russia to Fight a Campaign Like No Other." *The Scotsman*. April 23, 2019. Accessed Aug 17, 2020. https://www.scotsman.com/news/opinion/columnists/when-british-forces-invaded-russia-fight-campaign-no-other-yvonne-mcewan-547827

McMeekins, Shawn. *The Russian Revolution, a New History*. London: Profile Books, 2017.

Martin, David K. *"Teke's Russian Adventure 1917–1919."* Unpublished manuscript, 1965.

Moorehead, Alan. *The Russian Revolution*. New York: Harper and Brothers, 1958.

Rappaport, Helen. *Caught in the Revolution*. New York: St. Martin's Press, 2016.

Reed, John. *Ten Days That Shook the World,* NY: International Publishers, 1934.

Rhodes, Benjamin D. "A Prophet in the Russian Wilderness: The Mission of Consul Felix Cole at Archangel, 1917–1919." *The Review of Politics* 46, No. 3 (1984): 388-409. Accessed March 15, 2021. http://www.jstor.org/stable/1407221

Rhodes, Benjamin D. "The Anglo-American Intervention at Archangel, 1918–1919: The Role of the 339th Infantry." *The International History Review* 8, No. 3. (1986): 367-388. Accessed Dec. 11, 2019. https://www.jstor.org/stable/40105628

Smith, Gordon. "In Memory of Chief Yeoman of Signals George Smith, DSM, Royal Navy 1904–1928." Part 2: North Russian Expeditionary Force, 1919. Scrapbook Diary, Photographs, Mementos. The National Museum, Royal Navy. Accessed Nov. 10, 2019. www.Naval-history.net/WWIz05NorthRussia.htm.

Taylor, Clara I. "A New Era in Russian Industry." *The Survey.* Vol. XLI, No. 18. (Feb 1, 1919): 612–615.

Ullman, Richard H. *Anglo-Soviet Relations 1917–1921. Vol. 1: Intervention and the War.* NJ: Princeton University Press, re-issue 2019. orig. pub. 1961.

Online Sources

Demm, Eberhard. "Censorship." Version 2.0 updated March 29, 2017. International Encyclopedia of the First World War. Accessed Jan. 2021. https://encyclopedia.1914-1918-online.net/article/censorship

Dispatches Navy-History.net, http://naval-history.net/WW1NavyBritish LGDispatchesArmy1918-20.htm#31850

31850—2 APRIL 1920 NORTH RUSSIAN EXPEDITIONARY FORCE ARMY DESPATCHES dated 5 October 1918 to 1 November 1919

British Navel Dispatches: Allied Forces in North Russia

21 May 1918–30 Sept 1918 (Maj. Gen. Poole)

20 Sept 1918–28 Feb 1919 (Maj. Gen. Maynard)

1 Oct 1918–11 Aug 1919 (Maj. Gen. Ironside)

11 Aug 1919–27 Sept 1919 (Maj. Gen. Ironside)

10 Aug 1919–12 Oct 1919 (Gen. Lord Rawlinson)

APPENDIX A to DESPATCH No. 4. From Major-General Sir C. M. Maynard, K.C.B., C.M.G., D.S.O., Commanding Allied Forces, Murmansk. To General Lord Rawlinson, G.C.B., G.C.V.O., K.C.M.G., A.D.C., General, Commanding-in-Chief, North Russia. War Office, London, S.W. 1, 25 October 1919

APPENDIX B to DESPATCH No. 4. From Major-General Sir W. E. Ironside, K.C.B., C.M.G., D.S.O., Commanding Allied Forces, Archangel. To General Lord Rawlinson, G.C.B. G.C.V.O., K.C.M.G., A.D.C., General, Commanding-in-Chief, North Russia. War Office, 1 November 1919.

"WWI at Sea" Army dispatches with Naval operations. Part three of three. *London Gazette* editions 30462–32156 (Jan 1918–Dec

1920). Accessed Sept. 2020. https://www.naval-history.net/ WW1NavyBritishLGDispatchesArmy1918-20.htm#31850

History.com Editors. "American troops land at Archangel." A & E Television Networks. (Oct. 28, 2009). Accessed Mar. 2021. https://www.history.com/this-day-in-history/american-troops-land-at-archangel

London Gazette editions 30462–32156 (Jan. 1918–Dec. 1920). Accessed Mar. 2020. https://bentley.umich.edu/research/catalogs-databases/polar-bear/polar-bear-expedition-history/

Quarberg, Lincoln A., Editor "The Liberty Badger." Vol. XXXIV. Madison, Wisconsin: Class of 1920 of the University of Wisconsin, 1920. Accessed Feb. 2021. http://digital.library.wisc.edu/1711.dl/UW.UWYearBk1920

Smithsonian National Museum of American History. "Women in World War I: Correspondence." Accessed Mar. 15, 2021. https://www.si.edu/spotlight/women-in-wwi/correspondence

Film

"The First World War." Disk 4. Ben Steele and Jonathan Lewis, Directors and Producers. Hamilton Film Partnership, 2003.

Accessed for General Background Information

Arkhangelsk: https://russiatrek.org/arkhangelsk-city

Casualties: Report of United States Secretary of War https://net.lib.byu.edu/estu/wwi/memoir/aef_cong.htm

Spanish Influenza: https://www.cdc.gov/flu/pandemic-resources/1918-commemoration/pandemic-timeline-1918.htm

YWCA

The Association Monthly: The Official Organ of the Young Woman's Christian Association, Volume 12, Issue 5; and other issues.

War Work Bulletin of the YWCA, issues 17–96.

The Survey, a Journal of Social Exploration. Edited by Paul U. Kellogg; Assoc. Eds: Edward T. Devine, Graham Taylor, and Jane Addams.

[This magazine was published from 1909 to 1952 and ran articles and art relating to social and political issues. Graham Taylor, one of the editors, was attached to the American Embassy, Petrograd, Russia, in 1918.]

Index

C

D

P

Z

Acknowledgments

The archives of the YWCA of America and the personal papers of Clara I. Taylor and Elizabeth Boies Cotton are housed at the Sophia Smith Collection at Smith College, Northampton, Massachusetts. We are grateful to the staff at the archive for helping us locate and copy material for these volumes.

David K. Martin, Patricia's elder brother and Clara's grandnephew, wrote a manuscript in 1964 that was the original inspiration for us to tackle the project of publishing Clara's letters and diary. We dedicate this volume to him with our thanks.

Katrina Maloney thanks her friends who patiently listened to stories about Clara, the challenges of historical research, and the process of writing these books. Maureen Sullivan and Lily O'Leary were especially supportive during this multiple year-long project.

Patricia Maloney wishes to thank James R. Bradley, Professor of Classics (retired) of Trinity College, Hartford, Connecticut, for his encouragement and support.

About the Authors

Katrina Maloney, Ed.D., lives and writes in southern New Hampshire. She is a former professor of natural sciences and education. When not at her day job as a paralegal, she kayaks, reads, plays music, and gardens on her property facing Mount Monadnock.

Patricia M. Maloney grew up in Nebraska and came east to attend college. She and her husband John raised their three children in Connecticut. After retiring from her career as a Director of Christian Education, she travels, enjoys her lake cottage, plays the organ, piano, and clarinet, and sings in local chorales.

SELECTED TITLES FROM SHE WRITES PRESS

She Writes Press is an independent publishing company founded to serve women writers everywhere. Visit us at www.shewritespress.com.

Dearest Ones at Home: Clara Taylor's Letters from Russia, 1917-1919 edited by Katrina Maloney and Patricia Maloney.
Clara Taylor's detailed, delightful letters documenting her two years in Russia teaching factory girls self-sufficiency skills—right in the middle of World War I.

Motherlines: Letters of Love, Longing, and Liberation by Patricia Reis $16.95, 978-1-63152-121-8
In her midlife search for meaning, and longing for maternal connection, Patricia Reis encounters uncommon women who inspire her journey and discovers an unlikely confidante in her aunt, a free-spirited Franciscan nun.

Times They Were A-Changing: Women Remember the '60s & '70s edited by Kate Farrell, Amber Lea Starfire, and Linda Joy Myers. $16.95, 978-1-938314-04-9
Forty-eight powerful stories and poems detailing the breakthrough moments experienced by women during the '60s and '70s.

Queerspawn in Love by Kellen Kaiser. $16.95, 978-1-63152-020-4
When the daughter of a quartet of lesbians falls in love with a man serving in the Israeli Defense Forces, she is forced to examine her own values and beliefs.

Renewable: One Woman's Search for Simplicity, Faithfulness, and Hope by Eileen Flanagan. $16.95, 978-1-63152-968-9
At age forty-nine, Eileen Flanagan had an aching feeling that she wasn't living up to her youthful ideals or potential, so she started trying to change the world—and in doing so, she found the courage to change her life.

In the Game: The Highs and Lows of a Trailblazing Trial Lawyer by Peggy Garrity. $16.95, 978-1-63152-105-8
Admitted to the California State Bar in 1975—when less than 3 percent of lawyers were women—Peggy Garrity refuses to choose between family and profession, and succeeds at both beyond anything she could have imagined.

Printed in the United States
by Baker & Taylor Publisher Services